# BOMBER

## THE WHOLE STORY

Mark 'Bomber' Thompson played 202 games for Essendon Football Club from 1983 to 1996 under legendary coach Kevin Sheedy. He captained the side for four seasons. Thompson played in three premierships in 1984, 1985 and 1993. In 2000, Thompson became the senior coach of the Geelong Football Club, where he led the greatest team of all to the club's drought-breaking premiership in 2007, then took them to another flag in 2009. In November 2010, he left Geelong, returning to Essendon as senior assistant coach to James Hird in 2011. He was appointed senior coach for the 2014 season when Hird was suspended. He is now a Fox Footy panellist and works with emerging coaches.

Martin Blake has written on sport for 30 years, most of it with *The Age* in Melbourne. He has covered every VFL/AFL season since 1986 and has won numerous awards for writing on football, cricket and golf. He is a member of the MCG Media Hall of Fame and broadcasts on sport for the ABC and SEN1116. He is the author of *The Rise of the Swans* and *The Mighty Fighting Hawks*. Martin plays far too much golf and lives in Melbourne.

# BOMBER

## THE WHOLE STORY

MARK THOMPSON

with

MARTIN BLAKE

MICHAEL JOSEPH

*an imprint of*

PENGUIN BOOKS

MICHAEL JOSEPH

UK | USA | Canada | Ireland | Australia
India | New Zealand | South Africa | China

Penguin Books is part of the Penguin Random House group of companies whose addresses can be found at global.penguinrandomhouse.com.

Penguin Random House Australia

First published by Penguin Random House Australia Pty Ltd, 2016
This paperback edition published by Penguin Random House Australia Pty Ltd, 2017

10 9 8 7 6 5 4 3 2 1



Cover and text design by Adam Laszczuk © Penguin Random House Australia Pty Ltd
Cover photograph by Tim Bauer
Typeset in Sabon by Adam Laszczuk, Penguin Random House Australia Pty Ltd
Colour separation by Splitting Image Colour Studio, Clayton, Victoria
Printed and bound in Australia by Griffin Press, an accredited ISO AS/NZS 14001 Environmental Management Systems printer.

National Library of Australia
Cataloguing-in-Publication data:

Thompson, Mark, 1963- author.
Bomber : the whole story / Mark Thompson with Martin Blake.
9780143785231 (paperback)

Subjects: Thompson, Mark, 1963-
Australian football players--Australia--Biography.
Football coaches--Australia--Biography.
Australian football--Coaching.

Other Creators/Contributors:
Blake, Martin (Sports writer), author.

penguin.com.au

# CONTENTS

# PROLOGUE

It's time to reflect.

In professional sport, you go at a thousand kilometres an hour, and scarcely stop for an instant to think about the bigger picture. It is the nature of the business; slow down and you get run over. I played footy from the time I was a kid growing up in Airport West in the suburbs of Melbourne until I broke my arm when I was 32 years old, in my sixteenth season and worn out. Beyond that, I coached 18 straight years at Essendon, North Melbourne, Geelong, and then back at Essendon. That makes 34 years in the game. It did not end the way that I envisaged, because I was finished with coaching when I completed my 11 years at Geelong, only to be lured back to Essendon when James Hird was suspended and the club was in need.

But it is only part of the journey for me. I'm 52 and that's a big chunk of my life taken up by the game that I love, the game that shaped me and made me who I am.

The game put me in the company of great players and great people. I was lucky to play with all-time greats of the VFL–AFL: Simon Madden, Tim Watson, the Danihers, Roger Merrett, Mark Harvey, James Hird and under the legendary Kevin Sheedy, a borderline genius and mad professor of a coach who I learned so much from, as well as Denis Pagan, the two chief influences upon my coaching.

I coached Gary Ablett Jr, Jimmy Bartel, Matthew Scarlett, Joel Corey, Corey Enright, Steve Johnson, Joel Selwood, Cameron Ling and Paul Chapman, men who lived their own wonderful stories, bringing the premiership cup back to Geelong after so long. I am proud that Geelong not only won premierships but played football in an entertaining way; a style of footy that people said actually changed the game after some dourness and low-scoring had set in.

I celebrated five premierships as a player and coach and endured just as many serious disappointments, and at the end, during the long and draining Essendon–ASADA crisis, there was some bitterness and real angst to get through. I will have my say on that, but Essendon from 2011–14 is not the whole story, not even close.

When I was first asked if I was interested in writing a book, it had never occurred to me. I had been too busy trying to *create* a story, but then upon contemplation, I realised that there was a lot to be said. I have finished with coaching in the AFL; I am dubious about the system, these days, and my observation is that some of the fun has disappeared from the game for the combatants, as you will read later.

I consider myself a purist, a man of the people. While the politics of the AFL don't interest me, I still love the game. I love the purity of the head-to-head contest, the roar of the crowd, the idea of planning and executing a victory, risking failure, bringing young players into the game, the banter, the hits, the emotion, the skill. I wish that the game would belong to the people again, as it used to, that it was in the hands of the fans who barrack for their club for life, idolising their heroes, following the game like a religion.

I like to call it as I see it, rather than go with the pack. I hate group-think, it's just not my style. I have never been part of any boys' club in footy. I am an independent, which goes back to my youth, pumping petrol on the night shift at 15, running my own business at twenty-one.

So independent thought is a theme I've tried to maintain with this book. It's candid, and if there is criticism of certain individuals and organisations along the way, rest assured that it is not meant to be personal, rather constructive and honest. The idea is to set the record straight, tell my version of events, and let people decide what they think.

I make no apologies for saying it like that. It is *my* story, after all.

# 1

# BOMBA BOY

A lot of people are under the misapprehension that my nickname 'Bomber' came from my time playing football at Essendon, but I've carried that moniker for much longer, which is something only a few people know. It was given to me by my uncle Shane Goodrem when I was about eight.

Shane was more like a cousin, aged between me and my older brother, Steven, and the three of us spent a lot of time together. In our days of backyard footy in Airport West if the football disappeared over the fence into the home of the Russian lady who lived next door to us, it was automatically my responsibility to fetch it. The neighbour had planted an orchard, and she had two German Shepherd dogs, big, feral, angry animals, in place to protect her garden with malicious intent. What would happen was that my brother or my uncle – whoever was around – would hoist me up on to the fence between the yards, and then it was a race.

I would have to spot the footy, grab it and then find a safe spot as the dogs arrived, so after a while, I devised a little system where

I would snare the footy then jump into one of the fruit trees. From there, I would climb from tree to tree until I made it back to the fence and over to continue our football match, with those dogs growling and snarling at my feet.

First Shane and then Steven started calling me 'Bomba' after a character in *Bomba the Jungle Boy*, a series of books, comics and films about a boy who lived in the jungles of South America and Africa, chasing away smugglers and wrestling alligators in his lap-lap, swinging from tree to tree. The films, based on the series of books, came out from 1949 and starred Johnny Sheffield – the same actor who had played the character Boy alongside Johnny Weissmuller in the Tarzan films. The Bomba films were later reworked into a series of comic books in the 1960s, and I assume that it was these comics that were picked up by Shane and his mates around the time that they started calling me Bomba.

So that's where the name came from, and everyone ever since has called me Bomba, which morphed into Bomber, with the 'er' at the end. When I was coaching Geelong, a supporter with a love of the Bomba books sent me a copy with a little message, which I still have. As for the name Mark, well virtually no one calls me that outside of my mother!

I come from the north-west Melbourne suburb of Airport West, a little triangular pocket bounded by the throbbing Western Ring Road, the Calder and Tullamarine freeways, that at last census count had just short of 7000 residents in its 3.7 square kilometre area. It is a working people's area: the median house price is $600 000, relatively cheap by the crazy standards of Melbourne real estate with its growing list of million-dollar suburbs – 87 at last count.

Airport West has the distinction of being the only postcode in Australia containing the word 'Airport' without actually boasting a facility for aircraft. While it is a dubious honour, the place of my childhood does have a particular connection with not one but two airports. It was built, I guess, to service the old Essendon Airport, which is just across the eastern boundary. And Tullamarine, Melbourne's main airport since 1970, is seven kilometres to the north. There are dozens of factories and businesses along Matthews Avenue, just across the way from the original airport where the 59 tram starts its journey to the city. The majority of the people who live there are connected to either one of the airports through some sort of employment.

In fact, the name Airport West is a moot point itself. In 2009 the Moonee Valley Council took a poll of ratepayers to gauge support for a change after some agitation from local residents who felt the 'Airport' name carried a stigma, but only 40 per cent were in favour of a change, and the title remains.

It is typically suburban, neither wealthy nor poor. There is now a Westfield shopping centre with a movie theatre, a pub, and the TAA Museum, formed to commemorate the old Trans Australia Airways, which has been absorbed into Qantas. Children have the option of several primary schools and there's still a football ground, Hansen Reserve, where I used to play as a kid. Our family home is still there in El Reno Crescent but my parents sold up and moved to the country some time after I left home.

I am the middle child of three; Steven is two years older, and sister Katrina two years younger, and our upbringing was happy and very independent. Mum and Dad both worked hard for as long as I can remember. My father, Bruce, worked as a butcher for RJ Gilbertson's, the local butchery firm, makers of the famous

Don Smallgoods. Dad ran the butcher's shop in the strip at Mount Alexander Road, North Essendon, about five minutes from home, and my mother, Patricia, was a travelling representative for various bakeries, flitting around the supermarkets to make sure the products were presented in the right way.

Dad and Mum taught us Thompsons to stand up for ourselves. For instance, by the time I was around ten, I was given licence to catch the tram by myself down Keilor Road to Dad's shop in Essendon North village after school, where I would help him clean up and perform odd jobs before he closed up for the night.

I attended Niddrie Primary School, but my focus was elsewhere. Steven and I were close, and would race home from school and straight out into the street to kick the footy, or to play cricket, or to ride the billycart, the usual kinds of activities Aussie kids loved in the sixties and early-seventies. El Reno Crescent was quiet enough for us to play the games out on the road. I can remember the football taking a terrible scuffing from all those hundreds of games on the bitumen road surface.

We had annual holidays camping up at the Mitta Mitta River near the Murray in northern Victoria with the extended family, which we all loved. It was up in the mountains, very beautiful and we fished and played golf and swam in the river and the water courses. There was a slow river, a fast river, a warm river, a cold river and we would jump off ropes that had been tied on the trees and plunge into the water.

My early football was played across the freeway at East Keilor Football Club, where Steven had started playing, but by the time I was about nine we had both transferred to the much closer Airport West club at Hansen Reserve, just a short walk from home. Airport West had not been a strong footy club; in fact, it was only formed in

1961 and the senior team wasn't promoted to A grade in the Essendon District Football League until 1973, around the time I started there. The EDFL is a strong competition, one of the best in Melbourne. Airport West would not win an A-grade premiership until 1992, long after I had gone.

My parents and family settled in at the footy club quite quickly. Dad was the treasurer of the club for years, Mum worked in the canteen, and Steven and I both played juniors. We were a close family, and my parents were always watching me play football, supportive without being intrusive. It was perfect, the way that they handled it. Mum and Dad were not the kind of people who told me what to do the whole time, which I liked, and having had my own kids and coached sport since, I have come to appreciate it even more over time. The bad parent syndrome is something I grew to detest, with tennis being a good example of how it can go wrong. In sport, you need to play for the right reasons, and I played because I loved it, not because I was pushed to compete by anyone else.

I progressed from Niddrie Primary to Niddrie High School, but I was not a great student, content to do what I had to do, but no more, just muddling my way through school while enjoying my sport. I played a spot of tennis and a lot of cricket, bowling left-arm fast and reckless, and batting right-handed when I played with the Catholic boys from St Christopher's team on the weekends, winning a few premierships before the club folded. But my real focus was footy.

I was a Carlton fan despite living in Essendon's catchment area for players under the old zoning system, which dictated that players who originated from certain areas were required to sign and play for particular Melbourne clubs. My first memory of watching what was then VFL football was around 1970, when Alex Jesaulenko was doing his thing for Carlton, jumping on packs to take skyscraper marks. It was the year the Blues won the premiership in what could be the most famous grand final ever, coming back from 44 points behind Collingwood at half-time to continue that club's dreadful affliction of the so-called Colliwobbles. My family – more specifically Dad's side – were all crazy about Carlton, the power club of the time, and I merely followed the rest of them in loving the Navy Blues.

Of course, having 'Jesss-a-lenk-ooooo, you beauty!' on the team only helped force my hand, but the family also adored Bruce Doull, the famous half-back flanker with the headband, and rough, tough Jimmy Buckley, ruckman Peter 'Percy' Jones and Rod Ashman, the little rover. Carlton had the great Ron Barassi as coach, and would go on to win the VFL premiership again in 1972 in one of the club's greatest eras.

So I was always going to gravitate to footy over other sports. Never tall for my age, I could always play the game, and I never stressed over it; it came easily to me as a junior, even though I was an understated player rather than the centre of attention. In 1980, my last year with the club, I captained Airport West to an Under 17 premiership in the EDFL. Coached by Bruce Dillon, we defeated Glenroy in the grand final and the game was played at the famous Windy Hill ground, the home of Essendon Football Club at the time.

I also won the league best and fairest award, which was the first time I realised that I might be on Essendon's radar. One of the club's former players, Daryl Gerlach, came down and presented the award at Brimbank Park; I did not know who he was, since he had finished playing at Essendon in 1972. In 1980 there was no drafting by VFL clubs, rather they had their metropolitan and country zones, and of course, the Essendon Football Club had the rights to players coming out of that region, as well as on the other side of Melbourne in the Ringwood area, and the Wimmera area in north-west Victoria. As an Airport West boy, I knew that I would be zoned to play with Essendon.

Around that time I guess I started to get the feeling that I could play at the top level. At end of Year 11 at Niddrie High School I remember weighing up whether to complete Year 12 in 1981, or whether to go out and find a job. It was a defining moment for me, because the teachers wanted me to continue my studies and I knew that I could have done that, but I had worked part-time for quite a while by then, running a paper round and pulling petrol at a fuel station. When I was 15, I handled the night shift by myself at a petrol station in Keilor Road, Essendon, buying my own clothes with the money that I earned. Mum's notion was that if we wanted a certain brand that was more expensive, we had to do the topping up, creating that sense of independence.

I handled all my own money by then, and I saved up $3000 to buy a lettuce-green Holden HJ Kingswood when I was 17, a decent car for a teenager. When I turned 18, on 19 November 1981, I sat for my licence and I was mobile. By then, I was playing in the red and black of Essendon.

# 2

# LEARNING

## 1981–1983

Late in 1980, after Airport West had won the Under 17 flag, I received my first invitation by letter to go to Essendon Football Club. The Bombers had appointed Kevin Sheedy as senior coach, replacing Barry Davis, and had been in a dark time, missing the finals in Davis's last season forcing the club's hand in making big changes. Essendon had a proud history as an original member of the VFL, but since the grand final appearance of 1968 under Jack Clarke's coaching, had not contended for a flag. In particular, the 70s had been a dreadful period by the club's high standards. The Dons' most recent flag was in 1965 under the legendary John Coleman's coaching, and in the 12 seasons beyond the 1968 grand final defeat by Carlton, Essendon had played only three finals and lost them all. To find a worse stretch in club history you needed to delve back to the 1920s and 1930s.

The club had endured money problems, it was pushover-weak, it had made bad choices with selection of coaches, and mostly missed the September action. In 1970 and 1971, when Essendon finished just one rung from the bottom in eleventh position, these were the worst finishing places the club had endured in almost 40 years, since the wooden spoon year of 1933. All of which came to a head at the end of 1980 with the appointment of Sheedy as coach, a new president in Greg Sewell and a new general manager in Barry Capuano, both being former Essendon players.

Sheedy's arrival was big news; he came out of the hugely successful Richmond club as a player, where he won three premierships in 1969, 1973 and 1974 as a rough, hard back pocket player. Sheedy was young for a senior coach at only 33, and his hiring was unusual in the sense that he was an outsider. While it was not unknown for Essendon to go outside the club to find a coach, it was certainly not the norm. Generally, Essendon liked to keep it within, and the significance of this I would only glean later.

Davis, a 218-game Essendon player, three-time best and fairest and former captain as well as a local boy, had stepped down at the end of 1980. He was struggling with a full-time job in the Education Department as well as the coaching position, telling the players late in the season that if the Dons did not qualify for finals, he would move on. Interestingly, Essendon went after a full-time coach, approaching – among others – Allan Jeans and Ron Barassi, but the revered Jeans, coach of St Kilda's only premiership in 1966, was appointed by Hawthorn, and the legendary Barassi by Melbourne, in the same week. This left Essendon plumping for the untried Sheedy, who had spent 1980 on the Richmond coaching staff after his retirement as a player. Apparently he was being groomed for the position at his original club, only to be poached by the club he had supported as a boy, Essendon.

The VFL consisted of 12 Victorian teams and the notion of a national competition was still a few years away, although coaches and players were spending more time at the football club, almost to the semi-professional level. Sheedy was the league's first-ever full-time coach. 'I believe in playing football for premierships,' he told the media at his appointment in October. 'I'm setting out to get the best out of the players here.'

My arrival coincided with the revolution that came with Sheedy, and I remember the letter coming in the mail, and being excited as well as apprehensive about the future. Four players from that Airport West team – myself, Peter Latham, Rodney Kent and Craig Mackley – were picked up by Essendon as it sought out local talent to develop and nurture.

I played in the Under 19s under Graham Leydin's coaching, and my progress was steady. I played 13 games in the Under 19s that season, which was enough to win the best and fairest award, and I was elevated to the reserves team to play with the men later in the season. My first-ever reserves game was against Fitzroy, and I recall playing against Brian O'Keefe, whose son Ryan would become a star with the Sydney Swans much later. I copped a belting up against the men, but I seemed to be able to bounce back, and while I was never a rough kid, or a fighter, I found my way out of trouble from early on. It never actually *scared* me to be in that environment although I was young and small.

I played on-ball, in the centre and on a half-forward flank rotating through the middle. In those days we played at the suburban grounds like Glenferrie Oval against Hawthorn and Victoria Park against Collingwood and Moorabbin against St Kilda, as well as at the big grounds like VFL Park and the MCG. The Under 19 squad trained separately from the seniors, but when I was elevated to the reserves I trained as part of the senior group. Essendon had some names that were intimidating to me: Tim Watson was ensconced at the club, Ron Andrews was there, Simon Madden, Max Crow, Robert Shaw, Justin Madden, Phil Carman, Glenn Hawker, Merv Neagle, Terry and Neale Daniher and their like. While I was not physically scared on the field I remember being petrified about making a mistake at training when I was with the main group, not even wanting the ball sometimes.

Of course you do become accustomed to that feeling, but it takes a while, maybe a couple of years, and at Essendon, you were not invited to say too much as a young player. In 1981 the senior team lost five of its first six games under Sheedy's coaching, entering into a crisis which Sheeds thought he would solve by pulling on the boots again, despite having retired more than a year earlier. It was a thought process that showed how deep the trouble was within the team as it adapted to a new method, but he was persuaded not to follow through on that decision as Essendon rebounded.

The club won its first night premiership at Waverley in July against Carlton, with Tim Watson's amazing leapfrog over a fallen player and surging goal going down into the annals of the game's history. In a way, it was symbolic of what was happening at Essendon, with a group of experienced players like Simon Madden, Terry Daniher, Neil Clarke, Shane Heard, Paul Vander Haar, Garry Foulds and Tim, who was 20 and a few seasons into his remarkable career, ready to explode. They played finals that season, knocked out in the first week by Fitzroy, but they were coming.

I was terrified of Sheedy, who had begun to change Essendon, to Richmondise it, if you like. Sheeds came from the Richmond culture, the culture of Graeme Richmond, the Tigers' legendary former secretary, whose attitude was summed up in the documentary *100 Years of Australian Football*: 'It's fair enough to say that we played in a manner that was *kill or be killed*. That's how it was with us.'

Richmond had won the 1967, 1969, 1973 and 1974 premierships under this mantra with Tom Hafey as coach.

That cultural change was a big shock to Essendon footy club in 1981. Sheedy immediately demanded perfection on the track, and the players had never seen and never thought it possible to deliver on that level of demand. He wanted perfect kicking, kicks that moved the receiving player on to the football, he wanted clean ball-handling under pressure. If you were not up to the mark in a particular area, he would switch over and supervise that group at training. The Bad Boys' Group, we would call it.

Garry Foulds would just walk straight over to that group as soon as heard the signal, because Sheeds had it in for Fouldsy, who came from the 'Old Essendon'. Garry was a terrific player, who had completed seven seasons at the club before Sheedy's arrival, but he had a way of gathering 25 touches of the football in the game without getting a bruise, and the ball followed him. Sheeds hammered Garry, probably because he looked to being doing it so easily. Fouldsy would go on to be a 300-game player.

Essendon was like Garry Foulds. It was gentlemanly, it was nice, and Sheedy did not like *nice* footy. He had taken over from Barry Davis, who was nice, and under Davis, Essendon would have looked good, playing a nice brand. But Sheedy came from the Graeme Richmond school, and Richmond was not nice about football; actually, he could be vicious. It was terribly difficult for Essendon to embrace the change and right from the start, Kevin Sheedy had his detractors within the club because of the way he went about it. He did not enjoy the full support of the club.

Essendon was a conservative club that used to carry the moniker 'Same Olds' when it played in the early years of the VFL. The victory song back then used to run:

The Same Old Essendon we used to be,
The Same Old Essendon we are you see
At the end of the season, that premiership flag,
The Same Old Essendon will have it in the bag
For the Same Old Essendon are we.

That was Essendon, which did not adopt its current song 'See the Bombers Fly Up' until a supporter, Kevin Andrews, wrote it to the tune of 'Keep Your Sunny Side Up' around 1959. It was a conservative club and it had been overtaken by more innovative clubs in the 1970s.

What Sheedy brought on board had to be done, in my view. Essendon was a club full of friendly people, but it was treading water, and I think that the senior players picked up upon it when Sheeds arrived. They started to think, *This bloke knows what he's doing, and we might actually be a chance to do something under him.*

Sheeds had a booming voice and it rang out all over the Windy Hill ground on training nights. He would wear his boots and tracksuit pants out on to the track, and he had not long finished playing, so it added to the feeling that he was ready to smash you if the time arose. He was so tough, so ruthless in the way that he coached, hardest on guys like Foulds, Grant Fowler, Alan Stoneham and Alan Reid, the educated boys. Sheeds liked the tradesmen in the team, the working lads, having been a plumber himself as a young man – the 'bloody back pocket plumber' immortalised in Tom Hafey's oft-quoted line from his 1975 preliminary final speech.

Sheeds had grown up in inner-city South Yarra, one of seven children living in a two-bedroom apartment. The 1950s were tough times everywhere, so he had worked hard to achieve anything he had. Hafey told the ABC years later precisely why Sheedy had prospered at Richmond:

> He was in the team because he was a rough, tough diamond. Make no mistake about that. He would have upset some of his own teammates because of the tough attitude he had and maybe a dirty player. Yes, so I had many of them come back shaking their heads about the things that Kevin Sheedy did out on the ground. They were his own teammates.
>
> And I can remember when he was 18 I took him to Pentridge. He knew close on 30 people by Christian name. His best friend was doing about four years for armed robbery. I remember it so well. We all had lunch with the Governor, Ian Grindlay, who was a demented mad Richmond supporter. Kevin went in to the cell of his friend and he was there while we was with Ian. That's an absolute fact.

For me, it was new, the Sheedy approach, but it must have been even tougher for the players who had been there before. 'We were frightened of him back then and we had good reason to be,' wrote Tim Watson in an *Age* column much later. 'Most, if not all of us, were unsure about whether we would survive the first pre-season. It was physically and mentally the most demanding time I ever had in footy.'

He was more demanding on the white-collar men, like Simon Madden, and he took the captaincy away from Simon at the end of his first season, giving it to Neale Daniher. Fouldsy was a schoolteacher and so was Simon, Grant Fowler came out of the private school system and married into the Murdoch family and Alan Reid ended up becoming an ambassadorial staffer in China and a trade commissioner overseas. He cut them no favours at all.

He was under the spell of Graeme Richmond, the hotelier who ruled the footy club that carried his own surname with an iron fist for years. Sheeds actually brought Graeme out to speak to the Essendon players one night, which was cheeky when you consider that Richmond was at the heart of the infamous Windy Hill brawl of 1974, a fight that erupted as the players left the field at half-time. Graeme Richmond, who had leapt the fence to get involved, had been suspended for the remainder of that season over his part in that incident, one of the most shameful in league history, so he was not exactly Mr Popular at Essendon a few short years later.

Sheedy did not care a bit. He asked Graeme to the club for a reason and in five minutes, I could pick up what an amazing motivator of men this guy had been. He was only a small man but they followed him, Neil Balme and Ricky McLean and those kind of guys at Richmond, and I enjoyed listening to him. As to how Sheeds brought him in and out of Windy Hill safely, now that is a minor miracle.

That was the environment in which my league football career began, a club trying to change its ways, to become a ruthless winner. In my second year, 1982, I played a few games in the Under 19s but mostly as a half-forward in the reserves, coached by Bernie Sheehy, a man who had left-field, almost wild ideas about the game. Then in 1983 I made the senior list for the first time, selected for my senior debut for Essendon against Sydney Swans in round 1 at the SCG, on Sunday 27 March 1983. I was 19 years old.

Sheedy had recruited Paul Weston, an excellent tall defender from Glenelg, at the start of the 1983 season, but the clubs were haggling about a transfer fee. Glenelg wanted $175 000 and Essendon had offered less than $100 000, meaning that the dispute had to go before the South Australian National Football League (SANFL) Appeals Board. All this occurred as the season was beginning.

When Weston's clearance failed to come through for round 1, I was the next man into the seniors. Essendon had three debutants that day – forward Wayne Beddison from Dimboola, a willowy ruck-forward called Paul Salmon who was just 18, and me – and we lost by a point. The Swans kicked eight goals in the first quarter before we made a belated comeback. My memory is that I played okay, having 15 disposals, and then I played again the following week against St Kilda at Windy Hill, having 17 disposals and kicking my first goal. But they were my last senior games of the 1983 season; I hurt my knee and could not break back into the seniors as they forged their way into a grand final against Hawthorn, the first grand final appearance of an Essendon team since 1968, a long 15 years earlier.

I was back with the reserves for the latter part of the season under the coaching of Kevin Morris, another graduate of the Tom Hafey– Graeme Richmond school, who had played in two premierships with the Tigers in the 1970s. Morris was another part of the Richmondisation of Essendon, along with people like Noel Judkins, the recruiter, and Bruce Reid, the club doctor. Morris was a hard-nosed and honest guy who was good for me, and I also had some sprint training from Barry Foley, who was a Stawell Gift winner and an outstanding professional runner. The club was concerned about my lack of pace, and it did help me, like any good coaching does.

We were all happy as our team-within-a-team, a few of us popping up to senior level at different times, but mostly playing as a group. Guys like Merv Harbinson, Barry Besanko, Gary Sheldon were almost permanent reserves players, and I was really part of that group in 1983.

It was a big day for Essendon, with both senior and reserves teams reaching the Big Dance. Under Sheedy, the Dons had played finals in both 1981 and 1982 and been eliminated in the first week of September, so the players came hungry to take another step and win the club's first premiership in more than a decade. But they were humiliated by a wonderful Hawthorn team in the grand final, the 83-point margin being a new league record, overtaking the 81-point annihilation handed out by Richmond to Collingwood in 1980. It was the beginning of a very brutal and spirited rivalry between Essendon and Hawthorn in that decade.

I watched this unfold from the stands and almost certainly under the haze of alcohol, having played in Essendon's reserves premiership earlier in the day under Kevin Morris's coaching. We played Collingwood out on the MCG that day, and I remember playing okay. It was a team that contained some of the players who would graduate to the senior premiership teams of 1984 and 1985.

That team was:

B: Gary Sheldon, Doug Cox, Anthony O'Brien
HB: Mark Thompson, Ron Andrews, Shaun Duncan
C: Michael Thomson, Kevin Morris, Mark Eustice
HF: Merv Harbinson, Frank Dunell, Graeme Schultz
F: Steve Richardson, Andrew Callaghan, Wayne Beddison
Ruck: Paul Salmon, Alan Stoneham, Chris Waterson
I/C: Shane Irwin, Peter Banfield, Michael Davis

Essendon's first appearance in a senior grand final in far too long had ended badly, and Sheedy was not about to allow the moment to pass quietly. Although the reserves guys were celebrating, I do remember him barking at the senior guys at the function that night during his speech, in his ruthless way, telling them to wipe the smiles off their faces. He would not allow anyone at Essendon to be happy with finishing second, and I can still remember the fire in him, as I reckon everyone else in the room can: 'I don't want you to enjoy tonight at all. I don't mind you really getting out and having a dance, but look, if it never hurts tonight, Essendon will never win another premiership.'

Back then, there were 12 teams in the competition, 11 of them from Melbourne plus the Sydney Swans, who had emanated from the old South Melbourne club and been transplanted to the biggest city in Australia in 1982, my second year at Essendon. There was no draft, and no salary cap, and the expansion of the competition was only a figment of someone's imagination.

We were semi-professional players, most of us having day jobs. We trained four nights a week in summertime, plus a run on the weekend, so it was not necessarily easy, while in-season we would train on Monday, Tuesday and Thursday nights and then play on Saturdays. If you had been injured or you lost a game badly, you might train on Sunday, too.

The game was still a few years away from full-time professionalism, although Sheeds himself led the trend towards full-time coaching. He was also the first coach to bring football skills to pre-season training, instead of only running, which was a big change. Sheedy shocked everyone when he turned up in summer with footballs and worked on our skills, because prior to that, the coaches just ran the players until they dropped, trying to build up a fitness base. We still ran hard, *really* hard, but we also tweaked our skills and worked with our hands and we were encouraged to muck around with the footy over the Christmas break. There is no doubt that Sheeds was the first with that kind of thinking.

After Year 11 at school I had chosen to move into the work force rather than complete Year 12 studies, and I had looked at a job with Ansett as an electrical technician, and also considered a plumbing apprenticeship with the Gas and Fuel Corporation. In the end I chose an electrical apprenticeship, based just a few minutes from home. By then, I also had an inkling that I could make some sort of living from the footy. The combination seemed okay to me.

I had started my apprenticeship as a sparky in the same year that I began in the Under 19s at Essendon, and had to fit footy around the job as best I could, just like everyone else. It was awkward for the players, walking the line between the two masters of footy and job. I would sneak off from work at 4.30 p.m. to make training by the five o'clock starting time. The owner of the electrical business that I worked for was not a football person and he was hard on me, although he knew that I needed to get away to training. We might be out on a job with the one truck, and sometimes we were close to finishing the task, but I needed to leave for training, which caused an issue. I would have felt the same if I was in his position.

I did not last beyond four years with my original employer. I thought that he was using me as a tool to help promote his business with my footy profile, yet he would criticise me for not being fully committed to working because I always needed to get away and train with Essendon. Ultimately he wanted me to stay, but I would not. I said, 'No, I'm going, and I want to get on with it.' So I set up Bomber Thompson Electrics, and at 21 was working for myself. That was my style and still is. I have always preferred doing my own thing.

The work came relatively quickly. I started out with a few contacts that became a group, and I only wanted enough work to fill three-quarters of a day, so that I could get away to footy training, although it never turned out like that. The job suited me and business picked up. I would undertake commercial and domestic maintenance and new installations, a cross-section of work that covered me in the event that one aspect might dip suddenly. The big money was in the new housing estates that were popping up on the outskirts of the city – at Werribee, Mill Park, Taylors Lakes, Eltham – and we might wire six houses in a day, move to the next one, jump in the trailer and start drilling.

I won a contract early with Tempo Homes (who were building homes in Mill Park, in the northern suburbs) and then with Stockland (who were developing at Werribee), meaning that I had to step up. I had never wired a home by myself, and they wanted 100 homes done, so it took some courage to take it on, looking back now. I needed help, and I remember thinking, *I can't do this on my own.*

So I tried to persuade my brother, Steven, to leave his job and come into the business with me. He was an electrician, too, newly married, and he was nice and safe and secure, so he did not want to take the risk at first. Eventually, though, I talked him around. I said, 'We'll do it together.' That's how our partnership began, and we started to employ a few people, wiring new homes. It was eight hours' work a day followed by the slog at training under Sheedy, and I can remember always rushing and running late for training. At night, I would go home – I was still living with my parents – eat, sleep and get up and go again. Three days a week I might leave home soon after dawn and not be home until nearly nine o'clock at night.

It was hard, but that was how it was for league footballers back then, and sometimes it kept your sense of perspective, especially when it came to life and death. I saved the life of a workmate once, a guy named Greg Jones. Greg was not meant to be a sparky, as it turned out, because he would touch anything that was live, and he did not learn his lesson from earlier incidents. This particular Friday it was hot, middle of summer, and we were working at Ansett's bus division, a factory full of big welding equipment.

There was not much time left in the day, it was about 4.30 p.m. and Greg always wanted to finish up because he liked to go away for the weekend. Often he had planned a skiing trip. On this occasion we were wiring up the factory and the switchboard was huge, one of those boards where you have to walk in behind it to set the thing up, and you need two people to do the job. Greg had not chosen the right career; he touched a big busbar at the back of the switchboard and his hand locked on to it. A busbar, colloquially known as a buzz bar, is a thick, copper conductor in a switchboard that is made to conduct big amounts of electrical current. It was hot, we were rushing, and bang . . . his hand wrapped around it.

Greg was yelling, and he was choking so badly that his whole body was shuddering, which was like something out of a horror movie. He had about 415 volts going through his body and a lot of flow, like a river of electricity. It's low voltage but big current, and it was going to kill him unless I could get him off that conductor. I also knew that if I touched him, I would cop the shock myself.

Despite the panic, I noticed that he had thick woollen socks on, so I grabbed him around the ankles where I had some protection, and tried to rip him off the busbar, but I could not shift him. Plainly there was not much time to spare, which became obvious when his screaming slowed down and then stopped, although the shuddering did not. I was losing my cool.

Once I could not shift him by force, I raced around to the front of the switchboard to check if I could get through the locked door and shut the main switch off, but I pulled the handle of the door so hard that I broke it off. By this time, Greg was unconscious and while there were other people around, workers from the factory, they were frozen. It was an awful scene.

*What do I do now?* I looked around for something to smash the door to the switchboard and found a sledgehammer, and I was able to hack a small corner out of the door, pop it open so that I could get inside, and flick the main switch off. Greg dropped to the ground like a rag doll and that's when I completely lost it. We dragged him from behind the switchboard and I was screaming out, 'He's dead, he's dead.'

Fortunately, some of the other people who had gathered there told me to relax, one of them gave him mouth-to-mouth resuscitation while I called an ambulance. He spent a couple of days in hospital, but survived. He had spent maybe 20 or 30 seconds hanging on to that conductor, and the medicos told him it was amazing that he had survived.

That was his last day as an electrician. He moved to Albury, went into the motel business, and made some money. About six or seven years ago I went to visit him, and he told me for the first time that he reckons that he had an out-of-life experience; that he was unconscious yet aware of what was happening, floating through the house that he grew up in as a child, seeing his mum and dad watching TV in the lounge room. It was kind of spooky, what he said. 'I'm not making this up,' he said. 'It's real. It's what happened. And I need to tell you that.'

I had a few electric shocks in my life but nothing like that. I quickly learned to be careful and methodical on the job, a bit like the way I played footy.

BOMBERS
MARK THOMPSON
ESSENDON
AUTOGRAPH

BOMBERS
MARK THOMPSON
ESSENDON
25 of 132
SCANLENS

# 3

# THE PERFECTIONIST

## 1984

Essendon footy club was on the rise. Kevin Sheedy's words on grand final night in 1983 must have resonated throughout Essendon in 1984, booming around the flanks and dark corners of Windy Hill. 'I don't want you to enjoy tonight . . . *at all.*' The reality was that Essendon had not been ready to win a flag in 1983. Hawthorn was too physical, too tough around the ball. Colin Robertson knocked out Tim Watson and Essendon had no response.

But in 1984, that changed. Sheedy's harsh and cutting speech was not universally popular, and he has said since that Essendon people were unaccustomed to that kind of approach. He has also said that, had the result been different in 1984, he might have been sacked. But to me, looking from the distance of just outside the team, it probably needed to be said. 'Wipe the smiles off your faces.' Those words kept reverberating in our ears. I think that like so many teams, Essendon needed the acute pain of grand final defeat to drive the club forward.

Sheedy would not allow Essendon to be comfortable with just

making the grand final for the first time in many years. In 1983, the club had been content to get there, as Tim Watson observed in a column for *The Age* some years later when he described the scene in the rooms at the MCG before the grand final: 'I recall laying on the dressing room floor doing stretching exercises. As I tried to concentrate on what we had to do to win, someone walked across the rooms with big buckets of champagne on ice. If that wasn't a needless distraction, I don't know what is.'

The 1984 season was my breakthrough year, and I played 20 senior games. Centreman Leon Baker, who had come off a string of premierships in the WAFL with Swan Districts, had been lured across the Nullarbor. Paul Salmon was still just 19, and like me, had been tried for a few games in 1983, and he became a superstar until he suffered a serious knee injury mid-season. We had quite a new look, with rover Alan Ezard breaking in, and ruckman Justin Madden traded to Carlton. Clever forward Mark Harvey, the local boy with the shock of blond hair, also broke into the side and ended up kicking 28 goals in his debut season. Paul Weston came from Adelaide as a tall defender and the club had picked up Darren 'Daisy' Williams, who had debuted in 1979 then gone to Perth, an excellent on-ball player alongside Leon Baker. Sheedy wanted change; he knew that Essendon needed to be better.

We won the night flag again, and finished on top of the ladder with only four defeats in the regular season, overcoming the loss of Salmon, who had been an overnight sensation. In just his second season, the giant forward-ruck kicked seven, seven and eight goals in the opening three rounds of the season, and he had 63 in 13 rounds. Then Geoff Raines went across Salmon's leg in a smother at Victoria Park and ripped his knee joint open, and he missed the rest of the season.

We lost twice to Hawthorn in the ongoing rivalry that was developing, and played one of the great games in a semi-final against the Hawks, losing by eight points. It was the game where drug squad detectives were asked to take videotape of Hawthorn's huddle at quarter time and three-quarter time, because Sheeds had this paranoia about what kind of substances they were taking – a drug controversy in footy 30 years before its time.

Allan Jeans, a senior policeman by occupation, was none too pleased with the allegation, which turned out to be unfounded. While it made front page news, Hawthorn's players were shown to have been sniffing a mixture of ammonium and eucalyptus, and Essendon issued an apology. That incident coloured the Jeans–Sheedy relationship for years but in a way, it was typical Sheeds, and another example of the animosity that was developing between the two best clubs.

We hated Hawthorn, which had one of the great teams, let's be honest, with Leigh Matthews, a young Dermott Brereton, Chris Mew, Michael Tuck, Robert 'Dipper' DiPierdomenico et al. But we were edging closer to their level all the time, and pretty much everyone knew we were most likely headed for a grand final showdown for the second year in a row.

Essendon was a young team, sometimes called the Baby Bombers in the media, but we also had some experience, and those older guys were hugely important. Watson, Madden, the Danihers, Roger Merrett, Garry Foulds, Shane Heard, Glenn Hawker and Neil Clarke had been around for at least five years by 1984, and three years under Sheedy's style. I have never, ever forgotten how easy it was for us young players to come into that team. They just shepherded young players like me through, brought them along. And they had a reason to play, all of a sudden, and they were hungry.

Sheedy engendered the competitive spirit from his Richmond days, and we would have done anything for him as a group. We had an interesting mix of players: the Horsham/Wimmera group, with guys from our country zone like Merrett, Hawker, Heard, Neagle and Watson; then the Ringwood group, from our metropolitan zone, like Darren 'Daisy' Williams, Neil Clarke, Peter Bradbury, Paul Vander Haar, Salmon, and a bunch of guys from the local area around Essendon, such as Harvey, Madden, Foulds and myself. I was close with Harvey and Hawker, and Neagle; we liked to think of ourselves as the rebels of the group.

I started the 1984 season in the reserves, broke into the seniors for round 6 against Fitzroy, and played in the back pocket for the first time in my life. Two of our smaller defenders in Shane Heard and Neil Clarke were injured, Clarke missing half the season, and we needed someone to play on the small forwards of the opposition. That ended up being me, in a kind of sliding doors moment. I remember playing on Doug Barwick and Leon Harris against Fitzroy, and doing okay in that first game, but it was about finding a home for me in a very good football team.

I never minded playing down the back, even though it was not what I was accustomed to. I ended up playing against all the resting rovers that season, guys like Peter Daicos, Wayne Johnston, Leigh Matthews, Brian Royal, Terry Wallace, Tony Shaw, all great players. The first time I played against the great Matthews was an education, that's for sure, because he was utterly ruthless in a way I had not seen before. I was running away from him with the ball and as I handballed I went to ground – he was behind me and he ran right over me with a foot in the middle of my back!

In that same game, I was front and square, read the footy off the pack, and John Kennedy Jr came and pinned me. I went to ground,

I could not release the ball, and Matthews went whoosh, hit me right in the face. He was a great player, a competitive animal, just as Collingwood's champion Daicos was. I did okay playing against Daicos, the so-called Macedonian Marvel, but what I recall is that he just *never* fumbled. And he had this knack for going to the ball sometimes, and other times he would not, so you would think, *Why aren't you going to the ball?* Then all of a sudden it would pop out. He knew that it was coming out, I reckon!

Even though I had not played in a back pocket before, it was not totally foreign, because in Under 17 footy we had always played on an opponent. I had played maybe 40 games in the reserves with Sheedy at the club, and he had been a back pocket himself, and he taught me quite a bit, just the basics. I remember him saying, 'Stick on your man, son, then find opportunities to get the ball.' Sheeds was never happy for a backline player to just stop his opponent; he wanted us to attack as well, to find the football and distribute.

Hawthorn was doing that under Jeans, as well, setting up attacking moves from the back half, which was relatively new to football. Once we picked it up, Essendon probably did it better than Hawthorn, more systematically, and I can remember switching the footy to the open side, for instance, when kicking across goal was frowned upon. There was an incident that same year in which Graeme Allan, playing for Collingwood, cost the Magpies a game against Footscray by switching the ball and kicking it to Bulldog full-forward Simon Beasley, and it was considered outrageous to kick across goal, going against 100 years of convention. If you watch it on TV, you can hear triple Brownlow medallist Bobby Skilton, gobsmacked, in the commentary: '[Bulldog Jim] Edmond is saying to Allan what a *ridiculous* piece of play it was!' But it was changing, and we might have been the first team to execute the switch to create space, I reckon.

Sheedy used to call me 'The Perfectionist' because I liked to do everything properly, and sometimes he would call me 'The Tradesman with Values', because he liked to put little labels on people. Everything had to be in its box with me, as a player. I used to preserve myself; I was not one to go out and get ten possessions in the last quarter if the game was already sealed because I would already be saving myself for the next weekend.

I was not athletically elite and I was only 177 centimetres tall but I had some speed, and repeat speed, although I hated the 200-metre sprints and the endurance runs. So I slotted into the back pocket and I was happy to play where Essendon needed me without being one of those guys who harboured ideas of doing something better. I was a role-player, and I had found my role.

Mostly I held my ground, but the Hawthorn forward Ken Judge was one guy who troubled me. He stitched me up in the 1984 semi-final against the Hawks, and I lost my front tooth that day as well, courtesy of Dermott Brereton. It was just an in-play incident, nothing sinister, but I had a dirty day in my first big final, and I thought that I might be dropped for the preliminary final. Fortunately Essendon retained me in the side against Collingwood for that game, we smashed the Magpies and I played well, having 26 touches. So I had a good idea that I would hold my place for the grand final against the Hawks, who were sitting back and waiting for us as we wrestled with Collingwood out at Waverley.

It would be my first VFL grand final in Essendon senior colours, and it was quite a tough week, something I had never experienced in terms of distractions. In those days, Essendon would pick its team on Thursday night, announce it to the players, and we would have a dinner and hang out for a while, but we had to wait a long time for this team and it turned out that, as ever, there was a heartbreak story for grand final week. Tony Buhagiar missed out on selection while Frank Dunell came into the team. 'Budgie' had 23 disposals and a goal in the preliminary final, but it was not enough to win a place, and he moved to Footscray, never to play in the red and black again.

One story that is not well known is that I could easily have missed playing in that grand final. On the Thursday night before the final we had arranged to train at the MCG, rather than our usual Windy Hill, and my car broke down on the way there. I was driving on the Tullamarine Freeway into town when it gave up the ghost, and I had to let it roll up the Moreland Road exit ramp and leave it there. The obvious option was to catch a cab, but it was getting toward peak hour, and I could not get through to the taxi companies. A guy ended up picking me up from a phone booth at the side of the road, an Essendon supporter who recognised me. I said, 'Get me to the MCG as quickly as possible'. By this time I was running terribly late, and that guy knew the gravity of the situation. He drove through red lights, he broke land speed records, he did it all, and I finally made it on time.

That supporter saved my game in the grand final and possibly my career, because I was 20, and I doubt that Sheedy would have accepted any excuse for being late to training from such a young player. It was not as though I was on the same level as Watson and Madden and Merrett, and I fear Sheeds may have dropped me for the grand final. To round off the story, I ran into the guy who drove me to training quite a few years later at a club function, where he had bought my guernsey in an auction. I recognised him straight away and he knows full well that he played a big role in my career.

I remember being very excited that week, and finding a way to escape from the house a couple of times, because a lot of wellwishers were dropping in to Airport West and telephoning as you would expect. Melbourne in grand final week is a sight to behold but for the players, there is a football game to prepare for. I was terribly nervous the night before the grand final, in particular, because at 20 and in only my 22nd senior game, I was about to play on the biggest stage of all.

On grand final day the veteran Leigh Matthews kicked a goal within 30 seconds and pointed at his opponent, Billy Duckworth, with menace, as though to send a message that Hawthorn had come ready. The Hawks kicked the first four goals, a nightmare start for us, but typical of the way they operated; they liked to smash teams early and usually, they could manage it. This was the day that Sheedy sent a message out to Simon Madden to start a fight, just do anything to change the momentum. Simon, who admits that he cannot fight, belted Ian Paton with a lettuce-leaf punch and was reported, but typically of the day, the distractions did seem to have some effect.

We were 25 points down at half-time of that grand final, but I think we could all sense it turning, even when we were 23 points down at the last change. Sheedy thought that Hawthorn was spent, and he was right. We were running on top of the ground and we had actually had more scoring shots (20 to 18) to that point; it was only inaccuracy that had cost us.

The last quarter is a blur, one of the most exhilarating bursts of footy that you would ever see or be involved with. Sheedy swung players around like a crazy man, notably sending our centre half-back, Paul Weston, to centre half-forward as well as Billy Duckworth, a regular defender, to full-forward, and Terry Daniher, our centre half-forward, into defence. Centreman Leon Baker and Peter Bradbury, who was a knockabout half-back, went forward, too and Daisy Williams went into the middle on Terry Wallace, their great ball-winner.

The Weston shift was the big one; Paul had played in six losing grand finals before that day, five with Glenelg and one with Essendon the year before, and he was not about to let another one slip through his grasp. We just overran Hawthorn that day, and once the momentum changed, it was a tidal wave. It changed right from the first bounce of the final quarter, when Simon Madden popped the ball down to Daisy Williams, who kicked it to full-forward and Leon Baker, that brilliant player, snapped a left-footed goal that set us alight. Peter Bradbury snared the next one, sitting out the back of a marking contest, and still two minutes had not expired.

My moment came midway through the last quarter, when Tim Watson went raging down the wing and hit up Duckworth with a pass, and Billy squared the ball to me at 40 metres out, pretty much straight in front. We were still 11 points behind Hawthorn, so obviously it was important, and I remember that I was about to pass it off when Merv Neagle came running up, yelling, 'GO BACK AND KICK IT!'

Fortunately, I did what I was told, with a little fist pump to celebrate, not too much, but enough to let everyone know that we were on a roll. From the very next centre bounce, Daisy Williams pumped it forward from the middle again and Baker kicked his famous spinning goal to put us in front, beating a fallen Gary Ayres and David O'Halloran in the tackle. Essendon had kicked four goals in eight minutes of footy and we were in front, and unstoppable.

There are some memorable images of those moments: Baker high-stepping and Robert DiPierdomenico hitting Kevin Walsh with an elbow that knocked him senseless and would have earned him a long suspension nowadays; an Essendon trainer abusing Dipper as they carted Kevin off the ground. And Paul Weston, the five-time loser, kicking a left-foot goal and going crazy, with Lou Richards saying on the commentary, 'This premiership is Sheedy's premiership with these tremendous moves he's made.'

And then finally Tim Watson kicked a running goal to seal it, and headed toward the crowd to celebrate. We kicked 9.6 for the quarter, a grand final record for a final quarter, and the premiership belonged to Essendon for the first time since 1965.

Nineteen years is a long time between flags, for Essendon anyway, and the fans were delirious. I remember the dressing rooms being packed, and moving on to the function at a city hotel, but I don't think as a 20-year-old I quite comprehended what it all meant. Yet there were plenty of tears flowing that night, mine included, and the one thing that never leaves you is the excitement of the supporters, the passion that spills out on nights like that. I recall turning up at Windy Hill for a barbecue the next day, having kick-to-kick with some kids, and we had not been to bed at all.

So 1984 was a massive breakthrough for Essendon, which had a great history but a terrible humiliation from the year before to redress. Like every successful club, we had needed to take certain steps along the path before we were ready to claim the ultimate prize, and those steps test your resolve, make you appreciate the opportunities when they come. As for Sheedy, he was on a high, of course, and he enjoyed it as much as anyone, as he told the media, 'I won't be on the planet tonight. I'm an extrovert in a conservative community.' It was classic Kevin, that statement.

We headed off on the footy trip to Los Angeles, San Francisco and Las Vegas, and had some fun. At 20, I had made it a little too early for my own good, perhaps, because I was in a great team and that smoothed the path for a young player like me. I did know that

I could play the game, which is a big step for all players. When you are worried about your place in the team it is difficult to play to your best, whereas an automatically selected player can relax and give himself over to the team. I was working as an apprentice electrician, and I probably had not reached the point where I simply knew that I would be playing at that level, but I was close, and I knew that I had made the right decision to focus on football.

We had a pattern to the way we played at Essendon. The ball would come into the backline, we would get hold of it, sweep it across and we made sure we had people out on the open side. Sheeds was unconventional, and very creative. For example, he wanted the defenders to get the football and make opportunities rather than just defend dourly, and even though I played a lot of my career in a back pocket I averaged 20 possessions. That is what he wanted: two-sided players and people who could play at either end.

He wanted a lot of handball and he would say, 'Go to the ball, always have an extra', which would be the forerunner of what coaches today call 'the outnumber'. He would say, 'Take half-chances.' His voice was so piercing, so intense, it shook you to the soul. I will never forget that voice. He drew a lot of credit for that 1984 premiership and there is no doubt that the positional changes he made and the unpredictable placement of players that he would throw at the opposition were unique at the time. They changed the way that the game was played.

The point is, that thinking took courage to plan and implement, and a lot of people thought he was mad, probably some of his players included! When it did not work, he was savagely criticised by people with a conservative bent. But he was touched with a little genius, I have no doubt; he had been influenced by Graeme

Richmond and the butchery of Richmond's way, but there was a creative side of him that went *beyond* brutality.

We had long team meetings, and Sheeds would be there showing us video clips on the old VHS tapes, fast-forwarding and rewinding to find the right spot in a particular game. It's incredible to think of that now, in this age where players get their own edits delivered by staff, and coaches only have to ask for all the edits of, say, the stoppages in a particular game or from a particular opponent. Sheeds just had the numbers on the little counter on the video recorder scrawled down on a notepad to help him find the right moment in a game.

He had very little of the technology that the modern coaches are afforded to help him, and no full-time assistant coaches at all. He had this great ability to remain optimistic and positive, and it was not his style to barrel you if you messed up while you tried something different on the field, because Sheedy was never afraid to try the unusual and he liked his players to be the same. Importantly, he would back you even if it failed, so long as it was not especially outrageous.

He is a talented man, Kevin. Under pressure, that ability to resist the negative is so important in football clubs, with the public focus upon them and the tendency to overreact. And it is one thing to talk in optimistic tones; it is another to act it out, week after week. Kevin Sheedy could get himself up. That is his strength.

He was a premiership coach in September 1984 at just 36 years of age, and he was about to show that he had plenty more to offer.

# 4

# INVINCIBLE

## 1985

We had a great team at Essendon, well-led, extremely well-coached and thoroughly united with an age and experience mix that was perfect. In 1984 we had challenged Hawthorn a few times, fallen, then ultimately broken the jinx on the last day in September, and by 1985, we just *knew*. Like all the great teams, we just *knew*.

We went with largely the same side with the exception that Paul Salmon returned from his knee surgery late in the season, adding some further firepower. In the home-and-away rounds we beat Hawthorn twice, and the margin kept growing until we smacked the Hawks by 40 in a semi-final. The pendulum had swung right across in our favour.

Of course, we would end up playing them in the grand final again, for the third year in a row, but it was a different Essendon; a more confident Essendon. We had matured and we had only lost three games for the whole 1985 season. We had appropriated something of Hawthorn's self-belief, that knowledge that in all situations, the opponent can be reeled in. Stephen Carey, who had missed 1984, came into the team along with Tony Elshaug, Bryan Wood and Salmon. Merv Neagle, who was injured, Shane Heard and Frank Dunell all missed out.

The 1985 Grand Final featured one of the biggest brawls in league history, out on the wing under the Southern Stand. Hawthorn, I have since read, had vowed at their team meeting on the Thursday beforehand that they would not be physically intimidated, but it was not as though the brawl itself was premeditated. It started with a minor wrestle between Michael McCarthy and Leon Baker, but that turned out to be the trigger release.

Others came charging in, and there were some hard men in there: DiPierdomenico, Matthews, Brereton, Duckworth, Merrett. I was more than happy to dance around the outside, looking like I had something to offer! I had a wrestle with Richard Loveridge and got rid of him, and I think I planted myself in between Hawker and Gary Ayres, who were fighting on the ground. I was thinking, *Who's gonna hit me?* I remember Brereton putting his knee into Kevin Walsh's back, and Matthews coming in hard. Paul Vander Haar was in amongst it, too, and he could throw punches when he was serious. Fortunately I don't think anyone was seriously hurt, but it was quite a scene.

It was hatred, between the clubs, I have no doubt. We never socialised with Hawthorn players in that period; we played in three consecutive grand finals and while there was respect, we were not friends. I can remember much later going to Miami at the end of 1989 for a game against Hawthorn, a promotional venture for football in the United States played at a gridiron stadium, and it ended up in fighting. They had just won the grand final that year, and we played just to beat the hell out of them. Kevin Egan, our football manager, even had a blue with John Hook, Hawthorn's equivalent, in the race. I can remember Hookey yelling, 'It's only an exhibition.'

And we were saying, 'Stop whinging, Hookey! We're here to kick the shit out of you!'

As a club, we had challenged their physical superiority, and they did not like it. And that was what it was always like except that on grand final day in 1985, when Hawthorn had nothing more to give once the fighting stopped. We took a bit more than a half to get on top, but once the dam walls burst it was a biblical flood. We kicked 11 goals in the last quarter this time, beating our record nine from the year before, and 26.14 (170) to 14.8 (92) for the day, winning by 78 points in what was Leigh Matthews' final game. Can you imagine those kind of scores in modern footy? Dermott Brereton kicked eight goals for Hawthorn in a losing team, a mighty effort, but we had the spread of scoring options that Sheeds loved: Salmon kicked six in his first premiership win, Merrett five and Harvey four.

Kevin Sheedy was more an offensive coach, and we kicked some big scores, cricket scores. Eight times we topped 150 points that season, and the range of options was impressive. Harvey kicked 48 goals, Vander Haar and Merrett 46 and Terry Daniher 41, and we averaged 19 goals a game, because Sheeds took the view that 'if they kick 12, we'll kick 14'. He did like accountability; it was not as though he wanted us to allow our opponents too much space, and he did focus on the opposition, but he was happy to let the game open up.

Of course that is easy to do when you have the horses, so to speak. We were like Geelong in 2008, boasting that feeling of invincibility that you rarely get in sport. That year, we were trying to become only the fourth Essendon team ever to go back-to-back with flags, matching the team that won the 1949–50 premierships under the legendary Dick Reynolds, arguably the best Essendon teams in history. The thought of losing was never even an issue, though, for us in 1985. We finished three games clear on top of the ladder, and we *knew* that the flag was there for the taking. Plus, the older players had spent too many years waiting for the opportunities, and they wanted more; they were hungry.

Men like Tim, who was outstanding again in that grand final, and Leon Baker (28 disposals) and 'Nobby' Clarke (24) and Simon Madden were not about to miss their opportunities after waiting so long. I can remember Hawthorn playing Chris Langford (who would become an all-time great full-back) and Michael McCarthy in the ruck, and Simon giving them a clinic in ruck play on his way to the Norm Smith Medal. I also remember Allan Jeans saying that if he could transplant Simon into the Hawthorn team that day, the Hawks would have won, which is a good way of explaining exactly how good a player Simon was.

I played as a midfielder quite a bit that season as well as in defence, and kicked 14 goals, and while we had some specific role-players, like Shane Heard, I would fill a role, too, if required. When an opponent needed to be taken care of, I would go and take that assignment, close him down, and I felt much more comfortable in the finals having had the experience of the season before. I had 26 disposals and two goals in the semi-final against Hawthorn, and 20 plus a goal in the grand final triumph.

Our team was awesome, looking back. Our average age was 25, which was pretty much standard, with Bryan Wood at 31 our oldest player, and it was only Harvey and Salmon, both 20, and myself at 21 who could be considered young in football terms. We had great leadership with Terry Daniher, who I rate in the top three teammates I played with, alongside Simon Madden and Tim Watson. Terry was a fabulous centre half-forward but he was an even better captain, a natural leader who had taken the mantle from his brother Neale when the latter kept breaking down with knee injuries in the early 1980s.

Terry was a meat-and-potatoes footballer fundamentally, but he became a better player through hard work. He just made sure he was fitter than everyone, he would wear out two or three opponents, and he would tell them all about it. 'Come on, son, I'm goin' again,' he would say to them. 'You'd better be ready for it!'

In many ways, he was ahead of his time with his aerobic fitness and willingness to run people off their legs, but in other ways, he was a throwback to another era. For instance, you could never keep up with Terry if you went drinking with him. He might go to the doctor for some treatment on a Sunday afternoon and then he would be off for a drink after that, then get up at 6 a.m. for a run the next day, that was his modus operandi. He was an absolute star, and without him, I don't know if we could have won those two flags.

Terry set the pace for us, he pushed us harder and harder again, made us become more consistent. He was the guy who drove the standards, I think, just with his actions both on the track and in games, although I cannot in all honesty say that it was so much through his words, because he talked some drivel at times! He was not there for motivational speeches, although he would try, of course, making it up as he went along and hoping that he could pull it off: 'Fuckin' get in there, don't you stop runnin', don't you stop workin'.'

But it was his body language that brought you with him, kept you motoring ahead. He was always chipper, always positive – like Sheedy – forever up and about, and if you were struggling as a player, like so many people do at times, he would bring you up with him. He would give that player some attention, and he might say, 'Come on, let's do something about this!'

In the end, it is just plain optimism, and that sort of attitude is gold around a football club. You follow your leaders, and follow your influences, and if you have negative influences and pessimistic people, that bleeds through a club as well. Terry kept us together, he was a great captain. He would say, 'Straight to the pub!' And away we would go. We were close at Essendon, the closest team I played in.

Essendon had also become ruthless during this time, and Roger Merrett was a big part of that. Don Scott, the former Hawthorn captain, had written a story in *The Sun* calling Roger 'the Hit Man', and it hurt him, I know, but it was accurate as well. Sheedy would send us out to target opposition players, not necessarily to belt them, but if they got to the ball, we would go hard at them and hurt them. The only time I ever remember Sheeds going across the line in that sense related to Craig Bradley, the great Carlton midfielder, and that was because Bradley had signed with Essendon, then defected to Carlton, and Sheeds thought he had double-dipped on us. In any case, we could not get near Bradley!

There was a lot of talent in that team and great bravery too. Mark Harvey was dangerous, reckless, fearless, exactly who he was as a person with his boofhead blond hair. That's Harves, he was quite stupid sometimes in the way he put himself at risk, but he had everyone's respect because of his courage, and he was just exciting to be around.

He actually had no fear, Mark Harvey, which is unusual even in a hard sport like football. I had some myself, but that is not a bad thing at all, and that is common in most players. Later in his career he had injury problems; his bones were soft, so he broke a few with the crazy-brave way he went at the ball. Sheedy eventually had to shift him to centre half-back to let him run straight at the ball and protect his body a little.

Merv Neagle, one of my favourites, was pretty fearless. Paul Vander Haar didn't have much concern for his body either, the way he ran and jumped at the footy. 'Vanda' was an amazing aerialist and he played hard off the field as well, too hard, I guess. He had a huge amount of natural ability, he was big and a great kick. At 192 centimetres with a great leap, he was quite a presence as a tall marking player, and when you threw in Simon Madden, Roger Merrett and Paul Salmon, we had seriously dangerous marking targets up forward.

Off the field Vanda was a lad, he enjoyed that side of life. He was the head of the Rat Pack, of which I was considered to be a member, but he actually took it too far. Could he have been better with a more professional attitude and a little less drinking? Yes, probably, but he behaved like that for a reason, obviously. I can remember that he would get off the grog at times, he would try to do the right thing for a while and then his form would dip and he would say that he needed to be himself. It was the mindset that he had. Maybe he did not have confidence in himself as a player, but I think he was underrated if anything, a superstar player.

They were the times, in terms of off-field behaviour, because we were only semi-professional players. We worked hard on the track and played hard in the games, but most of us liked a drink and we often went to pubs. Saturday night was the drinking night, because we mainly played Saturday afternoons. Once, Sheedy had organised a pre-season training camp at Cerberus naval base down on the Mornington Peninsula, but Vanda, Billy Duckworth and Glenn Hawker indulged themselves in a pub crawl along the way and turned up late, so the squad voted to send them home.

Quite a few of us smoked cigarettes, hard as that seems to believe. I reckon there were about 15 of us in the premiership teams of 1984 and 1985 who would have a smoke, including me. It is a source of amusement nowadays. A few years ago Kevin Sheedy sent me a book he had written about great coaches, including the premierships that he had been involved in, adding a note: 'You'll enjoy that.' Flicking a few pages in, I saw what he was talking about: it was a double-page photo of the milling Essendon players after the flag on the MCG in 1985, taken from up high, and out the side of the pack is me, puffing on a gaffer! Needless to say, it would never happen today.

Talent covers a lot of inadequate preparation. In particular, guys like Tim Watson and Simon Madden were at the height of their careers. Tim turned 24 in 1985, and had been at Essendon for nine seasons. He was an amazing talent from the get-go. When he debuted in 1977, Tim was 15 years and 305 days old, and still at Essendon High School, having moved from the little town of Dimboola in the Wimmera. He was the fourth-youngest person to play a senior game in league history, the top three being from decades earlier.

So in 1985, Tim was a kind of veteran. He had amazing power in the legs especially over the first 15 metres; he could burst away from packs and stoppages and contests, a bit like you would see Chris Judd or Patrick Dangerfield do much later, and that is not common among players. Tim did not spend his days and hours with the team, he was not part of the gang or the Rat Pack or out drinking with Terry, but wow, he could play, and in the mid-80s he was at his crescendo, just unstoppable.

Essendon was innovative in those days, thanks to Sheedy, and to my knowledge, we were the first to employ the services of a sports psychologist of any sort, in the form of the big West Indian Rudi Webster. Looking back on that, it is quite unbelievable because a lot of people thought that kind of stuff was nerdy, but in fact, it worked really well for us. Rudi was not actually a sports psychologist at all, he was a radiologist from the island of Barbados! But I liked him and I did use him, as many of us did.

Rudi had come to Australia to work with the West Indian cricket team in the days of Kerry Packer's World Series Cricket, the late-1970s, and he remained in the country, eventually picking up work with Essendon as footy moved to get the best out of its people. The players who liked to talk to him would travel out to his house in Toorak, and he had his lounge room set up for a chat. Nobody was forced to go, and it was not serious psychology like you would see in football clubs today.

He used to do a form of hypnosis or meditation where he would ask you to count backwards from 100 or look at a spot on the wall, and you would drop into this state of selflessness. Rudi would say, 'I think we're going to play well. Kevin wants you to play like this, he wants you to make sure you do that, if your teammate does this make sure you pick him up.'

Rudi gave us some notes before the 1985 Grand Final, which began:

> The 1985 grand final can be considered as the deciding set in a three game match. The score at the moment is Essendon 1 (1984) and Hawthorn 1 (1983). The final set is a great challenge and if you win it, you will establish yourself as the better team.
>
> Victory will be influenced by:
>
> a/ Your CONCENTRATION – how well you focus and lock in your attention to your BASIC skills. The greater the impulse to ignore the basics, the greater is the need to concentrate on them. THE BASICS make up 90 per cent of your game. You will run into trouble the moment you IGNORE them or

EXECUTE them poorly. Distractions during the game can be used as signals to refocus your concentration to the job at hand.

b/ Your AGGRESSION at the BALL

c/ Your PATIENCE and PERSISTENCE. Never give in.

They were Sheedy's words coming out of Rudi's mouth, but all in a positive way, as I recall, and he would say, 'I know we're going to have a good day.' He would tell us what to say to ourselves if things were not working out, and I found it to be valuable. Rudi was a champion fellow, and really, it was another way in which Essendon jumped ahead of the pack.

Looking back, we were lucky that Hawthorn fell away in 1984 and 1985, because they were a great club. If Hawthorn had beaten Essendon in 1984, that would have been two flags in a row for the Hawks, and Sheedy might well have said, 'We're never going to win one with these blokes.'

That is how huge it was for Essendon, and for Sheedy. He was different to say the least, Kevin. I think that he drew pictures in his mind, a bit like a cartoonist would do, and there was so much happening inside his head all the time, because he was a sponge for information.

Sheeds would talk to anyone and everyone and he never stopped looking for *the edge*. But can you imagine if those radical moves he made in the 1984 Grand Final had failed? He would have been savaged in the public arena. We had already lost in 1983, and that would have been two consecutive defeats. Critics would have said, 'He has turned the team upside down and failed. What's he doing?' He could have been sacked then and there, but he ended up staying at Essendon, for a mere 27 years!

As for me, I had won the flag with Essendon's reserves in 1983, then two straight senior premierships, plus a night flag in 1984, making it four flags in three profitable years. I just thought that was what football was about, a little like Joel Selwood must have felt after he started at Geelong, winning three premierships in his first five seasons. But of course, the game has a way of coming back to bite you, as I was about to find out.

In the media, Essendon was being feted as one of the great teams. People talked about us having a dynasty in place, and the legendary Dick Reynolds went on record saying that this was 'the best Essendon side ever'. Alf Brown, the longtime *Herald* chief football writer, rated our team above the great 1950 Essendon line-up. It was all set up for a prolonged period of success, maybe a hat-trick of flags to start with. But how wrong could we all be?

NUBRIK
BRIK
NUBR
NUBRIK

# 5

# FALL AND RISE

## 1986–1990

Kevin Sheedy used to say that even premiership teams needed to improve a few per cent to keep pace with the game the following season, and the opening months of the 1986 season reflected that thinking. Essendon moved two popular players on – Stephen 'Stan' Carey and Peter Bradbury – who had been premiership men. It was not unusual to see league players having to find a new home, but the playing group struggled to see the need for such dramatic change, particularly when Sheedy had chosen to bring in Michael Richardson and Geoff Raines from Collingwood on good money as replacements.

Carey was the main fundraiser for our end-of-season trips away, and Bradbury was a salt-of-the-earth character, so the closeness that we had experienced in the previous two years went out the door with them. Carey, a tough backman from Tasmania, was only 26, and he was traded to Geelong after playing one senior game in round 6 of 1986. By round 8 he was a Cat, as shifting players during the season was allowed back then, but he only played seven more VFL games.

The same cruel cut happened to Bradbury, who had kicked one of the tidal wave goals in the last quarter of the 1984 Grand Final. In 1986 he played one game for the Dons in round 4, then by round 8, he was a Collingwood player. It was brutal and the players did not like it at all; it was an introduction to the modern game, in a sense, and confirmation that ultimately, Sheedy did not see Carey and Bradbury as top-line players.

Richardson and Raines never settled at Essendon; the players perceived them as being selfish. Raines had been a fabulous centreman in Richmond's 1980 premiership team, when Sheedy was an assistant under Tony Jewell's coaching, and Sheeds was an unabashed admirer. Raines had already been traded on from Richmond to Collingwood before he arrived at Essendon. Trading was the new way of footy, but at Essendon the players took a dim view of it.

Raines was not embraced, particularly by our fans, and it rubbed off on the rest of us. He lasted one season before he moved on again, this time to the new Brisbane Bears club. As for Richardson, he was a classy finisher who had actually played for Collingwood *against* Essendon in round 1 of 1986, then played *for* Essendon against Collingwood in round 12. He was gone by the end of that first season, also to the Brisbane Bears.

These were unsettled times for the game and the turmoil seemed to have an impact on Essendon. A lot of the clubs had financial trouble and in the background, the league wanted to go national as some kind of solution, having already shipped the old South Melbourne club out and rebranded it as the Sydney Swans and seen some success with that venture; the Swans were drawing crowds and had made an unsuccessful bid to lure Sheedy away from Essendon at the end of 1985.

The first national draft would happen later that year, and the salary cap was not far away, equalisation measures meant to help the likes of Fitzroy, which despite having a strong team, had talked about moving to Queensland. The VFL had already decided it would go national from 1987 with the inclusion of the Bears and the West Coast Eagles, who paid $4 million in licence fees for the privilege. John Elliott, as president of Carlton, had started the rumblings by attempting to form a breakaway national league a couple of years earlier, and with half the clubs technically bankrupt, it was clear that something had to give.

Essendon was caught up in all this in 1986. In the days after the second premiership was won in 1985, the Swans made their lucrative pitch to Kevin Sheedy to join them as coach. Simon Madden was on their target list at half a million dollars a year, too, and I can remember Simon the schoolteacher saying that the Swans offered him a school! I am not sure if he was joking. Both Sheeds and Simon rejected those overtures but in the following seasons, we would lose more valuable players and people as the new clubs sought talent. It would not be the only time in my football life that the expansion of the competition would cause me grief.

Ultimately, 1986 was a disaster as a premiership defence, from the angst over Carey and Bradbury's departures, to Tim Watson breaking down with the first long-term injury of his career, a knee issue, and Vander Haar breaking his leg. We went 12–10 and made the finals by the skin of our teeth. Out at Waverley in the dying seconds of the elimination final, Fitzroy's Mick Conlan found himself in the wide open spaces to kick the matchwinning goal and end our season.

Michael Thomson had been tagging Conlan really well all day, but when he lost contact, Conlan needed no invitation to bury us. A couple of weeks on, Hawthorn won another premiership, against the grain of what everyone felt at the end of 1985 when we had smashed them. The Hawks had shown great resilience and cleverly topped up their list to win that flag.

It turned for the worse for us. Essendon missed the finals in both 1987 and 1988, for the first time in Sheedy's reign, and injuries and turbulence bit hard. President Greg Sewell was replaced by Ron Evans, the former champion player, and general manager Barry Capuano left to join the league administration, replaced by Roger Hampson.

In 1987 I won my first club best and fairest award, the Crichton Medal, but the team only won nine games. Mark Harvey played just the one game, Tim Watson (who broke a leg) played seven and Vanda played eight. We only had two players on the list who made it for every game that year. Mark Harvey broke a leg three times, and when he suffered from weight problems in his comeback, succumbed to bulimia, the terrible eating disorder. Sheeds wanted low body fat and he was pushing us in that area, and Harves was a victim of trying to please the coach. Not even the locks on his refrigerator could stop him from eating, then regurgitating the food.

The injury curse was well and truly upon us. In 1988 I missed the whole season with a right knee injury that I suffered in a pre-season match at Windy Hill, the worst injury of my career. I was tackled from behind, and the knee just buckled, I needed a full reconstruction and I had to look on as we missed the finals and the resurgent Hawthorn won the flag. *Again.*

Sheeds lost the plot to an extent around this time. He was trying to force the issue but it would not work for him, trying things that failed, and recruiting guys who ended up playing 30 or 40 games but not quite making it. He was looking to extract another premiership tilt out of the 1984–85 list with some tinkering around the edges, but it is easy to forget that his position was under threat, a fact he has acknowledged himself.

Steven Clark and forward Bradley Plain are two of the kinds of players that I am talking about here. Clark, a rover, stayed for five years and 53 games before shifting to Melbourne, and Plain, a sharpshooter around goals from Tasmania, did six years without conspicuous success and ended up at Collingwood.

Sheedy was not at his best, and I did not think he handled the inevitable retirements that were coming all that well. At the end of 1988, Terry Daniher stepped down as captain and Tim Watson was appointed as our skipper from 1989. Terry did not want to step down, and none of the players who were approaching the end of their careers – Terry, Garry Foulds, Simon Madden, Vander Haar – were keen to move on. Garry was afforded the right to play his 300th game, but was dropped after that, and he hated it, and carried it for a while. My observation was that Sheeds did not know how to handle the ageing of a cluster of his stars from the two flags. I would learn, much later, how difficult this can be for a coach with the slow demise of players who have achieved so much under his watch.

As for Roger Merrett, he took up an offer to captain Brisbane Bears from 1988, a decision that devastated Essendon, quite frankly. It broke the spirit of the club when we lost Roger to the Bears and Merv Neagle, who had gone to Sydney at the end of 1985. The club was almost disrespectful of the players, I thought, in particular with Roger, who reportedly was offered the same money as his previous contract. We needed to fight to keep Roger; he was too valuable to let go, but Essendon is a conservative club, that is the DNA of the place. Barry Capuano, the general manager, was a hall-of-famer and a 1962 premiership player and he did so much good for Essendon, but he was also a traditional Essendon person, and he didn't like spending money. I think it cost the club, big-time.

Sheedy was also under pressure to keep his job after eight years at the helm. 'I knew that a view was forming that my time had come to an end at Essendon,' he wrote in his book *Sheeds: A Touch of Cunning*. 'I knew that in 1988 there were lots of discussions about my future. In the end, I believe that Brian Donohoe (chairman of selectors) and Neville Gay (a director) went to Ron Evans and said, "We have to keep this person."' Sheeds survived, of course; he was the greatest of survivors.

Tim Watson was a very different captain to Terry, although he was primed and ready to go, still only 27 and a champion of the game. He had come through a period of injury trouble and he played wonderful footy in 1989, as we made something of a resurgence, back into the finals. We were building again. Terry Daniher had been Essendon through and through, and he fostered that culture of 'Get off your arse and get into it.' That attitude kept resonating in his years as captain, whereas Tim was a thinker, he was smarter, more strategic, and more private. Terry was very public and if anyone was going to the pub, he was going with them, but Tim was not like that.

Tim won the Crichton Medal that year, but he was not quite in the league of Terry as a leader. Tim and I remain close, so I can say that he did not take people with him. He led by example. He was a good ambassador for the *club*, but Terry was a great captain for the *team*. Much later I realised there are different kinds of good captains, and that Gary Ablett Jr was like Tim, in the sense that he was feverish about getting himself right. Tim was not selfish in any way, but his method of leading was to get himself right and play great footy himself. That is exactly right, but some people see it as selfishness. It is not.

Almost inevitably, we crossed Hawthorn in a semi-final, the rivalry still bubbling because those three grand final clashes were still etched in the memory, and Dermott Brereton ironed out Vanda at Waverley Park. I can remember Vanda getting reported for hitting Greg Dear a few minutes after that collision, and then going to the tribunal and winning a reprieve because he said he had no memory of the incident. But Hawthorn smashed us in that game.

We had some new players by that season, the likes of Gary O'Donnell, Paul Hamilton, Anthony Daniher, Greg Anderson and Michael Long, and I was back up and playing after my knee reconstruction. It all came to a crashing end at the hand of Gary Ablett Sr and Geelong in the preliminary final, the great man kicking eight goals, and then Hawthorn went back-to-back in one of the most famous grand finals. We had to hand it to the Hawks, who by this time had played seven consecutive grand finals and won four of the past six flags. They were too good for Essendon, a better club than Essendon, unfortunately.

I put it down to the influence of John Kennedy Sr at that club when he was coach, and I think it still resonates today at Hawthorn. I've met him, he's a lovely man, an incredible man, so down to earth and just a beautiful man, and he left an enormous legacy at Hawthorn. He had a big voice, and he was ruthless. I remember hearing him saying something like, 'If we're playing a team and we're better than them, I would want to play and win by the amount we *should* win by. If we're playing the bottom team and we're 10 goals up at three-quarter time, they would expect to be beaten by 14 goals! So if we don't beat them by 14 goals . . .' He felt that if you played an inferior team, you were not showing them any respect if you did not beat them by the appropriate margin. He was about setting standards and not deviating, and I really admired him.

In 1990, the first year of the newly-named Australian Football League, it was Hawthorn's turn to hit the downturn. At Essendon, we had already seen our fall and rise, and now with a new-look team, we were back as a force. Really, we should have won the premiership; it was only a quirk of the finals draw that stopped us.

We won 17 games that season and finished on top of the ladder. I had one of my best years, eventually winning the Crichton Medal for the second time. But in those days, the top team had the first week of finals off, which seemed like a great advantage for us at the time. We had rounded out the regular season with a win over St Kilda, a game in which Sheedy took the opportunity to rest some senior players so that he could play all four of the Daniher brothers in the one team – Terry, Neale, Anthony and Chris – which was a first. Neale was retiring after an injury-plagued career, so this would be the last chance. It was a nice touch by Sheeds, one that was recorded for posterity.

On 8 September 1990, we travelled to Waverley as a team to watch West Coast play Collingwood in a qualifying final. The Eagles had finished third in their fourth season in the competition under Mick Malthouse, and they were a coming force. What happened next could not have been scripted.

Even though it was a close game – good for us – we wanted to leave a bit early to beat the crowd and get on the bus to find our way out of Waverley's always-choked car park. We heard that Peter Sumich, the Eagles' full-forward, had a shot at goal to win the game. Sumich, who would later become a century goalkicker, had marked in the forward pocket near the behind post, with less than 30 seconds on the game clock and Collingwood in front by a single point. The siren sounded as we filed out of the ground and I think someone heard it on a radio: 'He's missed.'

Sumich's shot had slid across the face for a behind, and the game had been drawn. All of which meant that West Coast and Collingwood would need to replay that qualifying final in a week's time and given that we were drawn to play the winner in a second semi-final, we would have to wait another week to learn who our opponent would be. It was a disaster for us; we lost all the momentum from the home-and-away games. I remember the feeling at the time, *Oh, no!*

By the time Collingwood won the replay in the second week of finals so that we would face the Magpies in a semi-final, it was 23 September, a full 15 days since our previous game of footy against St Kilda. For some of the guys who had been rested from round 22, it was even longer than that, and it felt like a whole month of inactivity. Needless to say, this was not ideal for footballers, who are programmed in a certain way, and to play regular games. But it is also worth acknowledging that we underperformed in those last few weeks.

Collingwood had a good team with Tony Shaw, Peter Daicos, Darren Millane, Gavin Brown, some terrific players, and the Magpies beat us in the semi-final, which put us further on to the back foot, pinching the momentum. We found our way through a 10-goal preliminary final win over the Eagles to reach the grand final, with me playing on Chris Lewis, a brilliant player with wild eyes, and keeping him in check. We were headed back to a grand final for the first time since 1985, but Collingwood was waiting for us and the Magpies had Leigh Matthews, our old rival from his Hawthorn days, in charge as coach, his first assignment as a head coach after taking over from the legendary Bob Rose.

It was a dreadful day, that 1990 Grand Final. I had broken a toe on my right foot during the finals, and was on painkilling jabs to play, and I performed badly, as did the team. I had to get my toe injected beforehand, and the doctors said that the effect would last until half-time, but the reality was that I could feel the pain about 10 minutes into the first quarter. I could not run, which was less than ideal.

Just on quarter time there was an enormous brawl which went into the annals of the game, a fight that included some of the club staff as well. I was at the other end of the ground and not involved, but I know that Gavin Brown, one of Collingwood's stars, hit Kieran Sporn, our utility player. Terry Daniher and Brown were playing on each other, and as they were running up to join the fray, Brown accelerated and smashed Sporn from behind. Kieran did not see it coming, he had 17 stitches in his head from the blow. Terry saw it happen, and he clocked Brown as retaliation.

Sporn was later suspended for striking Denis Banks, which may well have been the spark that lit the fire, with Sporn telling the *Herald Sun* a few years later that he had hit Banks. 'Banks gave me a bit and I went back at him. That's when Gavin Brown came in and got me, and Terry [Daniher] was coming in to support me.' As for Brown, he was knocked unconscious, and as the brawl cleared, he was laying on the ground with the Collingwood trainers. He copped a three-week suspension for hitting Sporn with what I thought was a bad act; it is true that Terry hit Brown as a response, but at least it was not from behind.

As the officials came on the field for the quarter-time huddle, Graeme Allan, the Collingwood football manager, had hit Peter Power, our runner, and Essendon's bootstudder, Graham Mendola, landed one on Allan. Eddie Hillgrove, the Collingwood team manager, became involved and so did John Synan, the Essendon doorman. My understanding is that Kevin Sheedy was heavily involved, too, and that Synan took the rap for Sheeds, at least that was the rumour! It was an untidy scene and the ramifications continued.

At half-time, Leigh Matthews made his way down on to the field to go up the race, and I was walking right near Leigh when he made his famous gesture to Daniher, grabbing Brown (who had returned to play) by the arm, and screaming, 'We'll get you, Daniher.' Collingwood just kept getting further ahead; we only kicked five goals for the whole day. Tim Watson, who was captain, wrote later, 'At times like this, you only feel contempt for the game.' It's true, too. This one hurt a lot.

There was the memorable scene at the end when Tim embraced Tony Shaw, who won the Norm Smith Medal and who led Collingwood magnificently on the day. Tim has spoken since about his admiration for Shaw, and I share it. He led like Terry Daniher would lead, dragging his men along with him.

The two-week break killed us, I have no doubt, and Sheeds erred in training us too hard toward the end, I guess because of the gaps in our preparation. But at that stage of the year we needed to keep our minds fresh, and our skills sharp. It is a draining year and when your body stops, like ours did over the first two weeks of the finals, it shuts down. It's like when you work really hard for a period then reach an endpoint, and you get ill. I know that I do. We had dead legs on grand final day because our bodies had already shut down. We could not run, and we ended up on the wrong side of history, as Collingwood celebrated the breaking of a 32-year premiership drought.

It was not exactly what we had planned for.

# 6

# LIFTING THE CUP

## 1991–1993

They don't hand out redemption tickets spontaneously in sport. All of us at Essendon were stung by the failure to complete the business in 1990, but the opportunities to atone would not come immediately. In 1991, we limped into the finals and went straight out at the hand of Melbourne, and I only played nine games for the season after breaking my arm. At the end of that disappointing season, Tim Watson decided to retire. He was cooked; he had played 15 straight years from his teens, and his body had taken a hammering as well as his mind. This left the captaincy vacant, and as vice-captain, I was asked to step up.

I don't remember there being much question about my elevation to the captaincy. It came naturally, and I guess that I had known for a while that it would happen. I was 28, I'd played 128 games including two premierships, I wanted to do it, Kevin Sheedy liked my style, and there was nobody else at the club who was a more obvious successor to Tim.

I was more of a Terry Daniher-style captain, although not in the sense that I would have everyone down at the pub drinking beers. I was about process, and hard work: 'Train well, do everything right, so that we *play* well.' I was a methodical player and that was me as the captain.

I looked at numbers to see who was going to win the ball. If I won it myself, I usually knew what I was going to do with the football, even before I got it. It was more about the brain for me, rather than the physical, although I was one of the quicker players on the list. We had a 20-metre time trial around that time and Glenn Manton recorded the best time (2.842), but my 2.867 seconds was up in the top handful.

Our list was evolving. In particular, Sheedy had begun his famous push to recruit more Indigenous players, something that would change not only Essendon but the game itself. The competition had been through a period of a few years where there was resistance to recruiting Indigenous players. Sheeds' plan started with Michael Long being drafted at the end of 1988, but by 1992 we also had Derek Kickett, who we had picked up in a trade from North Melbourne, and we had drafted Gavin Wanganeen from Port Adelaide. Sheeds could see that these guys would bring speed and dare and bravery to our team, and they did.

In 1992 we won 12 games but missed the finals, and around that time Sheedy decided he would take a risk and play youth. There was a strong sense of evolution that year, with Tim gone, and both Terry Daniher and Simon Madden went at the end of the year. All three ran a lap of honour at Waverley after we lost to Geelong in that final round, because Tim's retirement at the end of 1991 had gone without a proper opportunity to farewell him.

Quietly in the background, Sheedy was scheming. He had blooded a few younger players in 1992, notably a baby-faced James Hird,

Joe Misiti, David Calthorpe and Mark Mercuri, and legend has it that our horrible defeat in round 20 of that season by Hawthorn – a 160-point annihilation by the old enemy – convinced him of what had to be done. The old fox was trapped in a corner, and he is a dangerous man in that situation. Sheedy did what he has always done – he punted. In 1992, Essendon used 42 players, including 20 who played fewer than 10 games, searching for people who could take us forward, knowing that the loss of three greats would leave a gaping hole to fill.

Not everything worked. Sheeds could get things horribly wrong, like most coaches can, and the recruitment of Ben Doolan from Sydney was one example. Doolan came to us in 1993 as part of the new broom, but he did not play a senior game that season despite being paid more than any of us. He had left the Swans after just two years and Collingwood was keen; when Sheedy heard about this, he made sure Essendon swept in to sign Doolan, but the players were not happy, and I remember a bunch of us going into his office after training one night and taking him on about it.

I can also recall Mark Harvey having a lot to say about it, because we did not think that we needed Doolan. There was Sheeds, towelling himself down after having a shower, with his players hammering him. All these years later the irony that I can see is that Ben Doolan became a good Essendon man; he loved the club and tried his best. It was not his fault that the club paid him too much money.

Sheeds sometimes would act on a hunch, or through advice from a network of friends, and it could backfire on him. At some point, the game grew so big that you had to trust other people to make those decisions together, especially with recruiting and list management, but at one point he seemed trapped in the old way, where the coaches still managed the list. Having said that, he did correct the situation when we became the first club to employ full-time assistant coaches in 1992, and people like Neale Daniher, Denis Pagan (who moved to North Melbourne in 1993) and David Wheadon came on board. Ultimately, Essendon innovated under Sheedy.

The 1993 season started with no huge expectations. We had finished eighth in 1992, we had a lot of young players, and the great trio of Watson, Madden and Daniher had gone. We were around 50–1 odds for the premiership, and even the club was intent upon a rebuild of sorts. If we had made the finals we would have been relatively happy that we were on the right track, although Sheedy called it 'the year we are going to change the rules'. I recall him talking to me as captain early in that season, and saying, 'This is what we'll do. We'll play the kids.'

Nobody expected a flag, at least not as we started out, but it clicked for us, and the timing was perfect because it was what you might call a soft year in AFL footy. Hawthorn had gone into its downturn after a mighty era, and Geelong went off the boil, while West Coast, which had won its first flag in 1992, had the dreaded premiership hangover. And in stepped Essendon, the so-called Baby Bombers, ahead of our time, there is no doubt about that, coming out of nowhere.

We had eight wins through round 14, and we had a sniff of the glory. I can remember a night in the social club where we had dinner, and Sheedy came to me again. 'We're a chance,' he said. He was all over us, Sheeds. He was 'on' that year, and looking back, we had a great coaching panel, which helped. Pagan had come across from North Melbourne Under 19s, prior to coaching the Kangaroos at senior level, and he was outstanding. We had Neale Daniher, who had moved into a coaching role since retiring as a player, and who would go on to coach at senior level for a long time afterward, and we had Wheadon, an ideas man who spent a long time coaching at AFL level. Plus we had Danny Corcoran as football manager, a real professional in that role.

I was immediately a Pagan fan. When Denis came in 1992, it was the first time we had a formal game plan. We actually had our rules and game style written down so that we could refer to it, which was a first. I know that a lot of coaches over the years had written down rules and philosophies, but this was a proper game plan for Essendon. Denis is regarded as the first to use that expression 'game plan' that is so commonly used today in the footy world, and to my knowledge that is right.

Denis coached Essendon's reserves to a premiership in 1992, and he loved working with David Wheadon, too. Wheadon was unconventional with his thinking, and he would challenge certain ideas, and it was good for Pagan and Sheedy because even though he was out there on the edge, it gave them good foundations to work off, planted some ideas in their heads. He is a thinker, David, and a talented man. Sheedy and Pagan were from the Hafey way and the Barassi way and he helped bring them into the modern era and entertain different philosophies.

Neale Daniher was smart, and he was a documenter. His playing career had been ruined by knee injuries but pretty soon everyone knew that he had a lot to offer as a coach. He was into his software, and he created the video edits that we had started doing around that time, where you could bring up stoppages, for instance, or kick-ins, to study both what we had done and what the opposition was trying to do. This would prove highly significant at the pivotal point of the season.

The Baby Bombers tag came from the cluster of young boys who became regulars in 1993, players who in some cases would become champions. Dustin Fletcher was 18 and still at Essendon Grammar, and Joe Misiti, who could find the football, was also 18, but both would play most of the season in the seniors, including the finals. Mark Mercuri, beautifully skilled and clever, was 19. James Hird and David Calthorpe, who had played a handful of games the season before, were 20, and so was Ricky Olarenshaw.

In a throwback to the 80s, all of those guys with the exception of Hird had come from the local area and on top of that, both Hird and Fletcher had Essendon bloodlines. Dustin's father, Ken, was a 264-game Essendon wingman; James's father, Allan Junior, had played for the Bombers in the 1960s and his grandfather, Allan Senior, was an even bigger figure in the club who had played more than 100 games in the 1940s before becoming a committeeman, treasurer and president from 1969–75. The Allan T Hird stand at Windy Hill commemorates his contribution to Essendon. Fletcher came at the end of 1992 under the father–son rule and Hird was a bargain basement pick 79 in 1990, one of the best draft selections ever made by any club.

We put a group of senior guys around them – myself at 29, Paul Salmon, Gary O'Donnell and Mark Harvey at 28 – and threw the dice in the air for 1993, while Tim Watson had been coerced into a comeback after taking the 1992 season off. Ironically after his brief retirement he had been drafted by West Coast Eagles for 1992, but he never intended to play with the Eagles, who had flown a kite by using a pick on him. Half a dozen rounds into 1993, though, he grew his hair and came back to have one last crack. He was 32, not old in anyone's language, but he had played a lot of AFL footy.

He has said since that he had played for so long under Sheedy (from 1981 to his first retirement in 1991) that he could not find the necessary motivation to keep playing, but when St Kilda made rumblings about wanting him to play in 1993, Essendon did the right thing and made sure that if he ran out on a field again, it would be in our colours.

It was an even season – just 20 games, a quirk of that particular year – with no standout team, and we finished on top with 13 wins and a draw. The draft and the salary cap appeared to be biting for perhaps the first time after seven years in operation, because the seventh-placed team, Geelong, missed the finals but won only one fewer game (12) than us, the AFL using a final six at the time. Anyone could beat anyone else, so it seemed.

We lost the first final to Carlton, which was the first ever night final, played at the MCG. It was close, but Stephen Kernahan almost beat us by himself with six goals, and we went into elimination games from there. Nobody would have been surprised if we had fallen over, but we sneaked over the top of West Coast, the defending premiers, whom I think Sheedy regarded as the best team just a year after their first premiership.

Then in the preliminary final against Adelaide at the MCG, we were smashed in the early part of the game, and 42 points down at half-time. Adelaide, coached by Graham Cornes, was only in its third season in the competition, but the Crows had a seriously good team. They had Tony Modra, who kicked six goals that day, and Shaun Rehn, the ruckman, and Tony McGuinness and Chris McDermott, veteran on-ballers and hardened players.

Our midfielders were not defending that day. There was no pressure on the ball and down in the backline, the footy just kept coming over the top. I can remember late in the second quarter running into the middle and saying, 'Any chance you fuckers could pick up a man?' Even at half-time, I was yelling at them as we came off the ground. The change rooms were close together, and Mark Bickley, one of their on-ball players, told me years later that he could remember me howling at my teammates.

We should never have beaten them. But just like that, Darren Bewick jumped up and kicked four goals in the third quarter, and we got a run on. Michael Long and Gary O'Donnell tore Adelaide up through the middle, and Paul Salmon ended up kicking four goals. We reduced the margin to two goals at three-quarter time and eclipsed the Crows in the last, the signature moments being Andrew Jarman's miss from close range for the Crows, and Watson's remarkable late second-effort goal that sealed our place in the grand final.

Tim was physically shot, his ankles were no good, and he had not played especially well that day, but he had saved his best for last. After misfiring badly with a left-footed kick from half-forward that travelled about 20 metres off the side of his boot, Tim was so angry that he chased it down himself, pushed his way through a few players, collected the ball and looped it through from 40 metres. He just willed it through, a magic moment for Essendon and one that has been replayed a thousand times since. It was the sealer, and we had won a preliminary final from seven goals down at half-time, one of the greatest finals wins for our club.

Jarman's miss from the top of the square in the third quarter had proved pivotal, a fact he acknowledged years later in an *Adelaide Advertiser* interview:

> That haunts me. I don't have too many bad memories of my football career but that one will sit with me. It was a 15 to 20-metre kick. If I kicked that it would have changed the momentum back to us again. I bloody blew it. I had Mark Thompson ripping in to me after that kick. I can hear his voice now just giving it to me: 'You've cost them the game, you've cost them the game, we're going to win it.'

Legend has it that Adelaide coach Graham Cornes was interrupted at the end of his half-time speech by an ill-timed piece of flatulence from one of his players – Bickley has been accused of it – that might have had an influence. Teammate Matthew Liptak, speaking in the same article, put it this way:

> It was the most ill-timed release of gas. Cornesy was in the most serious mode, trying to get us up for the second half and we're all in the huddle. Musashi was the choice of supplement in those days and that was rumbling in Bicks' stomach for a while. He just let out this stink bomb and not only did it sound like his stomach was falling out but the smell that reached out just changed the demeanour of the half-time break. I don't know if that was the thing that bombed us but it changed the mood in there that's for sure.

It goes down as the fart that changed a preliminary final!

So Essendon had progressed to another grand final, to play Carlton, which presented a few issues, notably Justin Madden's ability in the ruck. Justin had been traded out of our club a few years earlier, because we already had his elder brother Simon, but he was a great tap ruckman, especially around this time, and he was 206 centimetres tall. He also had a terrific connection with Carlton's midfield group, and they did not lack quality in that area: Greg Williams, Craig Bradley, Brett Ratten to start with.

Our ruckman Peter Somerville would have a huge task, but so would Neale Daniher, because it was assistant coach Daniher's job to unlock the Madden hitting pattern, using the video edits of previous Carlton games. Ironically, Paul Salmon could have played ruck, and he was just as big as Madden, but Sheeds preferred to play Salmon up forward. We would end up losing 'Fish' to Hawthorn, where he became a great ruckman, unbelievably good with his tap work.

Then there were questions over selection for the grand final. Dean Wallis, who usually played as a tall defender, was available to play after injury, and Mark Harvey, who had turned into an outstanding centre half-back after beginning his career as a forward, was also expected to return from injury. Harvey would certainly come in if he passed a fitness test; Wallis was at the least an option.

This left Derek Kickett in the gun. It is a sad reality of every grand final that someone who deserves to be there will miss out. It happens every year, with every team, and there are always some tears. Derek was a dynamic player, and we drew great value out of him after he left North Melbourne, playing every game in the 1993 season to that point.

His form had faded in the finals, where Sheeds used him off the bench (and this was before the time of four interchange players), but he could do amazing things on the football field, and he had kicked eight matchwinning goals as recently as the last home-and-away game against Footscray, just a couple of weeks earlier. I loved Derek and his wife, Denise, and their beautiful kids, they were great people. I thought Derek should play the grand final, and I told Kevin Sheedy that.

But Derek missed out, and so did David Flood, a tall defender who made way for Wallis in the grand final. It was Harvey and Wallis in; Kickett and Flood out from the preliminary final team. At training during the week, Sheedy told me his intentions. The coaching staff knew that it was a big call, that it would cause some controversy because Kickett had played the full season, and I sensed that I was being brought on board as captain, because as the skipper

I sat on the match committee and helped pick the team. The notion was, 'We just need you on this one.'

But that night after Sheeds told me what was happening, I was completely taken aback, and distracted. I kept thinking as I trained, *I'm going to have to do something really tough here, something gutsy*. That was my style, not to hold things back, so I went and told the match committee after training that the players wanted Derek Kickett to play.

I said something like, 'Even though he hasn't been in good form, the players want to play with Derek. I'm representing the players, and they would prefer Derek to play.' So I had gone against Sheedy, which was a big moment for me after all those years. I always spoke my mind, but this was one moment when I wished that I was not on the match committee, because I never thought it was a great idea to have the captain involved in the selection process anyway. It was not much later that it was changed.

The reality was, the match committee of Sheedy and people like Brian Donohoe, the chairman, would pick the side without much input from me anyway, but on that occasion, they did ask me for an opinion, and to back them. I expressed that opinion and I lost the battle, although I was not necessarily alone, because I think that David Wheadon wanted Derek to play, too. Which is why it was so critical for Sheedy to get to me early, to push it through.

With hindsight, it might have been better for Derek to be dropped earlier, in the latter part of the season when he started to tail off. He had kicked 37 goals for the season which indicates that he was more than doing his job, but his drop-off in form was not addressed until very late. Sheedy would play Derek off the bench and call him 'the Storm Trooper' in the media, but in the three finals he had only kicked one goal and had totalled just 15 touches.

Making matters worse, Sheeds did not handle it well. He should have told Derek directly, and I know that he regrets that he did not. Sheeds said that what he chose to do that week was to tell five players – Kickett, Flood, Wallis, Michael Symons and Chris Daniher – that a maximum of two of them to play, and that they should be ready. He has insisted that he wanted to wait until game day, and that if it had been wet, Kickett might have come into the team. But when the team was selected on the Thursday, with Derek not picked, Kickett rang Danny Corcoran, our football manager, to find out what had happened. Danny told him to ring Sheedy, but they never made contact.

In his distress and anger, Derek did not attend the grand final at all. To this day I am not even sure if he knows that I backed him that week, because I have not had the chance to talk to him about it in depth. He quit the club and went on to play three good years with Sydney Swans, and while I have seen him once or twice since, he was polite and courteous but you could sense the tension and the change that had occurred. Derek was really warm and engaging when we were teammates, but we lost him, which was a pity.

Carlton had a much more experienced team than ours in the 1993 Grand Final; the games totals were 1717 for us and 2139 for the Blues. But Essendon had an edge to it that year, real speed especially through the brilliant finals form of Michael Long off a wing. He had been sensational in the preliminary final against Adelaide and he turned it on again in the grand final. From memory Gavin Wanganeen, who won the Brownlow Medal that year, said he had never seen a player complete a better finals series and it is a fair argument. On grand final day, Longy destroyed Carlton, with 33 disposals and an amazing goal on the run, and he ended up with the Norm Smith Medal.

Longy had been five years in the game by then, and he had grown in confidence to the point where he would take people on: 'Give me the ball!' I read that he had dreamt that he would win the Norm Smith Medal and Essendon would win the flag, and there was a bit of destiny about it all that day given that 1993 was the International Year of Indigenous People, he was the person who probably best represented the change in AFL footy toward recruiting Aboriginal players, and his uncle Maurice Rioli was presenting the medal. Not only that, Gavin had won the Brownlow.

Until Longy came in 1989, Essendon had not picked an Indigenous player since Norm McDonald, who had played at the club in the 1950s. Maybe the club had even been racist in its recruiting, but Sheeds took us into Darwin, embraced the Indigenous players and people, challenging the conventional thinking about Indigenous players, which went along the lines that many were difficult to handle and difficult to retain. Sheeds loved the raw talent and creativity that they brought to the game and to him, that overrode any other concerns. Once again, he took what might have been perceived as a risk, yet 25 years later everyone was doing it and look how the game has benefited from what he did.

Longy was dead quiet; he is still quiet, although he had a beautiful sense of humour when you engaged him, and he liked to sing a lot. He found the transition difficult in one sense, because he would sit in the sauna at Windy Hill in the early days to protect himself from the cold of Melbourne's winters. But in other ways he was the standard-bearer for all Indigenous players, and in 1993 he was at his peak. Beyond that he suffered injuries and, while he came back, he was not quite the same, but I will never forget him slowing down sometimes with the footy, he might do a little shimmy, and the game would virtually stop around him. He knew exactly what he was doing and he was brilliant with the ball; he did not need many disposals to hurt the opposition badly.

We were five goals up at quarter time of the grand final and Carlton never came any closer than that; we ended up winning by more than seven goals. Paul Salmon kicked five goals, and what a great grand final player he was! In the middle, our boys kept picking off anything that Justin Madden had his hands on, because Neale Daniher had unlocked the opposition hitting patterns so that our guys knew where it was going. I remember their players looking at each other as though to say, 'What's going on?'

Dean Wallis's selection ahead of Kickett was a talking point, but Wally made his impact with one hit on Milham Hanna, the Carlton utility player, in the second quarter. Wallis went right past me to get to Hanna and body-slammed him, and I just heard the thunder clap of the bump. It was an opportunity to hurt that Wallis did not allow to pass. He saw things differently to me, Dean, and he hit Mil Hanna flush. The Carlton player was stretchered off but he did come back on, although his effectiveness was curtailed by that one collision.

We had seven players under 21 in that premiership team, which is an awful lot, but what we had not factored in before the season was that they were really good, that group of guys. History tells you that. Fletcher, of course, became a legend of Essendon and so did Hird and Wanganeen, who were just 20. Mercuri at 19 played a fabulous grand final. They were fearless, those guys, and they stepped up on the day.

I had a good season, averaging 24 disposals as skipper. My style as captain was to be hard on the players if they did not live up to our standards, and the senior players like Salmon, Harvey and O'Donnell helped me. We had meetings where we would talk about driving the younger boys, making sure they did all the right things, on and off the field. We had no problem with that aspect; when you are an older player, you are more capable of pulling people into line. I can remember that our idea was 'Support them, but be hard on them.'

Sheeds had a great year in 1993, he'd pulled a rabbit out of the hat for that flag. He *knew* we had a chance quite early, and from that moment he was focused, which was not always the case with him. Kevin fluctuated quite a bit with his coaching, usually off the back of whether we were a chance to contend or not. There were the 'build' years, when he might wander off talking to people in the crowd at training, and the players could sense that drop in intensity, then there were the 'serious' years, with a strong contrast. He tried to build teams that could win premierships, not merely play in finals, and my god when he was on, he would be committed and intense, his eyes would be sharp. Nobody had a sharper eye.

The 1993 flag came by surprise, a notion articulated by our club president, David Shaw, at the celebration at the Hilton that night: 'We forecast that we could put a plan in place to win a premiership in 1995. This young team has shot those plans to ribbons.'

I had a quiet time on grand final night, I just wanted to enjoy it and I was so happy that I did not need to drink. In my speech, I praised Sheedy's performance, arguing that 'the little knocks make him stronger, and there's nothing more powerful than Kevin Sheedy when the odds are against him'. It was my third flag as a player, and the first time that I had lifted the cup as the captain, and I can remember Longy climbing up on stage at the Hilton that night and throwing false modesty out the door: 'Jeez, I played well!'

That was Longy, he could be a hilarious man, the first Indigenous player in a long time who came along and revealed parts of his personality, comfortable speaking his mind, and able to handle being the centre of attention. There were a lot of other great Indigenous players who came into the game around that time, but Michael helped change it for all of them by showing that he could thrive in an AFL environment, and just as importantly, Sheeds has been rightly lauded for what he achieved with Indigenous players.

Did Essendon make the right decision dropping Derek Kickett? It's a question that is often asked, even 20-odd years later. As I have said, there is a heartbreaker every year, and you could say the very same thing for David Flood that day, because Floody had played really well as a defender in the preliminary final. But David had only played four senior games for the season, and he was really filling in for an injured Mark Harvey, who was an automatic selection.

So it came down to Derek and the real question is: who would have missed out on selection for the grand final had Derek played? A few people have said over the years that Tim Watson could have been dropped, and it is true that Tim had a bung ankle and he was just about finished, managing only three possessions in the grand final. But really, I don't think it was ever going to be Tim who was dropped.

I think if Derek was to play then Dean Wallis would have had to miss the grand final. It was a risk by Sheeds, because Derek had won games off his own boot, even in *that* season, although he had struggled in the finals. On form, Sheeds was arguably right, and you do want to pick an in-form team for a grand final. The players will always want to pick their mates and keep the club harmonious, so it should be no surprise that we wanted Derek to play.

It is just a shame the way it happened, the fact Sheeds never got to Derek to tell him the how and why. But Dean Wallis did some nice things in the grand final, and the premiership cup probably vindicates what was a hard call. It was Sheedy's call to make, and all these years later, having coached, I guess I have changed my view slightly. At the very least, I can understand more clearly.

# 7

# TEACHER–COACH

## 1994–1999

I had never planned to coach. All the time that I played for Essendon, I was running my electrical business on the side with my brother Steven, and the plan was to put more time into that when I stopped playing the game. The change of heart came in my last year, 1996, when playing ceased to be an option for me.

I had turned 30 soon after the 1993 premiership win, and we had high expectations of more success, but once again Essendon could not manage to create the dynasty that was being forecast after the Baby Bombers' triumph. Carlton came again, and so did West Coast, and we were left behind, showing that it is not that easy to stay up in this business, or more accurately, it wasn't easy back then. In those times, it was left to Kevin Sheedy as coach of Essendon to set everything up, run the reviews, get control of the recruiting, whereas now, the coach would have it all mapped out for him, and clubs have the resources to help. Hawthorn and Alastair Clarkson are examples of that.

It certainly did not happen for us. In 1994, Michael Long broke down at the height of his powers, Tim Watson played just nine games and retired for the final time, and I could only manage 13 games myself because of injury as we slumped to tenth and missed the finals. In 1995, Longy came back and we played a couple of finals, but my body was screaming at me, and I only extracted 11 senior games, handing over the captaincy to Gary O'Donnell at the end of the season after four years in the position.

I wanted to retire at the end of 1995; I was set on giving the game away. I could not get out of bed with the same enthusiasm to play anymore and mentally, I was finished. Actually, I was embarrassed with the way I was playing, sent to the weakest of opposition small forwards all the time, and I started to worry about keeping younger, fitter players out of the team. This is when you know that your time is up, but Sheedy convinced me to play on in 1996 because I only needed six more games to reach the 200-game milestone. 'You deserve it,' he said. 'It's a big milestone. Just play the six, and if you don't feel like going on, retire then.'

Truthfully it did not mean so much to me then, but with hindsight, I am glad that he talked me around. I hit the double century in round 8 of the 1996 season against Footscray at the MCG, we had a win, and I kicked a goal. The players went out of their way to get the footy to me and Sheeds was great with things like that; he had a terrific sense of the history of the game. Only four per cent of AFL players reach 200 games on average, so it was a landmark worth crossing, no doubt.

Two weeks later in round 10, 1996, I broke my arm (for the second time) in a Saturday night game against St Kilda at Waverley, the infamous match when the lights shut down in the third quarter, so that everyone had to come back on the Tuesday to complete the contest. I guess it was a metaphor for me, those lights going out. I went to a contest and was hit on the same spot that I'd broken that arm earlier in my career, and it fractured, and I ended up getting reported for trying to tackle Nathan Burke with my leg, because I could not use my arm. It was about the last shot I fired as an AFL player.

With only half the season left that was always going to be the end of the road for me at a tired 32. So for the remainder of the 1996 season, I went into the coaches' box with Sheedy, although in reality, it was just so that the club could pay out my contract, to justify them paying me. I went in there for a quick look, and my mind was more on my business, which was where I was headed, so I thought.

About two-thirds of the way through the 1996 season, Mark 'Choco' Williams, who was coaching Essendon's reserves team, defected to Port Adelaide, which had been admitted to the AFL competition, as assistant coach to John Cahill. This allowed me to stand in as coach of the seconds. I was green; I can remember being 10 goals down and having too many players on the ground one day against North Melbourne, and the Roos' coach, Tony Elshaug, went off at me: 'You're cheating!' I said, 'Relax, it wasn't deliberate!' We made the grand final, but lost to North.

The seniors went to a famous preliminary final against Sydney at the SCG, when Tony Lockett's kick from 50 metres for a behind after the siren broke a deadlock and put the Swans into a grand final, eliminating the Dons.

With Choco out of the picture, I was offered the coaching job in the reserves full-time in 1997, which also made me officially an assistant coach to Kevin Sheedy, and I decided to try to fit it in with my business. The first thing that happened was that Sheeds went off overseas to upskill in Europe, undertaking a training course for two months, and he left me in charge of the training, which I found remarkable. I still cannot believe that he allowed me to take over in my first year!

Essendon had a lot of young players making their way through the system at the time: guys like Mark and Jason Johnson, Justin Blumfield, Chris Heffernan, Daniel McAlister, and these were the guys that I began working with. It was a few moments with Blake Caracella, another one of those gifted, young guys, that I think stimulated me as a coach for the first time, and looking back, I believe it was the first time that I might have had an inkling that I could be a career coach, as opposed to merely filling in.

Caracella, a smart half-forward, was close to selection in the senior team for the first time, and he could play, but when I took over from Choco he started to go backwards. Late in the 1996 season, I approached him and said, 'What's the problem?' And he told me that when Choco had been his coach, he had watched game tapes with him, bunked him up a little, and that he was missing that extra attention. I had no idea what I was doing at the time; I had only played under one coach and that was Sheedy, and I certainly had not been sitting through tapes with every player to that point. So I said to Blake, 'Come and see me.'

I started doing edits myself at nights and I gave Blake a few things to work on, and he was a professional, he did everything I told him. He was clever and analytical, and not surprisingly, he ended up coaching himself much later. At the time, he said, 'That's something I can use.' I just got a kick out of that, the first time I had experienced helping a young player along as his coach. I liked that feeling. In round 3, 1997, Blake Caracella was picked for Essendon seniors, and he was away.

I was like a mini-Sheedy in those days, which had started in my later years as a player. I did what Tom Harley did years later at Geelong when he was captain: I watched the team meetings, listened to the players and acted on the concerns. Sheedy was quite broad with his planning, he generalised a lot, so I tried to shore it all up, pull it together and make sure nothing slipped through the cracks.

I had some ideas in my head, and I knew how I wanted my teams to play. It was based around how we played in the seniors, loosely on Sheedy's style but with a little more emphasis on defence. In that first year I struggled with the time commitments, and I cheated on my business, because I quickly discovered that there was more time required as a coach than what was needed as a player. Players come and go and they can forget about the game; you can never do enough hours when you are coaching, and you cannot ever do the perfect job, there is always something else to do. Ultimately, you have to prioritise, and accept that you will never have perfect weeks, or perfect preparation, no matter how hard you try.

Before my second full year in charge of the reserves, 1998, I wrote a review for the club in which I said I had achieved about 80 per cent of what I set out to do in 1997. I had come up with a concept called 'EDG', pronounced *edge,* which was an acronym. The notion went like this:

EFFORT

– to pressure opposition when they have the ball

– to run and make an effort to Get and Deliver the ball

– force opposition turnovers, one-percenters

DELIVER

– being able to kick or handball to teammate effectively

– create another Get for our team

GET

– have the skills to win the loose and hard ball

– position yourself to Get the ball

– position yourself to Deliver to teammate

While I was still naive as a football coach, a lot of what I wrote in that report would stand for the whole time that I coached. I had identified myself in that report as a person who focused on process, rather than outcome. I wrote that I would prefer to see more competitive training drills, simulating game-day pressure, and that while this might make some of the drills look ugly at times, it would have a long-term benefit. These were points that remained with me.

I also lamented the fact that Essendon had endured a horrendous run of injuries in 1997 right throughout the list. This was a fact that had been addressed by the introduction of sports science staff from the Australian Institute of Sport at the club's behest to conduct a survey in 1998. I believed that the players were being overtrained, and once again, it was a point that I would make over and over during the ensuing years. My report read: 'After a disastrous 1997 season, I never want to be part of a club with such a high rate of injuries again.' I also commented that the young players needed nurturing:

> Having been a person with limited natural ability, everything I have ever achieved has been achieved through learning the appropriate skills required to perform at that level. It is very easy for me to break down the skills for these young men and to teach the basic techniques for their development. I think we forget sometimes the young men have so much to learn once they arrive at an AFL club. All their football careers have been quite easy as they have been the stars of the competition, i.e:
>
> – the biggest
>
> – the strongest
>
> – the smartest
>
> – the best endurance
>
> – the most skilful

> All of a sudden the players are amongst players of the same ilk so the player who is most likely to make the grade (AFL) is the player either who is prepared to work on re-educating himself, a player who is willing to learn a new way to play to succeed, but we must be able to provide the pathway or education for him to learn. My motto: 'Teach, don't command or judge.'

That last line is the most significant. I intended to become a teacher–coach, not a hot gospeller like Ron Barassi in the 1970s, or dozens of coaches before that. It was not my style; I wanted to bring people along with me, to nurture them and draw the best out of them, rather than smash it out of them with vitriol and threats. Malcolm Blight once said that when he played under Barassi, 'you played in spite of him', which was common in the times, of course. But times had changed, and that style was certainly not me.

I was talking a lot about Essendon needing to improve its delivery of the ball, and we had what I believe were the first Dream Team points at the club, which I developed with Ted Hopkins, the former Carlton player who headed up Champion Data, the company that provides statistical information to the AFL. I talked to Essendon about improving our information systems, and we had player ratings that took into account turnovers and the like, giving us some sort of measurement of player output. All of these things, including the EDG concept, were applied to the senior team as well as the reserves. At this time we also started recording training times, trying to get a feel for the loads that the players were carrying and trying to prevent injuries rather than reacting to problems. On the field, we preached maximum effort to get the ball back from the opposition, high pressure in defence.

We made the reserves grand final in 1998, my second full season, lost to Footscray, and looking back, I clearly had my teeth into the coaching business. As it happened, Sheedy was under the blow-torch again. Kevin had been coaching since 1981, a stretch that was unprecedented in the modern era, and while he had coached three premierships (eight, if you counted pre-season and night flags) he had overseen a team that missed the finals in 1997, then drifted into eighth spot in 1998.

In the first final of 1998 the Dons were immediately ousted by North Melbourne, leaving Sheeds vulnerable. Ron Evans as club president had saved him once or twice, and Sheeds was a good politician, which he needed to be. Somehow, he always found the numbers.

Sheedy and I fell out slightly in the latter part of that season as he wriggled in the discomfort of potentially losing his job after such a long time at Essendon, a little tension that fortunately, was mended a few years later. There was just too much pressure around the club that year, too much politicking and conniving behind the scenes, and I did not enjoy being around Essendon in 1998. Kevin and I ended up being pushed around as pawns by the powerbrokers, used against each other in a game of chess.

In the public arena, there was enormous scrutiny on Kevin and with me starting to make some gains as an assistant as well as being a former captain, it became fairly obvious for people inside and outside the club to join the dots. People started to suggest that Sheedy would be sacked and that I would take over as Essendon's senior coach. Quite truthfully, I wanted no part of it.

I had endured my rows with Sheedy, like all of the guys who had been around the club for a prolonged period. Usually, it would be towards the end of a playing career, and Tim, for instance had his time at odds with the coach. Usually it was Sheedy's time management, or lack of it, that frustrated me, because he was always late. He was always committed, but it was quite repetitive, the way he prepared the team, and I felt the whole process needed some tinkering, a spark-up. Match committee meetings went for too long, and it was too hard to keep yourself fresh as a coach. You need to be fresh; it's the only way to function properly in that role.

In 1998 as we struggled, I had people from the Essendon board approaching me about Sheedy, saying, 'What's going on?' And I said to them, 'It's fine, but someone needs to get to him. I *can't* get to him. Someone needs to get him to focus on the players, get back on board and give the players the best chance.' That conversation was meant to be private, but it was used against Kevin, and soon enough it was being said around the club that I was plotting against Sheeds.

The contrary was the case, because I had decided to leave Essendon. I think the board was looking to sound me out, just in case they took the decision to sack Sheeds, but I told chairman Graeme McMahon and chief executive Peter Jackson straight, 'Look, I'm not going to be at Essendon either way, whether you stay with Sheeds or not.'

I had reached the conclusion that it was time to leave Essendon, where I had been since 1981. The environment was not something I wanted to be around, and aside from that, I had decided that I needed to experience another club culture for my own personal development as a coach. Maybe I could have taken over at Essendon; I am not sure. But personally, I did not believe that I was ready, and I never wanted to take the job in those circumstances: the nailing of a three-time premiership coach and legend of the club.

In the end, I believe the club was right to keep Kevin Sheedy for all those 27 years. He did a huge amount for Essendon, with four premierships at a better strike rate than average. If you consider that there were 16 clubs in the AFL through most of that time, theoretically you should be able to win a premiership every 16 years in the AFL, on the law of averages, but Kevin managed four (1984, 1985, 1993 and 2000), not to mention the fact that in his time, Essendon became a huge enterprise and massively popular around the country. It was Sheeds who built up the membership, the sense of tradition, the history and the supporters' pride in the club after it had reached a low ebb.

And here is the thing: it was not just about the army of supporters that we built up back in the 80s or 90s. The fact is, those people have children and those kids become Essendon supporters, and that is what Sheedy built. He created what Essendon is today, a huge footy club in a national competition. That hits home for me all the time, because I used to ask people, 'Why do you barrack for Essendon?' And almost always, they would say something like, 'Because we watched you guys winning flags in the 80s.' That is his legacy.

For me, it was a big call to leave Essendon, where I had effectively grown up. I had been at Windy Hill for 17 years, since my teens, but the offers were out there to move on, with Tim Watson after my signature. Tim was going to coach St Kilda, his first coaching position, and he had asked me to be an assistant coach. I told Tim that I was interested, but then Denis Pagan rang, and we had a good relationship from his time at Essendon, prior to his picking up the North Melbourne senior job in 1993. Denis had coached the Kangaroos to a premiership in 1996 and they were a powerful unit headed up by the great Wayne Carey, and he had emerged as a wonderful coach after waiting so many years for an opportunity. I knew Denis well; I had been the captain of Essendon when he was on the match committee as an assistant to Kevin. We had a rapport, so I said, 'I'll probably take that.'

With hindsight, I think Denis Pagan knew that what I needed at that point of my career was an opportunity to coach, and to broaden my horizons, just as he had done when he went from North's Under 19s to Essendon as an assistant to Sheedy. He had been continually overlooked for senior coaching jobs and was pigeonholed as a junior coach only, which was ridiculous. But once he left North, his original club, came to Essendon and had some success there, he finally cracked a senior role after North sacked Wayne Schimmelbusch in the pre-season of 1993. Denis was an immediate success, winning the flag in 1996 and unlucky not to win another in 1998, when the Roos reached the grand final only to kick a deplorable 8.22 in a loss to Adelaide.

So it was a good option for me on many fronts, and I went across to Arden Street in 1999 as reserves coach and assistant to Denis, working with other assistants including Tony Elshaug and Norm Dare, who had coached Brisbane Bears. North Melbourne won the premiership by beating Carlton that year, achieving redemption for the lost opportunity of 1998, a second flag for Denis Pagan, and it was a great experience for me. Halfway through that year, I actually began to feel like I was ready to be a senior coach.

Denis was the opposite to Sheeds; he was about control. They were both winners, and that taught me that there was more than one way to win, and I probably picked a chunk of both styles. Denis could deliver classic sprays at players, that was for sure, but methodical and meticulous preparation was everything for him; it was incredibly thorough, the whole process. For instance, when he went to an upcoming opponent's game to study them, all the coaches had to go with him.

I remember taking my own TV and two video recorders and my whiteboard from Essendon to work in North Melbourne's temporary headquarters at Arden Street, where the facilities were infamously bad, a world away from what some of the clubs have now. North had no money and not many supporters, and the staff and players had to operate out of mostly temporary buildings. I did not even have a door on my office and the surrounds were not great, but North Melbourne had a culture, a spirit that was intangible, and it was incredibly strong.

I reckon it remained from the 1970s, the old Shinboner stuff, because they had so many old staff members who had been there for years. They were on a mission in 1999, and in the box on grand final day you could sense them dominating. Carlton was not a great team, probably should not have been there, and North smashed them.

Did Denis take on too much? The way it worked was that 'Trout' Elshaug was his number one assistant, there was a trust that had built up between them, so I knew my place was outside that circle, given that I was new. Denis asked me to take on some projects in that season that helped my development. For instance, North's contested ball counts had slipped, and I looked at some patterns of what was happening around the ball. Shannon Grant and Peter Bell were two players who were getting outside too much, and I was able to show them that with video and statistics. A few of them were slipping past the contest, because North was so good around the ball, they were anticipating that the contest would be won, and I showed them some embarrassing edits. Denis made me do it!

Another project concerned the game style and potential changes to the way that North played. Denis wanted to include some options of hitting up free targets as we went forward, which was not the usual North Melbourne way at the time. Denis liked the ball kicked long to Wayne Carey, who was such a great player that he would either mark or bring the ball to ground, allowing the swoopers like Brett Allison to work into the game by playing at his feet.

But opposition teams were on to this, and I spent a lot of time trying to prove to Denis that we needed to become less predictable to other teams. My argument was that if we kicked one short, or maybe every second time, it would be more difficult for the opposition to counter. He would say, 'There's no point changing something that's not broken. I'd like to [change], but I can't!' All the same, I would like to think a bit of what I was saying filtered through.

It was just fun to be there that year, to have really strong discipline through the club, with the coach involved in every single decision. Denis had to approve everything, whereas Sheeds liked to empower people to do their thing, like leaving me in charge for a couple months in my first year! Denis could never have done that; he could not have lived with himself if it went wrong. That variation in coaching style was good for me after so many years under Sheedy, and the mix of both methods is exactly what I learned that year.

That was the season that Essendon pushed up to the preliminary final only to be pipped by Carlton, on the day that Fraser Brown dragged down Dean Wallis at the pivotal moment to win the game. Essendon was really good that year, and I remember watching the game with Denis and him being worried about the Dons. In the end, he had no such concerns.

Coaching footy is a highly fluid business, of course, and towards the end of the 1999 regular season a bunch of jobs became vacant quite suddenly. Malcolm Blight, who had coached Adelaide to two premierships, quit the Crows, Jeff Gieschen moved on from Richmond, Ken Judge walked from Hawthorn and Gary Ayres ran out of petrol at Geelong after the Cats finished eleventh. There had been a domino effect, leaving those four jobs open, and my name kept cropping up in the media speculation.

Pagan knew that I was keen and ready, but North had finals to play, so he asked me to complete my applications and interviews as quickly as possible. He said, 'Look son, go and do it now, so there's no interruption during the finals.' Ultimately there were three clubs who expressed keen interest – Geelong, Richmond and Adelaide – and another, Hawthorn, which I was told also had an interest. From memory, the first interview was with Adelaide, but while I ran second to Gary Ayres in the end, it was a great experience for me, pitching up for a couple of interviews, even though I sensed that I would probably not get the job.

I had to prepare a dossier of what I planned to do at Adelaide, and while it was not the most professional-looking document, the interview went quite well. There was a good connection with people like Bill Sanders, the Adelaide administrator, and I gave them my own flowchart of decision-making within a football club along with a plan for how I would operate as head coach. I still have that document and part of it reads:

**WHAT STYLE OF GAME WILL I COACH?**

Efficient – won't be high possession, over-use team

Quick movement of ball – into 50-metre area

Direct in carrying ball in least amount of traffic

Defence rather than offence

Team to be very good in close

Players must be strong in the contest air/ground situations

Kick to leading forwards inside the grid area

Kick long to a contest rather than short

The interesting part of that is that when I went on to coach Geelong, people thought that I was an offensive coach, rather than a defensive coach, but that was never the case. In the 1999 document, I further wrote about my views on the game:

WHAT DOES MARK THOMPSON BELIEVE IN?

- Positive self-belief
- Doing things correctly
- Hard work – no easy way to be the best
- Honesty – direct but fair in relationships
- Reality – putting things into perspective
- Praise more than criticise
- Preparation rather than motivation
- Coach is responsible to teach and develop
- Developing leadership qualities
- Spending time with players – finding out the best way to get the best out of themselves

That section indicated how I wanted to draw players along with me as the coach, which became a big part of my mantra. In another section of the document, I talked about my philosophy on footy:

FOOTBALL TEAMS

- Defence – all players to value it
- Good strong backline – a team within a team
- Players with character and good values
- Flexible teams/players – capable of playing in various situations.
- Right balance of players – tough/skilful/young/experienced
- Core of team to have good endurance, reasonable speed and be of reasonable height – 5'11"/180 cm
- Must have special qualities if under 5'10"
- Large number of players capable of playing midfield fwd roles
- Using the bench positively impacts players

## DECISION MAKING PROCESS – "GAME SENSE"

*By*
**MARK THOMPSON**

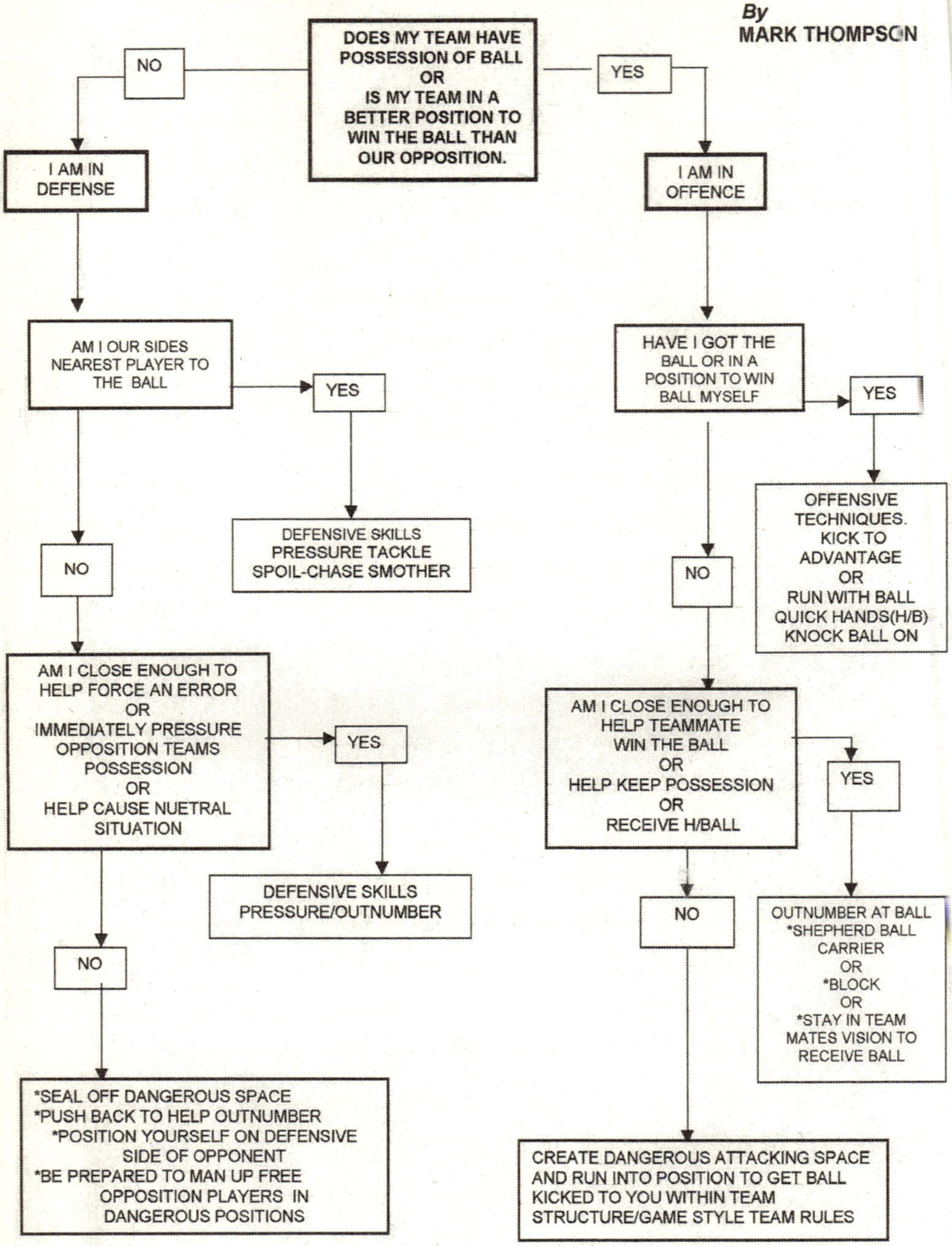

It is quite interesting looking back at that document more than 15 years on, because while I was not a fully-formed coach at the time, a lot of the ideas were already ingrained in me. I told Adelaide that I 'would need guidance with the media', because at the time, I was quite inexperienced in that area. I also described myself as 'a very steady person'. I had married Annette in 1987 when I was 24, and we had three children – Lauren was ten, Michael was eight and Daniel was five. I was typical of many footballers of my generation in that we settled down early.

As part of my preparation I had done a lot of study of previous premiership teams, and in terms of Adelaide's situation as the 1997–98 premiership team that had fallen away quickly, I talked to the Crows about what needed to happen next. I used the examples of Essendon post-1985 and West Coast Eagles post-1994 to show the patterns, and then I picked Adelaide's *next* premiership team, which included six players labelled 'recruit'. I suggested that only ten of the 1998 premiership team would remain as Crows players for the next flag.

In the meantime I was presenting similar documents to Richmond, and Geelong had also called, so it was a slightly awkward situation for me. I remember Bill Sanders ringing me from Adelaide and saying, 'We're offering it to Gary Ayres, but if he doesn't accept it, we're coming to talk to you.' I started to panic at that point, thinking, *Shit, I might actually get this!* When really, I felt that I was going through that process for practice as much as anything.

There were two interviews with Richmond. Leon Daphne, who was president of the Tigers, came to see me, and we met once in the board room at Crown with some board members. I remember one of them sporting a black eye, which was a little disconcerting, particular since I knew how it had happened!

In any case, by then I had met with Geelong, with whom I already had some familiarity. A year earlier, I had done an interview for an assistant's job there under Gary Ayres, and we met at McDonald's near Point Cook, because it was halfway for both me and the interviewers. Hence, my guess was that Geelong had me on their radar.

Brian Cook, the Geelong chief executive, made contact and a bunch of them came to visit me at my home in Greenvale, in the northern suburbs of Melbourne. As soon as I sat down with Cook and Frank Costa, the club president, I knew that they were people I could work with. I pulled out of the Richmond job, which Danny Frawley, the former St Kilda defender, grabbed, and Hawthorn hired Peter Schwab, a former premiership player, as its coach.

I completed the 1999 season at North Melbourne, playing my little part in a premiership, knowing that I would be the coach of Geelong from the 2000 season.

# 8

# A MASSIVE PUNT

## 2000–2003

Geelong was a mess at the end of 1999, and it is easy to forget that. The picture that was presented to me by Brian Cook, the chief executive, and Gareth Andrews, a board member, when they visited me at my home in Greenvale was not pretty at all. Millions of dollars' of debt was crippling the club, and the captain, Leigh Colbert, had walked out, which is highly unusual in football for an incumbent skipper. Colbert had signed with North Melbourne while Gary Ayres, who had taken Geelong to finals in three of his five years, was heading to Adelaide to coach the Crows.

The Cats had finished twelfth in 1998 and eleventh in 1999, miles from contending, and had an ageing list of players, with the highest-paid players either injured or not playing . . . or both. They were four years beyond making the 1995 Grand Final and already 36 years from their last premiership under Bob Davis in 1963.

All of this was explained to me with Brian Cook providing the detail of the financial situation, and a few days later I met Frank Costa, the club president, who had made his fortune in the fruit business. The ironic part of my optimism is that perhaps I ought to have been concerned about the club's plight, and whether I should be getting involved as a potential first-time coach. Because I never felt that at all; within five minutes of the first meeting I remember thinking, *Oh, gee, I like this. I like the way they're talking.*

They were good listeners, and they let me talk as much as they talked. Cook told me that Geelong's financial situation – $7.5 million of debt – meant that it had no choice but to rebuild from the bottom. The off-field changes had already begun, and in particular, the ANZ Bank, one of the club's biggest creditors, was about to accept 55 cents in the dollar to clear that debt. But Cook, Costa and Andrews had the same message: 'We have to rebuild, it'll take five years, but we can't say that to the supporters. We'll have to say that "it will take at least three years". And we won't win many games.'

Cook had just been appointed as chief executive, having spent nearly ten years running the West Coast Eagles, where the club had won two premierships and made big profits. He said to me, 'My philosophy is to recruit and develop our own.' And I said, 'Well, that's music to my ears, because that's exactly what I want to do. I want to train our own people up.'

The same went for Frank Costa when I caught up with him; we had an immediate connection. By this time I had sold my electrical business to my brother, Steven, because coaching was taking up all my time, and I could not afford to be away from the business so much. But to talk to someone as successful as Frank was interesting to me, and I quickly gathered that he was a *real* Geelong person. He spruiked for Geelong the city and Geelong the footy club, leaving the detail to Cook.

I liked Cooky's honesty and I liked his plan, so on gut feel, I took the job at Geelong. They gave me three years, to the end of

2002, and I did not even bother signing the contract they offered, beginning a long tradition of ignoring written documents that do not hold any weight. I trusted them, and what does a contract mean in footy anyway? They announced my appointment and there was a season launch, which I recall John 'Sam' Newman hosting. Costa and Cook, also recently appointed, had been joined by me in the triumvirate.

Geelong's list was tired, it was the tail end of a group that had gone to the grand final in 1995 only to lose to Carlton, the fourth runner-up finish in just seven years. In the trade period that occurred immediately after my appointment, half-back Michael Mansfield went to Carlton and ruckman John Barnes back to Essendon, his original club, while Liam Pickering, who had suffered two years of injury troubles, finished up. There had been a big run of retirements at Geelong, and the great Gary Ablett Sr had gone at the end of 1996 as well as Brownlow medallist Paul Couch at the end of 1997.

Veteran centre half-forward Barry Stoneham almost left the club as well, but I talked him into staying. I did not want all the senior players to bale out; so Garry Hocking (31) and Stoneham (32) stayed on. Guys like Tom Harley, Darren Milburn, David Wojcinski and full-back Matthew Scarlett had just arrived at Geelong, and more youth would come in the 1999 draft.

On 8 September 1999, Sam Newman was the face of the club's launch of a four-year plan entitled 'Stand Up and Fight', in which Brian Cook said Geelong would target:

- a premiership by 2003
- finals appearances in the next four seasons
- an increase in membership to more than 30 000, from 21 000
- a profit of $1.8 million by 2003

There was also the issue of debt, which Cook was addressing. The club brought in people from KPMG, the consulting group, to look at the books, as Cook recalled in an interview: 'They never said we were insolvent, but they were bloody close to it. We were the endangered species, there's no doubt about that.'

After two years with Essendon reserves and one with North Melbourne, I was ready to coach, but there is no way that I was fully formed, because no one can train you for the experience of being the head coach. The day after North Melbourne won the 1999 premiership I jumped in my car, drove down the Princes Highway to Geelong, and checked in for my first day's work, the first of many trips down that piece of bitumen.

Under the original plan, I thought that I would move the family to the Geelong area, but Annette did not want to move everyone to Geelong. Our two older kids were settled in Melbourne with their schooling. So I commuted, eventually renting an apartment there so that I could fall into bed if I had a late night at work, spending the other nights back home in Greenvale.

It was full-time, six days a week and sometimes seven, starting with the trade period and the national draft, and one of our first deals was to allow Mansfield his out to play at Carlton for pick 31 in the draft. We used that selection to pick up a forward named Paul Chapman from Calder Cannons in the TAC Cup Under 18 competition, which was some sort of deal! Perhaps it was a portent of things to come.

I went to the draft with Stephen Wells, our recruiter, and Garry Davidson, the football manager, and we picked up Joel Corey with pick 8, Chapman with pick 31, Cameron Ling with pick 38 and Corey Enright from the backblocks of South Australia with pick 47, the selection that was exchanged from North Melbourne for Leigh

Colbert. Looking back, it was a very good start, plus we traded to bring Cameron Mooney from North, where I had worked with him the previous year.

Mooney had played in the 1999 premiership for North as a young man, going without a single possession on the day, but I liked him, although I was keener on Brady Rawlings, their midfielder. North would not deal on Rawlings which put Mooney into the frame. I had seen Chapman testing at the draft combine and I was keen on him, but not so keen on Cameron Ling, a local boy from Geelong. Ling was not athletic, but we took him anyway, and as for Joel Corey, I came to refer to him as 'first man picked' at Geelong.

I had already rung Leigh Colbert to check if he would change his mind about leaving the club, but I was quickly learning about the problems of Geelong's culture at the time. He was an excellent player, and a good man, but Colbert told me that it was too late for him to change stride. To this day I don't know why he left Geelong at just 24 years of age because he never told me, but I have heard that there was angst within the playing ranks towards him, based on his appointment to the captaincy at such a young age in 1999 when he was unable to play a game because of a knee surgery.

I can see that, but on the other hand sometimes a player will just decide that a club is rubbish, and they don't really want to say it. You are not going to say, 'I'm leaving because this club is no good. I'm going to a better club.' This culture at Geelong was about each to his own. In a 1999 *Age* article, which I kept, former Geelong and Port Adelaide player Dwayne Russell identified it:

> At Port, you soon appreciated that brilliant players had gone before you, and brilliant players would come after. It was your job to maintain the club's standing. It was a lot different at Geelong. The club had a completely different history, to begin

> with. The bar had been lowered for so long, players had nothing in particular to maintain.

The writer of that article, journalist Ian Cockerill, observed that Geelong 'seemed to exist for the glory of its players'. Russell went further:

> We had an era – and I was part of it – where we had a selfish style. If we'd been more team-orientated and had a better philosophy about what was and wasn't acceptable, then I don't think those habits would have passed on to the next generation.

The Geelong I walked into at the end of 1999 into was a savage club, a ruthless club, too selfish a club, not the kind of club you would enjoy being drafted into as a young man. You would be left to figure it out for yourself. A lot of the former players were angry with the club because they felt they had been mistreated, I discovered. Steve Hocking, for instance, had been sacked on 199 games and he did not walk back into the club for a few years. I tried over time to get those guys back to the club, to embrace it again.

My style is about making people comfortable in a work environment, and helping people, so what had happened at Geelong was not the kind of culture that I wanted, and I am pretty sure Brian Cook and Frank Costa felt exactly the same. We had to find a balance between cleaning out the list on one hand, and making sure that supporters came to the football with some hope of winning on the other.

I knew it was going to take some time, if we were to give people time to develop, and fortunately the board was on side from the start. It is a highly emotional game, football, and boards want success quickly. Generally, they are not happy about having success in the fifth, sixth or seventh years, and coaches feel that pressure within a club. Some are lucky, because they get the timing right, but first-up coaches do not usually have that luxury. Most likely, they have gone into a club that is in trouble already, rather than inheriting a good team. So for me, it was a massive punt to take that job, looking back. We were not a great team nor a great club at that point.

Brian Cook told me that football department spending, which takes into account the salaries of players and coaches and all the football staff, would have to be cautious, but he added a rider: 'We won't have that big a spend in the footy department, but I'll promise you one thing, Mark, if we get money in and we start to reduce the debt and we get some spare cash, every dollar of it will go to football.' He was true to his word. At the time the AFL had its own kind of arms race with footy spending; clubs with cash were spending up big on coaching, recruitment, development and those kinds of areas which were not covered by the salary cap. Geelong had some catching up to do in that area.

Full-back Ben Graham picked up the captaincy, and we had one original coach in Alan McConnell, plus Ron Watt to coach the VFL team, then after Brendan McCartney was sacked from his assistant coaching role by Richmond, I rang him and asked him along. I had heard a lot of good things about Brendan and in five minutes' chatting I could tell that I could work with him as an assistant. As well as being a fine man, he had coached his own teams at Ocean Grove with success – four straight flags in the Bellarine league – before spending a couple of years in the AFL system.

When I first got to the players, I explained that there would be a big change to the way they played; that it would be a more balanced game between attack and defence. I showed them the ranking for defence in 1999, taken from the points-against total, and they were sixteenth and dead last, conceding 112 points on average. It was the history of Geelong, to play like that, to be all about entertainment. My plan was to bring a defensive edge but not lose the attacking flare, so I started at the back.

I talked a lot about defence and how we were going to win contested ball, and play a game that stood up in finals. Plus after all the tainted recent history of internal problems, I told them, 'We're here to help you and we're coming in with no preconceived ideas, no sets on people, no grudges. It's a clean slate.'

On the eve of the players starting pre-season training for the 2000 season, I gave an interview to Rohan Connolly of *The Age* in which I talked about my coaching philosophy. Looking back on that article, it is illuminating:

> I won't be a 'tactical' coach as such. I don't think I'll be throwing people around everywhere trying to play tricks . . . I don't think games are won with tricks. I think when it really matters most, in finals, you've just got to be solid; what really matters is that you are tactically smart, you match up all right, and you are playing a style of play which is going to stand up under any sort of pressure.

In the same article, I flagged my emphasis on interpersonal skills. I said that one of my strengths was in finding out how people operated, how they handled criticism, whether they needed praise for their work. And I made the point that while Geelong's players would be required to work hard, 'they've got to start to enjoy it, and that they *will* enjoy it'.

By the time the players came back, I was ready. I knew what I was going to say, and how we would go about changing the club, and it all started quite nicely. In my first game as senior coach, Geelong beat Fremantle in Perth, we won the first three games and six of the first seven before fading slightly. Tom Harley and Matthew Scarlett came into the defensive set-up, while up forward, Ronnie Burns, David Mensch and Adam Houlihan all kicked more than 30 goals that season.

We improved our defence (to eleventh in the AFL, conceding 104 points on average), but Geelong did not know how to defend or play on a man, did not know how to care for a teammate in the back half of the ground. It was woeful. Players would not come off their man and help out; if a Geelong player was exposed, with an opponent coming from behind, no one protected him, and he would get a knee in the back as a result. Plus, the midfielders had no defensive instincts, they did not know who they were playing on.

Against a top club we were shown up, and Essendon, the eventual premier and by far the best team in 2000, kicked 22 goals against us. Once the opposition had the football they just waltzed through to score, and I could not believe any of this. Remember, I had played in three flags in a decade at Essendon.

Even though we were still trying to find the right balance, we made the finals in year one, winning 12 of the 22 games, then lost an elimination final to Hawthorn by nine points. It was a decent start, and we had introduced some new players – Ling, Corey, Chapman and Mooney – who had all played some senior football in 2000.

The honeymoon was over pretty quickly, though. In my second season, 2001, Geelong fell away and missed the finals. We were in contention to round 17, just outside the top eight, but lost the last five games and missed out, finishing twelfth. We shifted away from what we had promised in a way, trading for Kent Kingsley as a forward from North Melbourne, Mitchell White from West Coast and

Justin Murphy from Carlton, and it was unsuccessful. Inevitably some of the older players disappeared: Stoneham at the end of 2000 and Garry 'Buddha' Hocking at the end of 2001.

Hocking was 32 and his knees were gone, and it was a test for me in the way that I handled his exit, because there was some controversy about this in the media and some uneasiness with the fans. Buddha was a much-loved Geelong player, and rightly so, but in 2001 we played him as a forward rather than on-ball much of the time, a decision which Mark Bairstow, Hocking's former teammate, called 'disgraceful' in an article in *The Age* in June. My response was measured. I said that we had spoken to Garry about retiring, and that we owed him the opportunity to make his own decision about the future. Buddha retired without too much angst, and I managed that particular test.

Fortunately we came back to the plan at the end of 2001 and had our best-ever national draft, grabbing Jimmy Bartel (pick 8), James Kelly (17), Steve Johnson (24) and Gary Ablett Jr with a third-round pick under the father–son rules of the time. But 2001 was a difficult year on the field, summed up by an *Age* article by Dermott Brereton, which I kept.

It went under the headline: 'Did Thompson make the right choice with Geelong?' Brereton argued that rather than coaching Geelong, I should have taken up the chance to coach Hawthorn. 'Geelong coach Mark Thompson must be wondering what has hit him,' he began.

Brereton had been on the sub-committee looking for Hawthorn's coach, and he pointed out that an approach had been made to me, and that I declined because I was in serious talks with Geelong. 'Thompson was the first choice of the three clubs in waiting at the time and, unfortunately for him at the moment, he has the weakest list and seemingly the worst culture of the three.'

Brereton's implication was that I had made a mistake in choosing Geelong, but deep down, I felt that we were on the right track. Late in my second season, Geelong's board offered me a new three-year contract for 2003–05, which reassured me that Brian Cook and the directors were comfortable with the progress. They had said all along – privately at least – that it was such a significant rebuild that it would take five years, and sure enough, it did take that long.

In 2002, Geelong won 11 games but just missed the top eight. Then in 2003 we lost seven of the first eight games, only won a total of seven for the season and finished twelfth. So in the first four seasons under my coaching, Geelong had only played finals once, and had finished fifth, twelfth, ninth and twelfth.

It was not a great result, but I didn't feel too much pressure because the board knew the plan; we had meetings and we talked about it. Brian Cook knew that, and he managed the expectations. With some of the veterans retiring we were left with virtually no experience, and we could have gone down the easy path of getting some top-ups to help, but I refused to do that. We had dabbled in that a couple of years earlier with White and Murphy, and I did not want to be a part of it anymore. Brian was strong on this as well; we chose to do it properly, and take our pain.

Off the field, Cook and Frank Costa were chipping away at a four-year plan. Geelong renegotiated its $1 million debt to the Australian Tax Office so that it could be repaid over five years. It did the deal with ANZ to cut that liability by almost half, and took up a new sponsorship with the Bendigo Bank worth several million dollars. The social club and the football club were merged, cleaning up that situation, and Ford, the major sponsor, was asked to bring forward payments to help with cash flow. They had worked a near miracle.

It was not as though we had fallen away badly on the field. We were competitive, but we would play the good teams like Brisbane Lions, who won the 2001–03 premierships, and they would beat us up. I would put all our young kids on their good players, and persist with that and we would last a quarter, then a quarter-and-a-half, then to half-time before we fell away, and that became a measurement for us. We had no choice in what we were doing and thankfully, the board held firm.

At the time, football was going crazy with revolving door policies, especially with coaches, and it is a method that I believe is terribly wrong. When the pressure comes on at a footy club, it tests the communication between football departments and boards, and normally, the coach is sacked. I agree with the notion of sacking people if they have not done their job, but first, you need to know if it is their fault, to check if they performed the task that they committed to do. Fortunately for me, Geelong was not into knee-jerk reactions like some other clubs.

My attitude was that we needed to go the draft, year after year, and train up the players in our way. Stephen Wells, the recruiter, was keen to explore trades along with drafting, and Stephen is really good at his job, but I was pushing the other way, for the kids. We had made mistakes with trading – getting the likes of Mitchell White from West Coast and clearing Charlie Gardiner to St Kilda, which I regretted – and perhaps I was burned by a couple of those situations, so I was not keen to explore too many trades from other clubs.

I demanded that Wellsy get the coaches involved and that we recruited players who fitted the club and fitted the game style. I trusted him, but I wanted to be involved, too. He would make the final call after the discussion – as long as they were the style

I wanted! We ended up agreeing even though it was not always easy to get to draft decisions. Often there were difficult conversations.

An example of where our recruiting worked was in 2003, when Matthew Scarlett won the Carji Greeves Medal at just 24. Scarlett had come in the 1997 draft at pick 45, being a father–son selection. His father, John, was a tough key position player who had played 183 games with the Cats, and in those days, clubs only needed to offer up a third-round pick to secure a father–son nomination.

In the 2003 season I used Scarlett on all the best opposition forwards and he was immediately successful. He held the Coleman medallist Matthew Lloyd to one goal in round 13, St Kilda's Fraser Gehrig to one in round 22 and the 2002 Coleman winner David Neitz of Melbourne to two goals in round 4. He would go on to become a Geelong all-time great.

Looking back, I have to laugh when I consider that I did not pick Scarlo in my first Geelong team, at the start of 2000. It was a pre-season game and I picked Hamish Simpson instead of him, and when Matthew asked me about it, I told him, 'We think he (Simpson) is a better option.' He disagreed, and I said, 'You'll have to prove that to us.' Ultimately, Simpson withdrew from the game with an injury, Scarlo played, and the rest is history.

We had also picked up Gary Ablett Jr and Jimmy Bartel, both of whom would proceed to become Brownlow medallists. I first saw Ablett playing for Victorian Country in an Under 18 game at Windy Hill alongside Steve Johnson, who we also drafted, and they were feeding off each other, streaming out of the middle that day. Gary was an obvious pick but he did take a while to settle into AFL footy, starting out as a small forward.

Even the process of signing him was difficult, I can recall. He was living at Jan Juc, on the coast outside Geelong, and even at that point he was concerned about terms, conditions, what certain elements would lead to, and what was guaranteed. It was frustrating for us, and there was a lot of work done before he said yes.

Gary was also incredibly shy, and petrified about the media, the fans and the whole scene of AFL footy, which I guess came from circus that went on around his father. Gary Junior knew it well; as a boy he had often hung around Kardinia Park on training nights and game days when Gary Senior was in the later part of his career. He wanted no part of that kind of scene.

Jimmy Bartel was a No. 8 pick in the 2001 national draft for us, a local boy who we knew had amazing hand–eye coordination as not only a brilliant footballer but a fine cricketer as well. He was under our noses with Geelong Falcons, and we went to see him at his home in the northern suburbs of Geelong, immediately learning something important about him.

Jimmy was quiet and shy up front, but strong, as strong as you can be when your father has left home and you have been the man of the house for quite a while. He barracked for Richmond, and he told us he did not want to be anyone's sidekick. 'Don't draft me to Geelong to look after Gary Ablett,' he said. And then went further: 'Don't draft me just because I am a local.' That was Jimmy Bartel, right there.

So in round 22 of a disappointing 2003 season, Geelong played St Kilda with only one player over 30 years of age, being wingman Peter Riccardi. That team included Scarlett at 24, Cameron Ling at 22, Max Rooke, Paul Chapman, Joel Corey and Corey Enright at 21, Steve Johnson at 20 and a trio of 19-year-olds named Gary Ablett Jr, Jimmy Bartel and James Kelly. Darren Milburn and Tom Harley swept across the backline in a good win over the Saints. The core of our team, the group that would take Geelong forward, was in place. Locked and loaded.

# 9

# RISING TIDE

## 2004–2005

When it happened for Geelong, it happened quickly. Of course our rebuild had been slow and methodical in the broader sense, but it was in 2004, my fifth year as coach, that it all clicked for us in a rush. The five-year build that myself and Brian Cook had spoken about in 1999 finally came to fruition. We made the final of the pre-season competition, losing to St Kilda, and finished top four in the regular season, eventually bowing out to Brisbane Lions in a preliminary final at the MCG, our first preliminary final appearance since 1995.

The Wizard Cup, as the pre-season competition was known then, was in March at the Docklands and Brent Guerra, then a St Kilda player, came off the square at the first bounce and flattened Cameron Ling. Guerra copped a three-week suspension but St Kilda, which had been drafting a team for the future like we had, was on a mission that night, and the Saints won their first piece of silverware since 1996, when they also had won the night premiership.

We were unfussed by that defeat, but concerned when we lost the first three games of the regular season to St Kilda, Carlton and Sydney, sliding to the bottom of the ladder. Patience was starting to run thin; Geelong's premiership drought had passed the 30-year mark, let us remember. But we held firm as a group and by the end of round 7, we were back in the top eight, and in round 13, we had a groundbreaking win over Brisbane Lions, who under Leigh Matthews were attempting to match Collingwood's 1927–30 feat of winning four flags in a row.

We had been chasing the Lions, trying to copy their style in some ways, and it was noticed that afternoon at Kardinia Park that this was something of a graduation. We had not beaten Matthews' team anywhere in their premiership era; not even since 1997. In a *Herald Sun* interview later that season, the recently-retired Lion Marcus Ashcroft told journalist Jon Ralph:

> They beat us at our own game. They won around the stoppages and ran harder than we did. As most teams do, they look at the best team of the previous year and try to model themselves on that, and I think Geelong, looking back to 2001, has tried to model themselves on the Brisbane team. I think that it showed in round 13 that they've come a long way.

Geelong defeated Hawthorn in round 22 to cling on to a top-four finish with 15 wins, vaulting from twelfth the previous season, completing a regular season in which we had not lost once at home. Excitement was building among our supporters, and undoubtedly we had the makings of a very good football team because we had been patient.

I had come from a club and from a coach who actually gave people time to develop, which was Kevin Sheedy's greatest strength. His genius was in his list management. At Geelong, we followed that model, and Cameron Mooney was an example of how it worked. Mooney's first season was 1998, and by 2004 he was starting to feel confidence in himself. We believed in him, and in most cases, players will make it if you have faith in them and they have the ability.

In footy, too many players are written off too quickly by coaches who want to see instant results. Coaches end up feeling the pressure from boards, who feel the pressure from the supporters. I was lucky at Geelong because I had support for the slow build right from the start.

Because of the debt and the long years without premierships, Geelong had never had the luxury of bottoming out for draft picks, as some clubs had chosen to do. It was in too precarious a position, because we knew all along that the club would be under tremendous strain if we disappeared too far down the ladder; the supporters would have dropped off in frustration. Around this time, Fremantle, Hawthorn and St Kilda were building again after going to the foot of the AFL ladder, but Geelong would have been wiped out had we gone to the bottom. As it was, we were able to remain competitive along with developing Brian Cook's plans to redevelop the stadium at Kardinia Park.

The dramatic improvement in defence is what I liked most of all in 2004, with our points-against down to 79, ranked number one in the competition, compared with sixteenth in the year before I started at the club. This was a huge step in five years, and offensively we were kicking 13 goals a game, seventh in the competition for scoring, which meant that the mix was good. The fast-ball movement had kicked in, which really came from Brisbane Lions, who were about contested ball, smashing it forward, running on to it. Their style was quite old school; Leigh Matthews had a simple brand and we were not far away from that model.

Our drafting in 2000–03 was paying real dividends. Cameron Ling had a great year in 2004, relishing his job as a tagger and winning the Carji Greeves Medal for the first time. Ling was only 23, Gary Ablett and Jimmy Bartel were 20, Steve Johnson 21, Paul Chapman (who exploded with 38 goals that year) and Joel Corey 22. Cam Mooney had developed and was still only 24 and Matthew Scarlett was a superstar at 25.

Geelong had profited from waiting for them to develop. Other clubs – Richmond was a notable example in that year – wanted the quick fix, and I hated this style of management. In one *Herald Sun* interview in July 2004, I said that the patience of the Geelong administration was the only reason I had held on to my job, and that the AFL was 'out of control, totally out of control'.

By season's end, Richmond had sacked Danny Frawley, who had taken the job with the Tigers at the same time that I joined Geelong, the end of 1999. The contrast in styles of management was duly noted, and at a press conference toward the end of 2004, a journalist asked me if I had any advice for the new Richmond coach. 'Just convince them they're not going to win the premiership in two years,' I said.

We were not too far away in that year. We lost the first final to Port Adelaide, when I remember that we were quite nervous, then beat Essendon, which pitched us against Brisbane Lions in a preliminary final, just one game away from a grand final berth. We lost by nine points at the MCG in a cracking game where we pushed the Lions all the way to the finish. I remember that we dominated the inside 50 count (59 to 40) but failed to convert properly, with Ben Graham (0.4) missing a few simple shots. Graham would not play another game in the AFL; he headed over to the United States to pursue his dream of becoming an NFL punter at season's end.

It was the game that Leigh Matthews felt probably cost the Lions the fourth consecutive flag, because the AFL made Brisbane play it in Melbourne, despite the fact that they had finished higher on the ladder than Geelong. At the time, the league was adhering to an agreement with the MCG Trust which demanded that at least one of the two preliminary finals had to be played at the MCG. Given that Port Adelaide had finished on top and hosted one preliminary final in Adelaide, it meant that the Lions–Geelong game was in Melbourne, and that Matthews' team had to travel again, a big factor without doubt. Lethal wrote in his book *Accept The Challenge* that he still felt sick about that decision. The AFL plainly agreed, because it changed the agreement the next year, and all finals are now hosted by the team finishing higher on the ladder, with the exception of the grand final, which is guaranteed to be played at the MCG.

We kicked 10.15 on the night, which is a gentle reminder of the importance of conversion, and here is the funny thing: I ran into Graeme 'Gubby' Allan, the Lions' football manager at the time, a few years on, and he told me that they believed Geelong should have won the game. I am not so sure about that, though, because deep down I don't think we knew how to close it out. With hindsight, we should not have been surprised at how it ended, because we were still learning.

Port Adelaide, coached by Mark Williams, won the flag, bringing Brisbane's amazing run to an end, and we watched the grand final thinking that we were a chance of going the extra step in 2005. A couple of weeks after the season, we were guaranteed to become one of the favourites when we produced a trade that brought All Australian ruckman Brad Ottens to Geelong.

Ottens was a star, we knew that. He had won his All Australian selection in 2002 as a raw 21-year-old, but he had hit a plateau, and Richmond was in turmoil after Frawley had been removed, leaving Terry Wallace to move in as coach. What we heard when he announced that he was coming to Geelong was something of a first, because Ottens said he joined the Cats for team success:

> The whole reason behind this was to enjoy my footy again, and I saw Geelong as the place that I could enjoy my footy and enjoy my life as well and live down there. They [Geelong] look like a really positive and stable club and that was something that really appealed to me.

Ottens would provide ruck support for Steven King, now captain of the club but battling persistent injuries. He was also more than capable of playing as a key forward, which had been an issue for us. It was the biggest recruiting coup Geelong had pulled off in years, and I felt vindicated by the fact Ottens actually *wanted* to come to the club.

We also had drafted Matthew Egan and Nathan Ablett, younger brother of Gary Junior and son of Gary Senior, giving us a young key back and key forward, and they would be introduced in 2005 as the evolution of the team continued.

In round 5of 2005 we defeated the defending premier, Port Adelaide, on their home deck at Football Park to make a statement about our intentions and our ability. We spent most of the first half of the season in the top four, then we lost four games in a row between rounds 17 and 20 and gave up a top-four berth, ultimately finishing sixth with 12 wins. We had regressed slightly from 2004.

Defence was the catch phrase of 2005 in the AFL, with the three interstate teams – Adelaide, Sydney and West Coast – all really difficult to score against, and all excellent teams. Geelong averaged 86-points-against, which was commendable, but slipped down the defensive rankings to fifth with the Crows at number one, conceding just 69 points a game. That is the kind of season it was; the AFL chief executive Andrew Demetriou memorably noted this when he criticised Sydney's suffocating game style early in the year:

> We don't tell football clubs how to play, but obviously we take notice of how things are going. And I guess I, like others, would like to see the Sydney Swans winning more games because it's a very important market for us. But I don't like at all the way that they're playing football, but that's just a personal view. I think it would be fair to say in the early part of the season we saw some games that weren't attractive, and I think they've been described as ugly.
>
> And probably there would a brand of football being played on the other side of the border which is not particularly attractive. Unless the Swans change that style of play, they won't win many football matches. I don't think there's anything we [the AFL] can do, because we wouldn't intervene. But I think unless there's a change in the manner and the style in which they play, they will lose more games than they win.

Demetriou would come to have that comment thrown back at him for years. Personally, I viewed the way Sydney played as *safe* footy, but they were an outstanding team with great talent, too, happy to grind out games at stoppages because they had great inside strength around the ball. They were terribly tough to beat, and as it happened, we ended up going head-to-head with the Swans at the SCG in a sudden-death final.

We had beaten Melbourne in week one of the finals to set that up, and it was a wet night in Sydney for the semi-final, the winner to secure a spot in the preliminary final. Needless to say, it was a difficult assignment, but we were up for it, and we played terrific football that night, taking on Sydney at their own game. The conditions made it even more of an attritional game than usual, not to mention the fact it was a knockout final, and almost every possession was contested.

Geelong led by 20 points at half-time, and Sydney had kicked only 2.6 to the long break. We were still 17 points up at three-quarter time and in a low-scoring affair, this looked a matchwinning lead, especially when we extracted the first goal of the final quarter to extend the buffer to 23 points. But the rest is history, as they say. It was *not* a matchwinning lead.

That game was ours. We owned it until the last three seconds, then it was ripped away from us by Nick Davis, Sydney's dangerous forward, and that defeat goes down as the most gut-wrenching I ever experienced at any level of football as a player or coach. It was a defining night for Geelong, and for me as a coach, and it coloured everything that happened from that moment on.

Davis kicked the last four goals of the game to win it for Sydney and end our 2005 season. The last of those goals, from a ball-up just 20 metres from goal, came with three seconds left on the clock and Geelong clinging to a three-point lead, and it still gives me shudders to think about it. There were excuses for Geelong; we were tired from a draining match, and Steven King had gone down with an injury, leaving Henry Playfair in the ruck, where he was not suited. But the fact of the matter is that in the pivotal moment of the whole season, we messed up. Nick Davis never should have been able to run through that stoppage area unmarked or unhindered, but that is what happened.

It was a set play by Sydney, not even close to a fluke, and I watched it unfold from the coaches' box and it was like death in slow motion. Our runner was already on the field; it was too late to get a message out to the players. In moments like that, the coach becomes irrelevant and it is down to the guys on the field; they have been trained for these situations, repeated over and over, and you trust that they will set up in the right way, the way that you have taught them to set the structure. But they did not.

Here is what should have happened: we needed to get players into defence for the 'outnumber' at the stoppage, to clog it up as much as possible. At the moment the field umpire called the ball-up in the goal mouth, that actually started to happen. I have watched it a zillion times on replay: there are 16, yes *sixteen* Geelong players in the picture as the umpire calls the ball-up, but then the Sydney players start waving their arms and walking away from the stoppage, clearing the area for themselves. And the Geelong players – their opponents – walk away with them, which is a mistake. A fatal mistake.

At this point, I was screaming in the box, and you cannot imagine a more helpless feeling as a coach. Sydney walked out a whole bunch of our players to utterly nondescript positions. Matthew Scarlett went with Barry Hall to the goal-line; you might as well be 15 rows back in the stand, and Tom Harley had gone (with Darren Jolly), Darren Milburn was out of there too, minding a man who did not want to go near the football. Sydney created a funnel wide enough for a bus to drive through, and Nick Davis came from the blindside, running straight at the Swans' goals.

By now, it is near despair for me. Jason Ball, working against a part-time ruckman in Playfair, taps it left, not even looking because he knows that Davis is on the burst. Josh Hunt, who is playing on

Davis, is chasing him hard but cops a block from a Swans player and falls a step behind. Davis grabs at the footy, but bobbles it, then hits it with a left-foot volley as Joel Corey tries in vain to smother. It loops through for a goal, and Anthony Hudson's commentary on Channel 10 goes into the annals: 'I see it. But I don't believe it.'

The point is, we knew the play; we actually *used* that play for our forward-50 stoppages in that year. We called it 'The Blitz', and our game plan from 2005 tells you all you want to know about set-ups for back-50 stoppages. The rule was to create the plus-one, a numerical advantage, and clog the game up, try to win the football. 'Never leave space for the blitz,' it reads. That is the paragraph that jumps out, the Nick Davis paragraph.

Under the most pressure they had ever experienced in their football lives, our senior players allowed themselves to be walked away from that stoppage when they should have stayed in the contest. They should not have allowed themselves to be spectators at the most critical contest in a final. It was the only way that we could lose that game from that position, and it happened. You cannot train for that pressure, and they failed the test. That is what they did, and that is what I was thinking as I walked across the SCG to the dressing rooms under the Noble Stand, very much alone.

I was angry, ready to smash someone or throw something, that is how angry, so furious that everyone left me alone, even the other coaches. You did not have to look too far to see the devastation of the players, and of the fans in the crowd. For Brenton Sanderson, a longtime warrior half-back, it was the end of his career at 199 games, one short of the double-century, and for the rest of us, it was season over. For Geelong, it was yet another near miss, the latest in the catalogue, and I cried, which is a rarity for me in footy. Most of us did.

In these moments, we could have disintegrated as a footy club, but what happened straight after that game was quite the opposite. I don't take credit for it, because the players and the entire club handled it in a certain way, but what I did in the rooms is one of my better coaching moments. I was ready to savage the players, but ultimately I did not. In fact, I said probably the best thing that I could have said. I knew from experience that in these moments, a coach can lose his players with a personal attack, or a blame game, and lose them forever.

I said something along the lines of, 'You tried your guts out. You didn't get the win tonight, but you know what? All we have to do, boys, is fix up three seconds and three points. We're well and truly on the way, boys.'

It was not easy to say that. I felt like going a lot further, but in the end, it was true, because they had done a mighty job, and if not for that one poor stoppage, our feelings would have been completely different. Footy is such a fine line sometimes. In the minutes before I spoke to the players, I had a Kevin Sheedy moment bobbing around in my mind. Most of what I learned from Sheedy was positive, as I have said, but this time I took something from a Sheedy error. When Essendon lost the 1996 preliminary final – coincidentally against Sydney at the same ground – to Tony Lockett's last kick for a point to break a deadlock, Sheedy hammered the Essendon players. I remembered it well; I had retired as a player, but it was my first season in the coaches' box with Sheeds.

The game had been similar in style and Essendon had made dumb mistakes at the finish, just as we had on that night, and Sheedy yelled so hard at the players that his voice was breaking under the strain of his tirade. No one could stop him; he was in a fit of rage, and I know all these years later that he regrets the way he approached that defeat. I did not want to go down that path in 2005. I didn't speak for too long, and we never reviewed the game, and the hard thing was, I still believe we were good enough to win the flag that year. Sydney, of course, went on to pip West Coast by four points in the grand final and it was a hard pill for all of us to swallow.

We went back to our city hotel that night in Sydney, and Alex Popescu, our patron and benefactor, put on a function for us. Everyone was there, and we stayed tight, and it was as good a night as you could have in the circumstances, and as the dust settled, I realised and Geelong realised that it *needed* to happen to us. We set about making ourselves what we called 'ballsier', we looked at ways to improve our confidence and probably for the first time, we put more serious effort into planning for stoppages, because it was a growing area of the game. I don't think we had a goal kicked against us like that for a long time afterward.

The pain dulls but never truly goes away, although I have reached the point where I can watch that game back, and talk about it, and when I do speaking engagements at footy clubs and sporting clubs nowadays, there is always a Sydney supporter in the crowd who asks me to run him through those moments and the Nick Davis goal. You don't forget something like that, which is as it should be, because when Geelong got another opportunity it was there in the back of the players' minds, driving them, just as it was for me as an Essendon player in 1993, thinking back to the heartbreak of 1990.

While our defeat was interpreted as yet another failure for Geelong, the reality was slightly more positive, and we all knew that. Because the phenomenon of the near miss happens to most clubs who eventually reach the top of the mountain. Our task was to get back on the climb.

# 10

# HELL

## 2006

The year from hell actually began with some strong optimism. Off the back of a strong 2005, albeit with a difficult finish, Geelong won its first silverware in 43 long years, defeating Adelaide by nine points in the final of the NAB Cup pre-season competition in March. Not since 1963 had the Cats won a senior premiership and you could see it in the players' reactions; they were jumping all over each other at the siren. Cam Mooney kicked three last-quarter goals including the matchwinner as we came from behind to win.

While winning the pre-season competition was not a priority, I felt there was a lot to take from that victory. In particular, the fact that the game was played in Adelaide, on the road, was important, because we were playing against the crowd as well as the Crows, who were an excellent team. We came through the test. The game was close, and we had come from behind, and the fact we had handled it was a good sign for us. I told the media the next day that the win would 'give us confidence knowing that whenever we play, whoever we play, wherever we play, we can win'.

But it was a mirage. When the regular season began, we lost seven of the first ten games, including three at Kardinia Park, and the club grew tense as only footy clubs can do when the losses mount up and the team unravels. I had also suffered in my personal life, with the breakup of my 18-year marriage to Annette during the first month of the season. This was a decision that I had taken myself, but it was difficult given we had three children. I knew it would hurt them.

I think what broke us up was the coaching. There is a toll that it takes, no doubt. My work was so demanding of my time and I felt like I was being pulled in two directions. I had the professional challenge of coaching, which was all-consuming, and the demands of family, and I knew I wasn't doing a great job of being a family man. Annette hadn't wanted to move from Melbourne, and right back when I started commuting, I hated it. There were roadworks – they were widening the Princes Freeway to four lanes – and there were holdups every day that slowly drove me mad. One night a week staying in Geelong turned into two nights, and then I started to like having my own space. After a long day at the club I could have a long shower, I could leave the mess in the kitchen and clean up later, I could watch whatever I wanted on TV. It sounds selfish, but playing and coaching elite sport makes you selfish. Sadly, a lot of marriages don't survive.

They all took a sacrifice, the whole family sacrifices. The kids were getting teased about Geelong, and my situation. I never put any expectations on them, but we would go to footy or go to tennis and the kids can feel what's happening with you.

The kids have grown up and fortunately they've found their own way, all independent people. Lauren completed a marketing/business degree and works in marketing for Bell Potter, the brokerage service; Michael runs a drive-through bottle shop where he started work at 18 and won the owner's trust to take control of it, and Daniel is still studying. He plays football at Aberfeldie in the Essendon league and spent some time in the TAC Cup with Calder Cannons. I think he will end up being a good player. I can see myself in him a little, the way he plays, although he is much bigger than me.

Maybe I have not been father of the year to my kids. People do sacrifice their own lives for their kids, but I chose a different path or in a way, that path was chosen for me. It was a big decision, but like a lot of people, your work takes you away from other things that you want to do, but you do it for a reason. And that reason might be a burning desire to give your all to something, without compromise. At least I know that when I leave this world my kids will be adults and they will reap some benefits from my work. They might even think, *He wasn't a good dad, but he helped getting my house paid for*. They mean the world to me, my kids, and maybe I can be grandfather of the year!

Meanwhile at the football club there were issues that bubbled up behind the scenes, notably the differences that myself and others in the football department were having with our fitness coordinator, Loris Bertolacci. Loris, who had competed at international level as a hammer thrower and shot-putter, had been at Essendon prior to joining Geelong in 1998, back in my time at Windy Hill, and we had been mates then. But at Geelong things had been testy before 2006, because Steven Hocking, manager of training services, and I both thought our running and skills programs were not right.

Loris survived a review at the end of 2005 and over the off-season he was probably feeling alone, because he knew our thoughts. The football department wanted to take more control, Loris wanted to do it his way, and I was finding it impossible to work with him.

Then in April 2006 he was sacked, and he took legal action over his dismissal that was later settled.

In June, a review we had commissioned with the Victoria University looked into our conditioning program over the previous two years. Hocking and I were concerned that the players were not fit enough to run out games, and the report appeared to confirm what we had thought. It said that pre-season running was down 47 per cent in 2006 by comparison with 2005, and that in-season skills were down 35 per cent.

The VU report was pretty clear: 'According to the raw data analysed when comparing workloads completed by players in 2005–06, on the surface it appears that substantially less work was done leading into the 2006 season.'

Bertolacci had a different view, which he expressed later that year:

> Since I was dismissed by GFC about a month ago, there has been speculation in the media about the reasons for my dismissal. People have speculated that there may be a connection between my dismissal and player injuries at the beginning of the season and the current fitness of players.
>
> The fact is that, at the end of last season, decisions were made at senior levels in the club about the length, frequency and content of pre-season training. One initiative was to limit training to one session per day. There was also a decision to send some players into a 'boot camp' style training program in November which directly resulted in a disruption to the training program. As a result, and due to a number of players recovering from surgery in respect of serious injuries from the previous season there was a lack of fit players available to participate in the skills training in the December–January period.

> When it came to the NAB Cup we had a squad of about 27 fit players. It was only with a concentrated effort from the players and the fitness and medical team that the club was able to successfully compete and win that competition.
>
> While I did not endorse the decisions taken in relation to the pre-season training, I do not believe that this was a factor which directly affected my dismissal. The immediate reason given by GFC for terminating my employment related to discussions between myself and club officials about the selection of a player who was recovering from injury. As the content of these discussions may well be a key issue in court proceedings, I do not wish to be drawn into further comment on these matters.
>
> As we are now going into round 11, I would expect all players, other than those who have been injured, to have reached peak fitness. I believe that the club has a very strong team and they will perform more strongly in the second half of the season. I wish the players every success and wish to thank those people at GFC who have continued to support me.

There are a lot of theories as to what went wrong at Geelong in 2006, and why we went backwards. We were not fit enough, we were overrun in games, we lost a lot of close games as a result, and we had too many injuries. Loris was about upper body strength and weight training and not enough running was done. In my opinion, inadequate fitness levels were the number one problem. It was not the only reason, and we all had to take some responsibility, but I had it at the top of the list. Loris deserves credit for building up those young players over a few years, but in the end my relationship with him went sour; it was not a united workplace. We made a hard decision, which is the way footy goes when you are trying to get better.

Meanwhile in round 10 against West Coast at Kardinia Park, we suffered the most humiliating fade-out of all, a defeat that resonated for quite a while. Geelong led the Eagles by 54 points in that game, with 18 minutes left in the third quarter, and we were still 36 points up at three-quarter time, but West Coast launched a last-quarter avalanche and Adam Hunter came off the bench to kick the goal that won it for the Eagles. It was that club's biggest-ever comeback from a deficit at three-quarter time and one of the biggest in VFL–AFL history.

That was the way that the season went. We lost three games by fewer than ten points, dropped out of the running for the top eight with two rounds remaining, lost to Hawthorn in round 22 and ended up finishing tenth, more than two games out of the finals. Needless to say after the optimism of 2005, it was a disastrous downturn and it almost cost me my job as coach.

Geelong went wobbly in mid-August, the first time I had witnessed that in six years with the club, and in response, I also was moved to consider my position. Brian Cook called a review of the operations of the club, which I saw as being too public and too inclined to apportioning blame. I went on holidays to Hamilton Island immediately after the last game of 2006, unsure if I would see out the last year of my three-year contract in 2007.

Brian Cook ran the review, which went for six weeks and of course, was accompanied by the noise that football creates, a cacophony of speculation that ran off the charts, most of it about my own future. Cook said to me the day before I left that he wanted to interview me as part of the process, but I told him that I intended to enjoy my break.

'Just come back and have a chat to us,' he said.

I said, 'No mate, I'm on holidays.'

He said, 'We'll pay for it.'

And I said, 'No, I'm not coming. You're gonna wait now. You made me wait all this time.'

My attitude was pretty feisty. While it was widely reported in the media as Geelong considering whether to continue with me, I was quite close to quitting, too, of my own volition. I went to Hamilton Island thinking that I no longer wanted to work with those people because, to me, I had done exactly what we set out to do at Geelong, to build from within and create something strong and sustainable. Why would I want to work with Geelong when I had delivered on my word, then all of a sudden a little pressure comes along and they want to throw the towel in?

I knew at the time that at least two directors, Doug Wade and Gareth Andrews, wanted to see me gone, which is not in dispute. Wade was asked about this on Fox Footy's *Open Mike* in 2013 and he answered: 'Pretty much, we thought that, yes. [But] we were convinced otherwise . . . It was going to come to a vote but we felt that [sacking] wasn't the right thing to do at that time.'

At the time there was a lot of rumour-mongering about my own personal situation, and questioning of whether I was distracted by my marriage break-up. There were suggestions that it was impacting on my ability to coach the team. A lot of it was unfounded; personally, I was okay. It was not that difficult to coach through that situation, because by 2006, the club was set up and running.

I do think that some people judged me because it was my decision to leave the marriage. Nobody makes a decision like that on a whim, but in society, the scuttlebutt just snowballs, gets bigger and *badder*. There were rumours that I was having a relationship with my personal assistant, for instance, which were completely wrong. I was living pretty much full-time in Geelong and what happened was inevitable, but I ran away for six months and hid from it, when what I probably should have done, with hindsight, was stand up and explain myself. I should have told people that you don't leave a marriage to hurt your wife or kids, you leave because it is finished.

I still did not know whether I would continue coaching Geelong by the time I returned from Hamilton Island a few weeks later for a 7 a.m. meeting with the board in Melbourne. The meeting was convened at one of the board member's legal offices in William Street in the city, and I had already warned Cook that I would walk away if any media turned up. Walking into the meeting, I told them right up front, 'I'm not sure that I want to work with you.'

There was a fair degree of anxiety in the room, but I kept going, told them they would be weak to break down at the first point of tension that we had confronted at Geelong. 'How badly are *we* going, because it's not just me that went badly, *the club* went badly. How badly are *we* going, and the *club* going?'

I had heard from certain people what they intended asking me, so I threw this back at them. I knew that they were leaking to the media; it had become a public event.

'I know exactly what you're going to say to me this morning. Want to hear from my mouth? You want to know if I've got the passion to do it? Is that right?'

They said, 'Yeah.'

Entering that room I was not sure how I felt about going on, but they did ask me, and I said, 'Of course I've got the passion.'

After that, it settled down, and on 25 September, Geelong announced that I would be continuing as coach in 2007, and that Tom Harley would replace Steven King as captain. I left that whole process a hardened football coach, my skin a bit tougher, having survived what was almost a public execution.

A few things had happened in the lead-up to the meeting, notably that the players saved me. I have no doubt about that. When Brian Cook talked to the senior players, I know that they backed me to continue, and that was critical. Without their support, I think that I would have been sacked, but they pretty much told him that I was delivering a consistent message and that I treated them well. That is where moments like the Sydney final in 2005 are important; you blow up after a game and you can pay a price later on.

But I had not lost them, and Matthew Scarlett made a phone call to Mike Sheahan of the *Herald Sun* in September 2006 that emphasised the point. Scarlett is a straight shooter, and he told Sheahan that he would walk from Geelong if I was sacked, creating a headline for the back page of the newspaper the next day.

Cook, who had interviewed 60 people as part of his review, emphasised this point when he made the announcement that I was continuing: 'Of all the people that I interviewed, to a person, there was a belief that Mark Thompson was a good coach, had been a good coach, and that his strengths were in teaching and developing players.'

Around the same time, I had also sought some advice and counsel from friends, the most important of which came from Rob Hulls, the Victorian government minister and a great Geelong supporter who is also a good mate. Hulls told me, 'Go out and coach, be yourself, do it your way, whether you fail or succeed. Do it *your* way.'

I took that to heart as we moved forward, and while I spoke to a few other people, it was Rob who really hit home with his message. I have said since then that I thought the review was too public, too hard on the coaching staff who seemed to be in the gun for a long period as we waited for the verdict. This doesn't only refer to me;

all the assistant coaches and the 30-odd staff were on tenterhooks as well. The whole club was impacted.

But the changes that came as a result of it were good results for Geelong, I acknowledge that. The club hired Neil Balme as general manager of football, coming out of Collingwood and replacing Garry Davidson, and Balmey and I found that we could work together. Balme had been ruck coach at Essendon when I played there, and he had coached Melbourne for a few years, but I didn't know him all that well. The first day, he said, 'Listen, I'm the footy manager, I'm not here to coach or judge you. I'm here to make it easy for you. You coach your way.' I liked his style.

Steve Hocking, a good man and a person I respected, who was already helping set up the fitness area, was upgraded to football operations manager. Part of Cook's review said that I was doing too much outside the coaching area, which was true, when you think of the fights I had been having with Loris and the interest I needed to take in the physiotherapists, the doctors and other staff. Having Hocking and Balme meant that I could achieve this and leave matters like contracting to other people whom I could trust.

Dean Robinson came in from Cronulla Sharks to do the weights and rehabilitation, and Paul Haynes from Adelaide Crows to do conditioning, and he was terrific with his energy and his positive ways. Chris Bradshaw had previously been hired as the doctor, having completed a stint with Fulham in the English Premier League soccer, so our set-up was better, and I went back to coaching. It was back to the players for me, which is how I liked it.

I wrote a letter to Cook on 13 September, soon after the review was completed. I noted that the club wanted me to do more hands-on work with players: 'In relation to these issues, I am more than willing to do more coaching duties than management/administration.

Having someone to look after the many areas will free enormous amounts of time to achieve this outcome.'

I advocated for the retention of assistant coaches Leigh Tudor and Andy Lovell, although ultimately I lost out in the case of Lovell, which left the way open for Brenton Sanderson to come back as an assistant after a year under Choco Williams at Port Adelaide. Cook wanted the training services area to be bulked up, with Steve Hocking to organise that, and I encouraged the club to employ a full-time development coach, rather than expect the current assistants to perform that role. Summing up, I wrote in my letter:

> Lastly, this year has been a disaster from early in the year all the way through to this point. We have not performed anywhere near our potential and when looking for answers, obviously a big finger has been pointed at me. It is understandable in many ways but I still believe this club can climb back up the ladder very quickly without drastic measures having to take place.
>
> If and when the board decides the outcomes for our poor performance and before expressing any of your decisions to the public or media could you please discuss with [me] personally the details of your proposed changes. If I am to coach the Geelong Football Club, as coach I really do need the right to accept and endorse the proposed intended changes, otherwise it will be seen by many as the coach not being able to have control over principally what he is employed to do.

The review affected my relationship with Cook for a time; that could not be avoided in the white-hot environment of an AFL club, and we did lose some personal engagement that had been there before. But I have not harboured a grudge. I knew that we had good outcomes, and I respected the fact that someone else could have been given a chance to coach. I also knew that at another club, the change might have happened to satisfy the mob. It has been happening for years in footy. Look at Stan Alves, who coached St Kilda to a grand final in 1997 and was gone at the end of 1998, a year on. Who makes these decisions? It is a joke.

One of the major changes that came out of the review was the arrival of Leading Teams, the leadership organisation, which was the suggestion of Neil Balme. Leading Teams, started up by a schoolteacher named Ray McLean, had enjoyed some success at AFL clubs, notably with the Sydney Swans in the Paul Roos era, fanning out to Hawthorn under Alastair Clarkson and some other clubs.

First used by McLean at Central Districts in the SANFL in 1993 with great results, Alves picked Ray's program up at St Kilda in 1996 only to see it fail to catch on, then when Roos took over at Sydney in 2003, he ran with it. The results were on the board. Sydney won a flag in 2005 and almost another in 2006 and their culture was being talked about, so other clubs looked to use the Leading Teams method, the Hawks, Collingwood, Melbourne and Western Bulldogs among them.

I was in favour of it and even happier when Gerard Murphy came into the club as the facilitator, because I quickly had a rapport with him. We did not follow the Leading Teams model strictly; in my view, whether it works is more about how good the facilitator is, and Gerard was good, there is no doubt. It is about their ability and the timing of the messages, and I could see what he was on about: open communication in the workplace so that issues were not allowed to fester, the encouragement of dialogue rather than having bosses who made their staff scared of them. What you do not necessarily want is work environments with *no* conflict, with no trust, no conversations, no accountability, no responsibility, no results.

Leading Teams has what it calls 'peer reviews' where players and coaches are required to sit in front of their teammates and hear evaluations of their performances and their work practices. That's the part of the program that has proven controversial and it is quite a tricky area. For instance, when Jason Akermanis was playing with Western Bulldogs, he was furious that he was told by teammates to stop performing his famous handstand after victories. Barry Hall has said that it went 'too far' at Sydney, where he was criticised heavily by his own teammates for being reported too often and eventually left the club and finished his career with the Bulldogs.

But we said to Gerard that we wanted the players to talk to one another, without being *too* confrontational. Yes, we wanted the honesty to come out, but not in a way that people would react badly to, because we were not ready for that. So we all prepared to face the music in 2007. We were about to hear some highly interesting views from within.

Slazenger
SIMONDS
Ford
GFC

# 11

# DEATH OR GLORY

## 2007

Geelong came back in 2007 to appreciable change. Personally, I was emboldened by the fact that I was back to pure coaching, and intent upon trying to do it my way, as Rob Hulls had suggested. I resolved to make the team more aggressive with the football, a kamikaze attitude that we devised to get through the congestion that other teams were creating. It was my eighth season as head coach, I had a year's contract to run, which meant that if we had played badly, I was gone. So it was death or glory for me, which in some ways, was a good thing.

Our early sessions of peer reviews with Gerard Murphy uncovered some deep issues. Within a few weeks the players had told me that I needed to stop focusing so much on what the opposition was doing; suggested to Gary Ablett Jr that he was not working hard enough; asked Cameron Mooney to stop getting himself reported and suspended and insisted that Matthew Scarlett curb his late-night drinking.

Most of the themes that came out of those truth sessions related to off-field behaviour and training standards, but it also became clear that the players did not know how to talk to each other. Fortunately Gerard did an excellent job of following up on the themes that were raised, which is hugely important.

Gary Ablett's case was interesting, because he was upset about the criticism that was made of his preparation. In a nutshell, the players thought he should be training harder, whereas he thought he was already working hard. In his own eyes, he was probably looking after his body, because Gary knew his body really well, and by 2006 he had been playing excellent footy.

The players thought that sometimes he skipped training when he could have been on the track, and Gerard explained it in a way that brought him around. In the end, Gary said, 'I'll give it a try. Everyone has to give a bit, so I'll give it.' And he started staying on the track for longer.

Matthew Scarlett's situation was quite simple. The players told him, 'You know the rules, you know what time you have to be out of the pub! It's no good for you to know the curfew is one o'clock, you kick everyone else out and then go back inside for another drink!' Scarlett, too, took it on board and responded.

Cam Mooney had been suspended from playing four times in 2006 and the players had had enough of his ill-discipline on the field. He copped their wrath, too, and like the others, he took the criticism as fair and constructive. He proceeded to have a great season.

So three of the big personalities of the team had all been pulled up within a few months of us bringing Gerard Murphy in to help us. I did not escape the peer reviews. I had to sit in front of the players to hear their feedback, and what they thought was plain: 'Stop talking the opposition up, make it more about us.'

I took that on board, as well as the second major point they made: 'Come out of the cave a little earlier when we lose.' It was a fault of mine that I could sook when we played badly, and you can be overly critical in that state of mind. The players also wanted me to improve my communication; to ensure that I talked to *everyone,* even those on the periphery.

The Leading Teams model favours a leadership group rather than leaving all the responsibility to a single player, such as the captain. Nowadays every club has a leadership group but it was Ray McLean who started the concept, and the model is similar for most organisations. Together as a group you create a 'trademark', which might be one or more words, capturing the way you wish the rest of the competition to view your team. At Sydney in 2003, for instance, it was HARD, DISCIPLINED, RELENTLESS. The Swans certainly followed through on that. At Melbourne, the Demons had a catch phrase: 'Anything it takes.'

Beyond the trademark, there are what are called 'expected behaviours', which is a list of dos and don'ts, fundamentally, as to how you play and how you carry yourself. The peer review sessions that happen afterward are about measuring how each individual stands up against the trademark and the behaviours. If they have not measured up, they are supposed to be told, not in a personal way, but constructively.

Open and honest communication is key; it is not about potting people, just maintaining certain standards and being clear about what they are. I immediately liked the method at Geelong, because myself and the other coaches were sick of being the policemen, and at the time, we did have a problem with off-field behaviour and in particular with too much drinking. In 2007, the problem was solved.

So Tom Harley headed up our leadership group, and they were quickly called into the firing line with a decision to make about

Steve Johnson. Stevie J had been an issue for Geelong for quite a while. In 2003, he had broken both ankles trying to jump off a wall to get himself into the Torquay pub, and in 2005 he was arrested for being drunk and disorderly outside a nightclub in Geelong, so he was already on quite thin ice. Then early in January 2007, when the players returned from their break, it emerged that he had been arrested and locked up in his hometown, Wangaratta, for drunkenness during the festive season. We had put Steve out for trade the previous year, after the earlier incidents, and Collingwood was close to taking him. By this time, he had played some good footy in patches, but he was unprofessional with his off-field behaviour.

As it turned out on this hot Christmas Eve, he had been for a long bike ride, had more than a few beers with some mates at the pub, and left to crash at a friend's place where the others would meet him later. He sat down in a chair on the back verandah and promptly fell asleep. The only problem was that his friend had moved! When the new owner got up in the early hours of Christmas Day, he called the police to have the gentleman sleeping on his property and affected by alcohol promptly removed. Steve was charged with being drunk in a public place. Worse, he had not told the footy club anything about the incident for more than a week after returning to training for 2007.

Tom Harley and the leadership group suspended Johnson for the first five weeks of the season and sent him off to train with the VFL group under Leigh Tudor, which I thought to be a harsh penalty. I know that Steve did too, and I told the leadership group that, but they were looking at the bigger picture. They saw it as a line in the sand moment and with hindsight, it was – not just for Steve Johnson, but for the football club itself.

The club put out a statement:

Geelong forward Steve Johnson has been suspended by the club from the senior playing group indefinitely.

All of Johnson's training will take place with the club's VFL squad under coach Leigh Tudor and he will not be invited back with the senior squad until such time as he proves that his attitude and behaviour have changed and that he is willing to be a responsible and contributing member of the club. Johnson's suspension from the senior group will be reviewed no sooner than the sixth round of the season.

'The club has not taken this decision lightly,' Geelong's general manager of football operations Neil Balme said. 'Steve has been given numerous chances and it is fair to say that he is now down to his last opportunity to prove that he wants to stay with the club.

'We understand that young people make mistakes in all walks of life. This includes AFL players. We do believe in allowing people to grow, learn from their mistakes and mature.

'We have provided ample opportunity for Steve to display the behaviour that we expect from all of our players. The ball is now firmly in his court to prove that he is worthy of a return to the senior group.'

The club decided to sanction Johnson following his recent arrest for being drunk in a public place and his decision not to inform the club of this latest indiscretion. The player leadership group was given the responsibility of working through this issue and their recommendation was accepted by the club.

Johnson was informed of the outcome and accepted the view of the club and his fellow players.

Stevie picked up a part-time job in a real estate office and swore off the grog for the year. He was not even allowed to train with the senior group, let alone play, and it hurt him, but importantly, he took it on the chin, as Tom Harley acknowledged in a *Herald Sun* interview:

> I can tell you after it was all handed down, I was livid and Steve was livid. At no stage did the leadership group consider this to be a watershed moment for the club. To us, it was all about Steve's wellbeing as a person.
>
> We didn't want Steve to be the guy perched in the corner of a pub in Wangaratta saying, 'I could have been this' or 'I could have been that'. It was about the individual first, the fact that we were able to get some football outcomes out of it as well, that was a bit of a bonus.

I remember Stevie coming to me halfway through his suspension and angling for a reduction, pointing out how fit he was and how well he was responding. He trained hard and did the right thing in that period, but the leaders were not going to back down on that, and nor was I. And once that incident happened, I think the senior guys realised, *Shit, this is the standard now. If I do it, this is what I can expect*. It was a big penalty but it actually got through to Stevie, and it was a significant moment for Geelong.

Tom Harley was already proving himself to be a revelation as captain of the club, an all-round good guy who said all the right things, yet who was no pushover for anyone. Tom had been at Port Adelaide in 1997 and 1998 and played one senior game before the Power cleared him, so he knew the harder side of the game, and he had made himself into a decent player in his eight years at Geelong. He trained hard, he was intelligent, and he could have those awkward conversations with people around the club that others might have found difficult.

He was a good conduit between the players and other parts of the club, where Steven King, his predecessor, was not really that person. Kingy had suffered horrendous injuries, missed a lot of footy, and was probably happy to step aside, and Tom Harley quickly stepped up as what I would call a good club captain. The players wanted Tom, and I was happy to go along with it.

We needed someone who would work hard to get the behaviours right, because the game had changed into a far more professional code than it was before, and I was concerned about the way that we trained. We were patchy, quite inconsistent, and the energy levels depended upon how the players were feeling, and that would filter through to how they played.

There were quite a few other changes at Geelong in that off-season as well. We drafted Joel Selwood with pick 7 in the national draft, which was one of our rare early picks, due to the fall down the ladder in 2006. Joel had only played a handful of games for Bendigo Under 18s in 2006 and there were concerns over his knees, but I think it was a cautious approach by Bendigo. That club took a long-term view to protect him, and they did the right thing, although it meant he was drafted a little lower down the pecking order, which was to our benefit.

We looked at Joel and Travis Boak, and Boak went to Port Adelaide with pick 5, which gave us no issues when our name was called out. We all loved Joel, including Stephen Wells, the head recruiter, who carries a huge responsibility, especially at these times. The recruiter can end up with egg on his face in that job, and even that day, I can remember having breakfast with him and we were tossing it around, all around our first pick and what might happen if so and so goes here or there. We were not even sure that Joel would still be available after the other clubs had the first six selections in the draft, and my memory is that Wellsy suggested at breakfast that we should look closely at Boak, and me and Brendan McCartney nearly jumped over the table. To this day, I'm not sure if he was winding us up or serious, but in the end, it was an easy decision because of Port' decision to grab Boak.

We also introduced Travis Varcoe to the team in his first season as well as Mathew Stokes, and Tom Hawkins, who would play almost half the season as a key forward and a work in progress. The other big step forward was taken by Nathan Ablett, a player who I loved watching and working with.

Nathan had been playing at Modewarre, a little town outside Geelong, with his mates, but we convinced him to come down to the club and join his elder brother Gary in 2005. It took a full two years to coax him, with Frank Costa being involved and Gary Junior giving us a hand, too, because Nathan originally had said that he did not want to play in the AFL. He had played seven senior games for Geelong in 2005, and another seven in 2006, but in 2007 we planned on using him at centre half-forward throughout the season. I rated him extremely highly; actually, I thought he was a potential superstar of the game.

Nathan was completely paranoid about media interest in him, to the point where he would walk off the ground at Modewarre if a car marked *Geelong Advertiser* turned up. He actually did that, so we did our best to shield him when he arrived at Geelong; we did not expose him to the media unless it was done in-house and under control, we kept him from the autograph hunters and tried to take baby steps. It is not easy in the AFL, with the huge public and media interest in the game, and Gary was good with this, too. He was not too pushy or demanding of his brother, he was quite respectful.

Nathan was a beautiful man, just sweet. And as a player he

was 6'5" in the old language (192 centimetres), he was quick, he could kick either foot, and he could do amazing things. What people forget with Nathan is that what they saw in the brief time that he graced AFL footy was pure, it was straight from Modewarre, and we had not had the time to develop him. He loved being around the club, playing with mates, but he hated the scrutiny, hated the public interest in what he was doing for a job.

I felt comfortable with all the changes off-field, and the players immediately liked having Dean Robinson and Paul Haynes in charge of the conditioning. Straight away we trained harder, just as I had wanted, and it felt like the football had taken some ground back from sports science at our club. We had a lot more ball work in the pre-season, which was a focus, and we also had a tweaked game plan.

West Coast had beaten Sydney by a point for the 2006 flag, and the games at the top end were attritional struggles, low-scoring and dour in those years, 2005 and 2006. Adelaide also strangled opposing teams. Those teams were hard to play against. What we did was a response that went against my principles, in a way, because I had defence-first as my mantra and the players knew that.

But we did some training over the summer along the lines of, 'Let's come up with something.' The principles were to get numbers to the ball, and for the player with the footy to give the first, easy option to someone under less pressure than himself. It was designed to help players out of the congestion and get the ball into free space, the emergence of the kamikaze game style that we would come to be known for.

What we created was meant to beat the flood and the slowed-down games. It was interesting, when we lost in the semi-finals of the 2007 NAB Cup during the pre-season. Brisbane Lions flooded back on us, but we left the players to work through it because we expected it. We knew that it was coming not only on that day, but for the rest of the year. We had practised running the ball from defence in the pre-season, and the next step was executing it under pressure, which we could not manage that night, but the composure that we were seeking was not too far away.

We played high risk, high reward, and I was almost conceding to Geelong what that club was. It was embedded in the culture of Geelong that it played attacking, bright football, Geelong liked to *entertain*, and it had an attacking backline, typified by the way the Cats played under Malcolm Blight in the 1990s. So in the end, after seven seasons, I gave in to that and we made it all about adventure.

I had never considered that style of play to this point, because to me, football was about what you practised and what you did, it was about the process. But certain teams have an element about them, a style that sits well, and Geelong liked to attack. So we attacked, which was not my natural way to play. And at the same time, we hung on to what we had built in terms of a strong defence, with the likes of Matthew Scarlett, Tom Harley, Darren Milburn, Matthew Egan and Corey Enright.

It was not necessarily a new idea to attack from the back – Hawthorn were doing it in the 1980s, for instance – but it was a significant change for us. And it turned out to be a nice blend, because we already had the defensive structures in place. We never let go of the principle of defence-first, but we did open up the games and allowed players to attack through the middle of the ground once they won the football.

Early in the 2007 season we lost to Western Bulldogs, Hawthorn and North Melbourne, three of the first five, which was not the greatest start. The North Melbourne game at Kardinia Park in round 5 was a watershed moment in the season, the game that it turned upon, because the Kangaroos flogged us early. We ended up only losing by three goals but it was a disastrous result. It was the game where Paul Chapman came out to the media and made some tough comments about the way we were playing:

> We're picking and choosing when we want to play and there's no excuses. Our first half was pretty bad and our second half was very good so it's not a matter of just being flat on the day or not being hard or not using the ball well, because we showed that we can do that it the second half.
>
> You'd have to say it's individual blokes. I think at the moment, we've probably got some passengers and we can't afford to carry them. We need 22 blokes who are going to live your values and die for your team. If you think about it, it's war, it's our little war. I know it's not, it's only a game of footy. But we need everyone to contribute and you can't have blokes picking and choosing and deciding when they want to go and when they don't want to go.
>
> It's not just this year and it's not just last year, it's been around for a while and it's something we're going to have to change as a side. You can't just be happy playing, getting your money and having a good lifestyle or whatever it is. You've got to go out there and do everything you can to win, and that's what it's about.

Our own internal meeting after that North Melbourne game had been brutal, because other than Chappy and Joel Selwood, a kid coming out of a dream, most of the players had struggled. Joel's performance that day was about the only positive; he had one of those days when he said to himself, *I'm not waiting for them.* He was awesome, especially for a kid in his first season.

But as a team we were 2–3 and the walls were closing in. People were expecting Geelong to fragment, I think, and when I got the players in the rooms straight after the game that day, I said to them, 'Righto boys, there's 100 media people out there, [my press conference] is going to be broadcast all over Australia, what do you want me to say? Am I going to cover your arses?'

In those team meetings – and I know that I have been on the other end of them with Kevin Sheedy – you just try to get in a position where the coach cannot make eye contact with you, keep out of harm's way in case you are singled out. But Matthew Scarlett sat exactly where he always sat, in the centre at the back, and he never took his eyes off me. I still remember that, even though everyone else's eyes were darting around. He just looked at me, like a man, and he said, 'Tell the *truth*. Tell it the way it is.' And I asked, 'What *is* the truth?' The truth was that, like Chappy said later, we were picking and choosing when we committed, we were not respecting the opposition and we were not being hard enough on each other.

We thrashed it around, and by the time I faced the media, I knew what I was going to say. 'We didn't respect the game or our opposition. We were mentally weak.' All of which, along with Chappy's comments, drew the headlines about Geelong, as we found ourselves the story of the moment again.

That was the turning point for Geelong. The so-called line in the sand game. In round 6 against Richmond at the Docklands, we started moving forward again. Steve Johnson had completed his internal suspension, and he came back into the side as we hammered Richmond by 157 points. It was as though the players wanted to get something off their chests; the Tigers were the victims that day as we compiled our third-highest score in club history.

We kicked 35 goals, one of the highest scores in AFL–VFL history, and we were mean and nasty for the whole game, led by Gary

Ablett. Nathan Ablett kicked four goals and so did Tom Hawkins in just his fifth senior game, as we tried to give the 18-year-old some experience. Stevie Johnson came back a different man. The suspension had been a hard pill to swallow for him, but he was so gifted that he had got away with a few shortcuts through his life, and now he'd been stung. I know that he hated training away from the main group, not being around the club, but he did his time, came back and had a great season.

We found ourselves on a momentum swing that would take us to a 15-game winning streak that lasted all the way to round 20 against Port Adelaide, and there were big margins and high scores as the game plan kicked in. We beat St Kilda by 10 goals, we beat Port Adelaide by 56 points in Adelaide, we beat Brisbane Lions, our old nemesis, and proved that we finally had their measure. We beat Adelaide Crows in a game where only 18 goals were kicked, showing that the numbers-back strategy was not bothering us too much, and in three straight games from rounds 16 to 18, we kicked at least 20 goals every week.

We had sneaked up on everyone and delivered this game style that no one had played against before, and they were almost spooked by it. There is a shock factor when you come up with something new; a little advantage that you can grab. Individually, things were also panning out, with Brad Ottens enjoying the benefits of a full pre-season for the first time in several years, which was important for us.

Darren 'Dasher' Milburn logged his 200th game against the Lions, sneaking around in his efficient way and mopping up. I think Dasher had a record at Geelong in this period of getting 35 disposals while running only 6.8 kilometres; that's how efficient he was and how well he could read the play. He just knew where it was going, and he did not waste a bean of energy. Sometimes he would play like that and the fitness people would say, 'That's not good.' We would say, 'What do you want him to do, run twice as far and get 70 possessions? It's not going to happen. We should be teaching our players to run less.'

Some of the newer guys were improving too, the likes of Mathew Stokes, a little man who went against one of my preferences. I have never been a fan of smaller players unless they offer something really special, but Stokes became a good overhead player anyway, because he was smart enough to control the ball drop, covering for his lack of height.

In May, Frank Costa had changed his mind and decided to continue on as the club president. Frank, who had started just before me at Geelong, had promised his wife Shirley that he would walk away in 2007, but he said that he had 'unfinished business', and it was certainly a boost for the club. It gave us stability, it gave us respect. People were loving the Geelong game style, and acknowledging that we had a real chance.

In my letter to Brian Cook after the 2006 review, I had spoken about the need to improve our development of players, and we had Brendan McCartney and Brenton Sanderson helping out with that aspect, which gave me time for the pure coaching that I loved. I'd given up some administration that year, stopped fighting with the fitness staff, and we now had productive meetings.

It all came together, and by round 19, we had the minor premiership wrapped up. In round 21, there was a hiccup when Port Adelaide pipped us in the last ten seconds to break the streak of 15 wins, Dom Cassisi's goal giving the Power the win, ironically after Gary Ablett (his opponent on the day) had put us in front immediately before that. A lot of people had been talking up the club record

I grew up in the north-west suburb of Airport West in a close family. We were happy and encouraged to be independent. That's me with Dad on the left.
(*Private collection*)

I was into all the usual kind of activities Aussie kids loved in the sixties and early seventies. We took annual holidays camping up at the Mitta Mitta River in northern Victoria with the extended family, which we all loved. (*Private collection*)

The Thompsons. I'm about 13 here, with Steven and Katrina. (*Private collection*)

I played a lot of cricket, bowling fast and reckless and winning a few premierships with the Catholic boys from St Christopher's team. (*Private collection*)

By the time I was about nine, I was playing for Airport West at Hansen Reserve, just a short walk from home. Never tall for my age, footy came pretty easily to me as a junior. (*Private collection*)

In my last year with the club, I captained Airport West to the under-17 premiership in the Essendon District Football League. The presentation was at Brimbank Park. (*Private collection*)

In 1980 I also won the EDFL best and fairest award. Not sure about those shorts, but they were the only kind you could buy at the time! (*Private collection*)

I was elevated to the Essendon reserves team to play with men late in the 1981 season. This is one of Mum's snaps from the early eighties, at Victoria Park. (*Private collection*)

## 1984

The grand final parade down Bourke Street was a very fancy affair in 1984 – I'm in the back with Garry Foulds. (*Private collection*)

Mum asked me to drop by and say hello to the family and friends gathered in the car park at the MCG before I played in the grand final – hardly the ideal match preparation by today's standards. (*Private collection*)

**1985**

Essendon players, officials and media on the MCG after we won the 1985 flag; at the back of the pack is me, puffing on a gaffer! Needless to say, it would never happen today.

We had a great team at Essendon, led by Terry Daniher. We went back-to-back in 1985, and won a couple of night premierships along the way. *(AFL Media)*

**1990**

We won the pre-season Foster's Cup in 1990, the first year of the newly named AFL, and looked forward to continued success that year, with Tim Watson as our captain. But Collingwood was waiting for us, coached by Leigh Matthews, and it ended in tears. *(AFL Media)*

**1991**

Pre-game warm-up, resembling dance moves! There are four Essendon captains in this photo: Simon Madden (1980–81), Terry Daniher (1983–88), Tim Watson (1989–91) and me (1992–95). *(AFL Media)*

I rate Terry Daniher in the top three teammates I played with. He was always chipper and would bring players up with him. *(AFL Media)*

# 1993

Harves and I took our kids in the car with us in the grand final parade in 1993.

James Hird was one of the Baby Bombers, winning a premiership in his first year, 1993. He and Ricky Olarenshaw were just twenty. *(AFL Media)*

1994

# 1994

By the end of 1995 my body was screaming at me and I handed over the captaincy to Gary O'Donnell. *(AFL Media)*

# 1995

# 1996

Sheedy convinced me to play on in 1996 to reach the 200-game milestone. With hindsight, I am glad that he talked me around. (*AFL Media*)

In 2002 I was included in the Champions of Essendon team. It was an honour to be alongside teammates like game changer Michael Long. Dick Reynolds welcomed us. (*Private collection*)

Sheeds 1985

Pagan 1999

The two chief influences on my coaching were Kevin Sheedy and Denis Pagan. Sheeds was a mad professor of a coach, while Denis Pagan was about methodical and meticulous preparation. They were both winners, and that taught me that there was more than one way to win. *(AFL Media)*

2000

**2001** When we were young! In my first two years we picked up some great talent, including Corey Enright, Paul Chapman, Cameron Ling, Max Rooke, Steve Johnson and James Kelly.

**2005** I loved watching and working with Nathan Ablett – he could have been as big a superstar as Gary. It's a great regret of mine that we couldn't keep him at the club. Round 21 against the Eagles at Skilled Stadium, 20 August 2005. *(AFL Media)*

**2005** Our semi-final loss to the Swans in the last three seconds goes down as the most gut-wrenching I ever experienced at any level of football as a player or coach. It was a defining night for all of us. SCG, 9 September 2005. *(AFL Media)*

**2006** We finished tenth in 2006, a disastrous downturn. I was unsure if I would get to see out the last year of my contract. Round 22 loss to Hawthorn, Telstra Dome, 3 September 2006. *(AFL Media)*

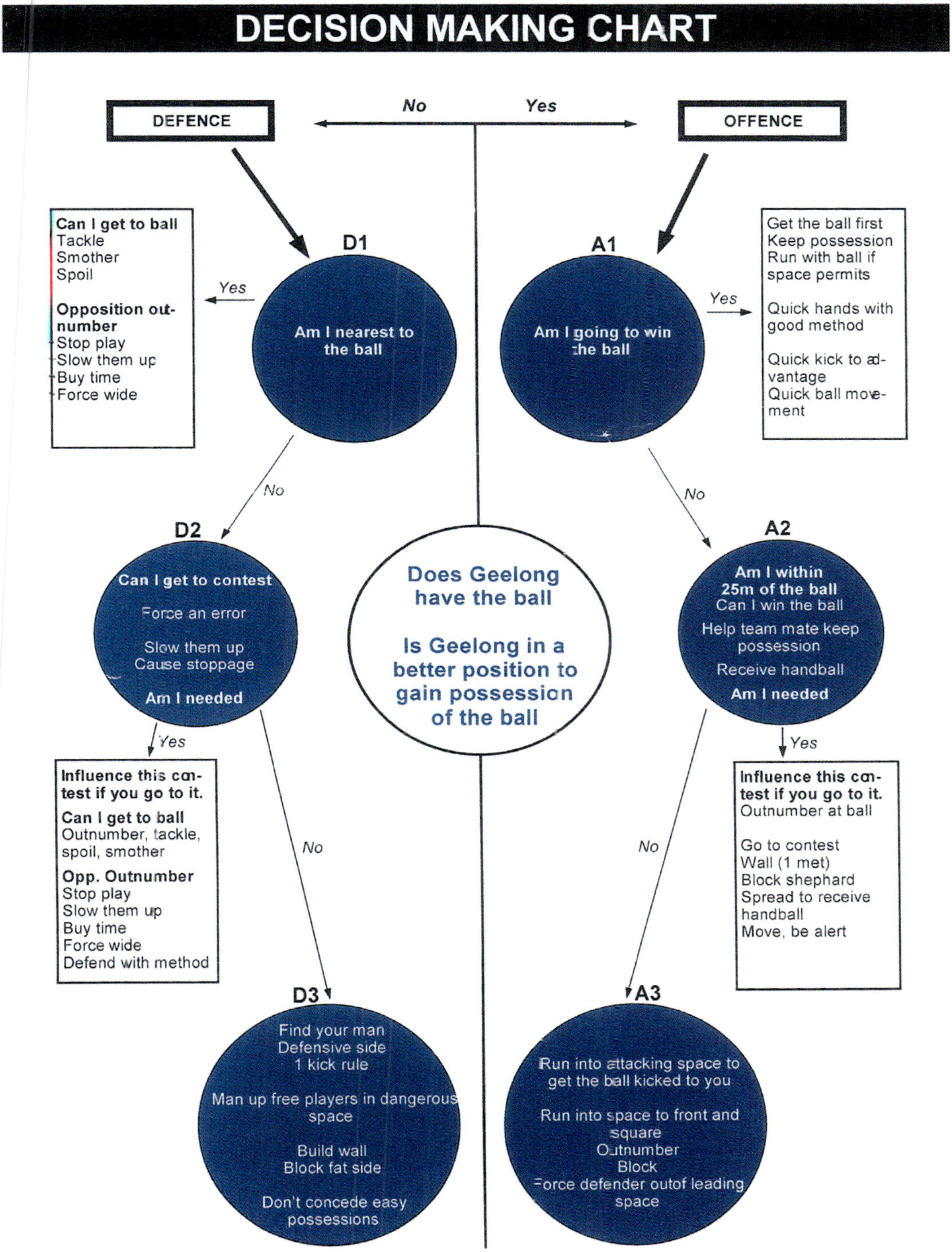


At Geelong, I refined my original decision-making flowchart from 1999 (see page 98). A = attack and D = defence; for more detail see page 208.

**2007** The team that broke the Geelong premiership drought.

**BACK:** James Kelly, Josh Hunt, Matthew Scarlett, Nathan Ablett, Brad Ottens, Steven King, Steve Johnson, Andrew Mackie, Joel Corey, Cameron Mooney, Corey Enright, Jimmy Bartel, Darren Milburn. **FRONT:** David Wojcinski, Paul Chapman, Gary Ablett Jr, Shannon Byrnes, Tom Harley (c), Cameron Ling, Max Rooke, Joel Selwood, Mathew Stokes. *(Sean Garnsworthy/AFL Media)*

It takes a lot of good people working together to win a premiership, and Brian Cook and Frank Costa are two of the best. MCG, 29 September 2007. (*Lachlan Cunningham/AFL Media*)

My kids – Michael, Daniel and Lauren – joined the grand final celebrations in the rooms after the game. (*Private collection*)

I slept with the 2007 premiership cup, happy in the knowledge that I was a premiership coach for the first time. This is one of my favourite photos – our little dog, Bindi, sitting inside the holy grail. (*Private collection*)

On the Sunday, Tom Harley and I presented the cup to 30,000 deliriously happy people who turned up at Kardinia Park. I had the best day of my life every day of that week. (*Lachlan Cunningham/AFL Media*)

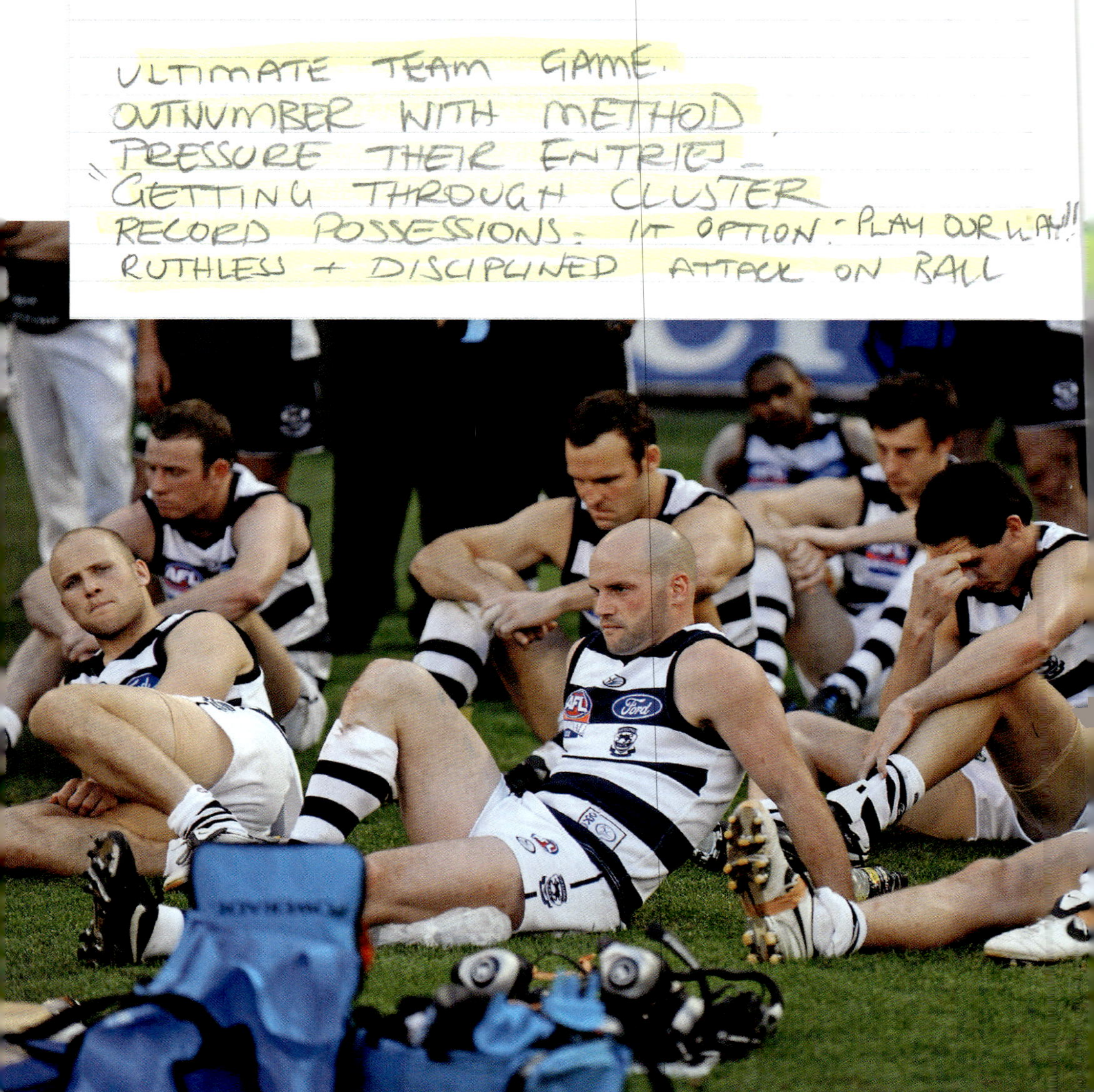


**2008** We were probably at our best in 2008, but we weren't good enough at the Big Dance. We had the right plan but we didn't execute it. MCG, 27 September 2008. *(Sean Garnsworthy/AFL Media)*

# 2009

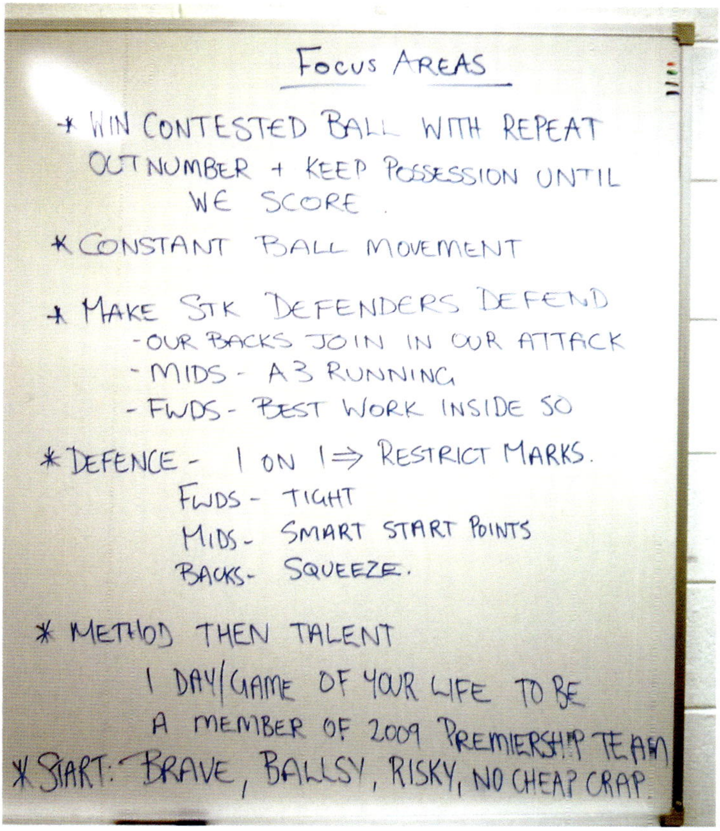


The game day board in the rooms – the key messages for the early meeting on the big day were pretty simple. (*Private collection*)

Quarter-time in the 2009 Grand Final against the Saints. It was a titanic struggle, but I always felt like we could win. (*David Callow/AFL Media*)

As Tim Lane called it, 'For the Cats . . . vindication has arrived.' Club legend Bob Davis presented the cup. *(Michael Willson/AFL Media)*

**2010** My last home-and-away game coaching the greatest team of all; I was cooked. We beat the Eagles at Skilled Stadium, 28 August 2010. (*Lachlan Cunningham/AFL Media*)

**2011** I was rapt when Geelong won the 2011 flag under Chris Scott. My leaving had invigorated the club, and I still feel a strong connection with the Cats. (*Andrew White/AFL Media*)

MID-SEASON 2008, KIMBERLEYS

NYC 2008

BARCELONA 2010

I made a point of going away every year just to explore the planet a bit and get to know other cultures. I needed to be away from the all-consuming world of football, to refuel.
(*Private collection*)

END OF SEASON SNOOZE, LA, 2008

LONDON 2008

RIO 2012

VIETNAM 2013

AT THE BOTTOM OF MACHU PICCHU 2011

**2011** James Hird had good, experienced assistant coaches around him: (L–R) Dean Wallis, Simon Goodwin, Brendan McCartney, Sean Wellman and Shannon Grant. Media conference at Windy Hill, 7 December 2010. *(Lachlan Cunningham/AFL Media)*

Hirdy had never coached before and I was to be a kind of mentoring figure in the background. In round 1 we beat the Bulldogs at Etihad Stadium, 27 March 2011. *(Michael Willson/AFL Media)*

## 2012

Dean Robinson was hired as high performance coach in August 2011, a decision that would have huge ramifications. Training at Victoria Park, 2011. *(Michael Willson/AFL Media)*

## 2013

Club president Paul Little announced on 10 October 2013 that I would be Essendon's head coach for 2014 only, replacing James Hird until his suspension was complete. *(Lachlan Cunningham/AFL Media)*

The events of 2012 and 2013 took a pretty heavy toll on all the people involved, as a sponsor's sign liked to remind us! Training at the True Value Solar Centre, 18 December 2013. *(Darrian Traynor/AFL Media)*

**2014** Footy had ceased to be fun for Essendon players in 2013, and we had to try to change that. We got off to a good start with a win in round 1 against North Melbourne at Etihad Stadium, 21 March 2014. *(Lachlan Cunningham/AFL Media)*

In round 2, we had a narrow loss to reigning premiers Hawthorn. Dustin Fletcher, on my right, was in his 22nd season with Essendon – we were 1993 premiership teammates. Etihad Stadium, 28 March 2014. (*Michael Willson/AFL Media*)

In 2014, I was more open than I had been at Geelong. I wanted to give something to the fans, give them real value for money. We beat Collingwood by 64 points in round 17 at the MCG, 13 July 2014. (*Michael Willson/AFL Media*)

Overall, 2014 was one of my best years of coaching, especially given the circumstances. We lost the elimination final against North Melbourne, but there were many positives for Essendon. This was the end of the road for me, and I was proud of my work. MCG, 6 September 2014. *(Michael Willson/AFL Media)*

of 23 straight wins from the 1952 and 1953 seasons, which I did not want us to be involved with.

And ultimately that game at Kardinia Park set us up nicely. It was finals-type footy, Port was one of the strong contenders, and the loss was a little wake-up call that we needed to do everything right. Geelong rounded out the 2007 season with another win over Brisbane Lions at the Gabba, leaving us with 18 wins and clear top position, but it was a bittersweet night in Brisbane because Matthew Egan fractured the navicular bone in his right foot early on.

Egan was a great story for us. He had been an elite tennis player, rather than a footballer, as a boy growing up in the town of Sunbury and his coach was honest with him: 'You're probably not going to be making a living out of tennis.' So he switched to football, played Essendon district league footy with Oak Park, and then had a run at Essendon, where Col Hooper, the club's former runner and current interchange steward, was his uncle.

The Bombers moved him on and James Kelly, who also hailed from Sunbury and was his closest mate, urged us to pick him up, a rare instance of one player virtually recruiting another. Initially he played VFL at Geelong, where Ron Watt, the reserves coach, worked hard with him, and we selected Egan with pick 62 in the 2004 national draft, a couple of years after he had started running around in the reserves. I can remember there was not much support for him at the end of his first year at the club, before he was drafted, and I had a strong conversation with Stephen Wells, who was initially doubtful, and Brendan McCartney, who had pushed me to watch Egan's tapes closely. Brendan was strongly in favour of keeping Egan.

It was a close-run thing. We also had Scott Thompson, the current North Melbourne defender, playing in our VFL team, and we were keen to take him, but what I liked about Matthew Egan was that he was very rarely beaten close to goal. I said, 'We don't have enough people who have the temperament to play deep, isolated, by themselves. It's the humiliation, the fear of humiliation.'

Everyone was worried about his lack of speed if he was isolated back there, but he did have great agility from playing tennis. In the end, I asked Wells to hand the tape of Egan to John Peake, who was second-in-charge of recruiting. 'Let him make an assessment,' I said. So I had failed with Wellsy, but I had another crack, and when I got to work the next day, John Peake was the first person that I saw. He said, 'I didn't realise how good [Egan] was!' I went back to the recruiting meeting and said, 'I think we should take him.'

So we all loved Matthew Egan's progress. He would be named an All Australian in 2007, so good was his performance from centre half-back, but on this particular night in Brisbane he landed awkwardly in a marking contest with Jonathan Brown, his opponent, and came up lame. He would never, ever play another AFL game, which is an extraordinary thing to say.

You would never have thought that an ordinary marking contest would cost you your career, but that was the reality for Matthew Egan. Not that we knew the full prognosis immediately, and publicly, we said that he remained part of our plans as we entered the finals. With hindsight, I knew that he could not do that.

I actually recommended to Matthew and the doctors that he forget about the 2007 season, go away and get ready for 2008, but they would not give up. We were a chance to win a flag, and I went along with that, even though I was doubtful. As a coach, you have to learn from these things, and you cannot make the mistake of being too sentimental. Make that mistake and it will kill you as a coach. And you cannot reinvent the wheel; sometimes it is just nature occurring, as sad as it was for Matthew Egan.

# 12

# GREATEST TEAM OF ALL

## 2007

As the 2007 finals approached, the usual banter surfaced about Geelong's traditional failure to finish the job, with all the recent history coming up for discussion. Brian Cook did one newspaper interview in which he talked about Geelong being too comfortable with a modicum of success, but I knew that those sort of comments upset Geelong people.

I did not like speaking in that way, because Geelong had *always* been a successful team, always in the finals, and I knew that before I took the job. Geelong had great teams and a great history, albeit with a string of relatively recent grand final defeats (five in a row in 1967, 1989, 1992, 1994 and 1995). In my view, those defeats, especially the four under Malcolm Blight's coaching, created a perception that did not reflect the overall history.

We had nine All Australians named in 2007: Matthew Scarlett, Darren Milburn and Matthew Egan in defence, Jimmy Bartel and Gary Ablett in midfield, Steve Johnson and Cameron Mooney as forwards and Cameron Ling and Joel Corey were both on the bench.

I was named coach of the year.

Ling had been wonderful as a tagger, a completely different role from what he was brought to the club for, which was to play as a forward. He saw an opportunity in that role of running with the best midfielder on the opposition team, and he was perfect for it. As a coach, you tend to say, 'Fifteen of the 22 I won't have to worry about today.' Cameron Ling was one of the 15; you might tweak what those guys are doing, but you really do not have to coach them at all.

The figure of nine was a record for a single team's representation in the All Australian team, and it reflected our dominance, while Joel Selwood's amazing first season saw him win the Rising Star award, too. There would be more individual honours over the next couple of weeks, but what remained was for us to finish what we had started.

In the qualifying final at the MCG against North Melbourne, all that angst from 2005 and 2006 came out, and we won by 106 points, a flogging for the Roos. We were able to bring Jimmy Bartel back from appendicitis for the game in place of Egan, and he was brilliant, while we played Paul Chapman as a deep forward, and he kicked five goals. He was a bigtime player, Chappy, along with Jimmy. A big final actually gets those guys into a head space where they are at their best, a bit like Luke Hodge and Jordan Lewis today, for example. Chapman just naturally went to the ball and in big games, he and Bartel would stand up.

We smashed North in the second quarter with seven goals, but I was angry in the coaches' box, which was probably nervous tension. I was thinking, *We're a good team, we're going to win this, and here we are*. The victory gave us a week's rest and a direct route into the preliminary final, which would be against either Collingwood or West Coast, and I remember Ken Hinkley and Brenton Sanderson going off to Perth to see those teams play in the semi-final the following week.

Meanwhile there was still chatter in the media about Matthew Egan's situation, and I acknowledged to the reporters that Matthew thought himself a genuine chance to play in the preliminary final, which was true. But I did not let on what was in the forefront of my mind: that Egan would have to jump through significant hoops before I would risk playing him, because there was too much at stake.

The Magpies rolled over the top of the Eagles in Perth behind Dane Swan (38 possessions and 2 goals), who would give us some cause for thought about an opponent. So Collingwood graduated to the preliminary final, to be played on a Friday night at the MCG. Meanwhile there was an issue bubbling in the background, because Geelong had secured a deal with the Victorian Government and the Federal Government for funding of a rebuild of the stadium at Kardinia Park to the tune of $28 million. It was a fabulous thing for the football club, but the government's people wanted to announce it at a media conference on the day of the preliminary final, and they also wanted me at the conference, which was crazy.

As it was explained to me, either I went to that press conference and sat up the front, or the funding was not happening, which was a big call on a preliminary final day for the coach of a competing team. I was not keen to say the least, but I had to do it, sitting up alongside Peter Costello, the federal treasurer at the time. In the end, it was worth the trouble for the sake of the redevelopment and what it meant to the club, but to say I was distracted would be an understatement.

Mick Malthouse, coach of our opposition, was on to it. He said in the media when he heard about the press conference that we were not serious about our footy, a little jab in the ribs for us. Collingwood had been to the draft and was building a team that would win a premiership a few years on, with great youth in Scott Pendlebury and Dale Thomas to go with the more established Dane Swan and an ageing Nathan Buckley, who was 35 and playing his final season. The Magpies had finished sixth on the ladder, five games behind Geelong, but had proven to be the surprise of the finals, beating Sydney then going to Perth and taking out West Coast. Collingwood would be no pushover.

It turned out to be an epic game and in the end, five points was all we had in reserve before 98 000 people, one of the biggest-ever preliminary final crowds. I never felt like it was quite that close from the box, but Collingwood just would not go away, pegging Geelong back and taking the lead in each quarter after we had started well, and the game was like that, to-and-fro all night.

Because of their place in the finals system as the penultimate game, preliminary finals are often played in the head. For the players, it is difficult to stay in the moment when the prize at the end is a place in a grand final, and that is how we played in that final against Collingwood. I believe our players were thinking, *I've got to give everything tonight to make sure we win the game, but once we've won the game I have to look after myself for next week.*

So we would kick away, then give up the lead, and then the players would think, *We've got to do a bit more now*. Mathew Stokes showed his value with three first-quarter goals as we sneaked away, but Collingwood was brave on the night. Even in the last quarter we moved out to a 11-point lead late when Gary Ablett sharked a goal from a boundary throw-in and a nice tap-out by Brad Ottens, who had a huge night. That looked to be the sealer, but Tom Harley made front-on contact with Anthony Rocca in a marking contest soon afterward, Paul Medhurst kicked the resulting goal to bring it back to within a goal the difference, and just inside the last minute of play it was a 50–50 game. When the siren rang, Collingwood was in attack again.

I had been forced to defend Ottens in his early years at Geelong (remember the 'all of you' press conference where I lambasted the media for criticising the ruckman?) He was magnificent in the ruck that night, and I recall a Joel Corey smother late in the game that saved us, too. That was trademark Corey, who I'd come to refer to as 'first man picked' in my team. The excitement of the players was obvious, as the grand final position was confirmed and many of them were qualifying for the first time. We did not have a single player remaining from the last Geelong team to reach a grand final, against Carlton in 1995. We were in a great position; clearly the best team, with the task of executing on the day.

Grand final week arrived, and it was as normal as we could make it, which is to say not all that normal. Fairly early in the week I spoke to the players about the historical aspects, in particular all the discussion about Geelong's recent poor record in grand finals – the five consecutive defeats that the media was throwing around. It was an issue that needed to be addressed, I felt, and my tone was along the lines of, 'The past is the past. It has nothing to do with how we are going to play, and the team that we are going to play.'

Subconsciously though, I think we all felt a subtle pressure. It was the reality we confronted as we waited to see who we would meet in the grand final, which turned out to be Port Adelaide, with whom we had played that titanic game at Geelong during the season. The Power had come from twelfth in 2006 to finish second in 2007, a remarkable achievement by Mark Williams and his men, and they had thrashed North Melbourne by 86 points in the other preliminary final in Adelaide. Port had a fine centre half-forward in Warren Tredrea, and some real star players in Chad Cornes and Shaun Burgoyne, and they would be dangerous, as we had seen when Cassisi stole that win for them at Kardinia Park earlier in the season.

We had a couple of selection issues but all that was set aside on the Monday night as we donned the monkey suits and attended the Brownlow Medal. Gary Ablett Jr was the heavy favourite, having completed by far his best season in terms of numbers, averaging 26 touches a game and adding 26 goals, but on the night it was Jimmy Bartel who took home the medal, sitting alongside Gary at the function, the dark-headed beating the blond!

Jimmy deserved it, just as Gary would have, with similar numbers and that ability to impact games when it counted. He had a great season, but it was a tricky night, because we had other things on our minds. I remember that after the medal count the winner is required to attend a party that is put on for sponsors and AFL people in another room at Crown. A few of us went in there, but no one really wanted to be there; we wanted to get into bed and get some rest so that we could prepare for the grand final. It is a big deal for a player winning a Brownlow, and for his club as well, but I cannot help but think that it would be a lot more fun if you were not playing in the grand final a few short days later.

The other issues of the week were, in order of importance, Mark Blake and Mark Williams. On the Sunday before the big one, our VFL team won their grand final and Steven King, our ruckman, came through the game nicely after returning from injury. I wanted to play Kingy in the seniors provided he proved his fitness and his sharpness, but that would necessarily mean that Mark Blake, who had played most of the season filling in, would have to be dropped. We were never going to play three ruckmen, and Brad

Ottens was close to best-afield in the preliminary final, so he was a walk-up start.

Blake had played 22 of our 24 games to that point and was part of the team; King had just five senior games. Blake was 22 years of age, he was fulfilling his role, and he was durable, although he had some flaws as a young player. King was 28, a 12-year veteran and former captain of the club, and a fine player at his best. It was one of those tough decisions that a coach has in grand final week. It was the Derek Kickett situation revisited.

Midway through the week we made the call as a match committee, but it was divided. My notes show that it was 3–3 with me having the casting vote. These things are always tough, but the basis of my decision was that Mark Blake was young, he had not played well in the earlier finals, and I thought that he was feeling the pressure. I thought he was getting tight; it was my gut feel and at least part of it was based on my own first finals series as a player at Essendon in 1984, when I was so nervous that I almost played myself out of the senior team.

It happens to young players under the pressure of keeping your spot in the team, and Mark had been dropped (leaving King and Brad Ottens as the rucks) after the round 18 win over Richmond, returning for round 21. There is a critical moment in a player's career when he knows that he is a part of the best team, and it allows him to be himself, to move away from that mode where he protects himself. Mark Blake had not reached that point.

Brendan McCartney, myself and Steve Hocking went up to Mark Blake's house in Grovedale after match committee on the Wednesday night to tell him that he was out of the team. I still have the table that we drew up with Blake on one side, and King on the other, with their strengths listed under the topics: accountability, ruckwork, possessions, follow-up, help down back, hook role, with a tick or a cross for each category. It had been quite a long debate, because Blake had some support.

In any case, Mark had already smelled a rat. We tried to call him, could not get hold of him, and decided to go to his house and tell him face-to-face. Mark lived with his mother and his sister was visiting, and we copped flak from the moment that we walked in.

We didn't realise it then, but the news was out by the time we arrived, which is the way AFL footy works. When we rang for Mark, we spoke to his mother on the phone, saying something like, 'We want to come up and see Mark.' And she said, 'You don't have to, he already knows what's going on!' We also asked her not to talk to anyone before we arrived, but she was so outraged that she apparently picked up the phone again, ringing a radio station in Melbourne and telling them that her son had been dropped from the Geelong team for the grand final.

So the welcoming committee was not all that friendly in Grovedale, it has to be said. At one stage, the three of us ended up sitting in the living room on our own; the family had left us to fry and we were looking at each other thinking, *What do we do now?* It was extremely awkward, but it had to be done, and I am comfortable that we did the right thing by turning up out of appreciation and respect for Mark.

We tried to explain the situation. 'It's a long-term plan, and Mark's part of the plan longer term,' I said. But Mark was angry that he was to miss a grand final after playing so much of the season, and who could blame him? As a coach, you delist people, drop people, cut off their lives, and it is just part of the job. Mark Blake had a good season, although we probably played him a few times when he didn't deserve a game as well, but no one is going to be happy to be dropped for a grand final. Mark's father, the former Geelong ruckman Rod Blake, let us have both barrels in a *Herald Sun* interview, indicating that his son would consider leaving the club:

> I seriously don't know what he'll do. I think Geelong has handled him exceptionally poorly and it goes back before the grand final, for God's sake. I would understand if he left and I'll tell you why I understand if he left: I think the Geelong Football Club failed him miserably and it concerns me they'll actually do it to somebody else.

I was concerned about the way Mark played against Collingwood in the preliminary final; in fact, I thought that Collingwood had come back into the game in the moments when he was playing in the ruck, with Ottens resting. Having spoken to a few players, I also knew that they were keen to have Kingy playing in the grand final, and that had an influence on my thinking, because 2007 was the season in which we started listening to the players' views a little more. I reckon the writing was on the wall after the preliminary final, and in the end, you make the call because you are getting paid to do it, and you are responsible for it.

Mark Blake was not the only player who would watch the grand final with a sense of longing. On the same day as King got the nod, we ruled out Matthew Egan, who had made a last-ditch attempt to get up for the game despite his broken foot. I had been doubtful all along, but he was upset when we told him. The doctors were involved, and I had developed great faith in Chris Bradshaw's word in these matters, because he was a guy who could make a hard call. He was decisive and clear, not a procrastinator, Chris.

Matthew Egan was dirty on us, and that is why he ultimately left Geelong, in my view. He hated the fact that his mates went on winning premierships and he missed out on the chance, it hurt him and he was angry with the world, even though he was happy for his mates. He would never play again, and he ended up taking legal action against the club over his injury.

By Thursday night, Geelong as a city was approaching hysteria. There were 12 000 people at Kardinia Park for our last training session, but I could sense that our players were not overly nervous, the week had gone nicely, albeit with some difficult decisions to make, and the players did not go over the top at training, despite the temptation to do so.

Choco Williams kept banging on about Geelong's past and mentioning the weight of the 44-year drought since the club's last premiership, which made for good media fodder. He also mentioned our defeat in the 'unlosable' final, against Sydney, two years earlier, as something of an omen, but deep down, I just felt that it was a bit of desperation on his part. So I did not respond, and I let him talk, because I knew that it was about him trying to get inside our heads.

We had to focus on what we could control. We had our work done early in the week, and then just let it unfold, with all the distractions that are inevitable. There was the grand final parade, for instance, but by the end of grand final week, I thought we were fairly relaxed and ready for the game. We let them absorb the hype and excitement, because ultimately, that is part of playing in a grand final. It's what a player steps out on the field for.

I could hardly have been more confident about the result; I was absolutely convinced that Geelong was ready and that we would win. Port Adelaide was a good team of course, and had won six consecutive games to reach the grand final, but for us, it was about bringing the best out of ourselves, it was about a process rather than an outcome. We were clearly the best team, and all we had to do was get the players to feel confident and comfortable, and to execute. So I slept comfortably.

Outside of the parade and the Brownlow, we did nothing different, taking a business-as-usual approach. I didn't bother with special guest speakers or special themes to drill into the players. A lot of coaches have done that in the big week, thinking they need to do something special. It is not my style, and perhaps it dates to my time as a player. I remember Kevin Sheedy showing us the famous vision of the protester standing in front of the tank at China's Tiananmen Square in 1989, certainly an inspirational photo but not necessarily to our taste. Tim Watson had piped up later, 'Does Sheeds know that the bloke got run over, he got squished?'

The notes that I handed to the players that week recorded that five players had injury concerns, which realistically was not too bad for a grand final. Tom Harley was tight in a hamstring, Andrew Mackie had a cork, Steve Johnson a shoulder AC joint problem, Cam Mooney a bruised back and Paul Chapman a groin strain. The notes identified Port as an outside running team and called upon our players to 'restrict opposition UP (uncontested possession) from half-back'.

Clearances were a big indicator for Port's success, with Shaun Burgoyne in particular being significant. We identified Cameron Ling as the best man to play on Burgoyne, in his customary role as the man to put out fires. Max Rooke would take the dangerous Chad Cornes if and when he came into the middle of the ground, as Cornes liked to do despite usually playing around centre half-back.

Port liked to fold back into a zone defence with players like Peter Burgoyne drifting across then setting up to run from there, and James Kelly's job would be to play as a defensive half-forward, picking up Burgoyne, who liked to zone off and create. Our notes on him read: 'Make him defend.'

THEME - COVER ALL EXITS
THEY RELY ON STOPPAGES
TO WIN GAMES.

**5. Stoppages**

Forward 50

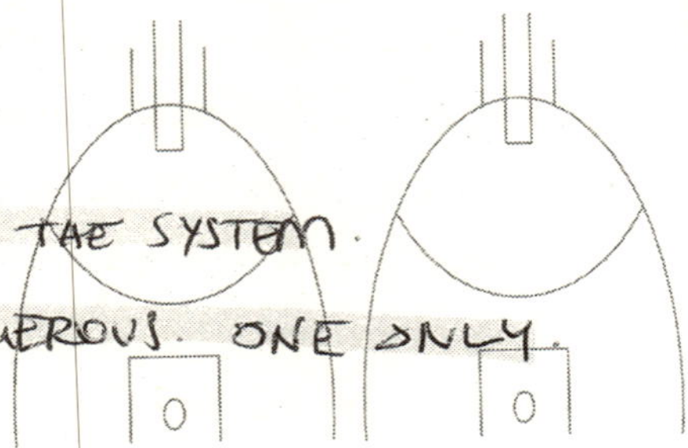

TEST THEM ~~EARLY~~ EARLY

GO IN WITH 8

STAGGERED WALL - BACK THE SYSTEM.

(29) 18, 25 CORRIDOR - DANGEROUS. ONE ONLY.

**6. Midfield**

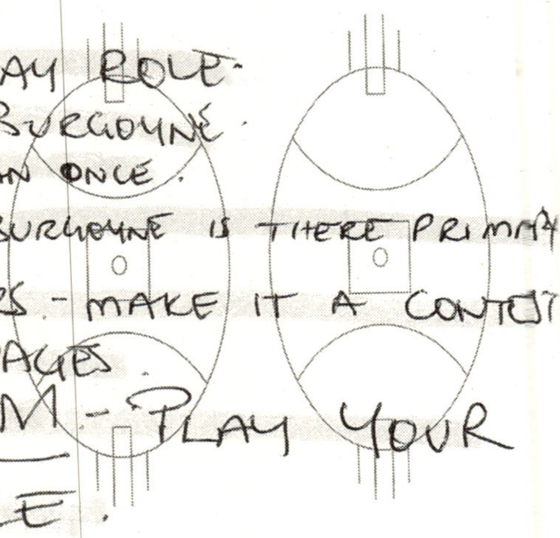

4th FORWARD MUST PLAY ROLE.
NOT OF (7) P. BURGOYNE.

C. CORNES ONLY 3RD MAN ONCE.

45 - SECONDARY AS S. BURGOYNE IS THERE PRIMARY

LOOK FOR BIG NUMBERS - MAKE IT A CONTEST
REPEAT STOPPAGES.

TRUST THE SYSTEM - PLAY YOUR
ROLE.

**7. Backline**

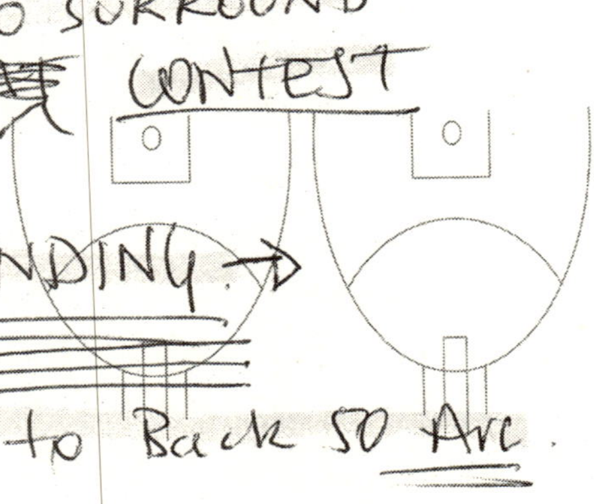

HUGE NUMBERS ~~AT~~ TO SURROUND CONTEST

CHAIN OUT

JOIN IN DEFENDING →

4th Forward up to Back 50 Arc.

There were only a couple of specific match-ups or run-with roles; when I started coaching, I would have long lists of match-ups, but by 2007 it would only be a couple of important pairings, which reflected the way I was coaching at the time. We worried about the way we wanted to play, primarily, around this time, and the notes show that we wanted to play the style that we had perfected in that season:

**RUN + CARRY – KAMIKAZE**

The defensive mindset exists in those notes, too. We wanted manic forward pressure, and we would refer to forwards at the time as 'flies', buzzing around the opposition and haranguing them:

**EVERYONE IS A FLY – VALUE IT!**

The moment finally came and Geelong's attempt to win the flag for the first time in 44 years began with Max Rooke laying a brutal tackle immediately after the first bounce. There was a statement in this, a sign that Geelong would not be tentative this time around. Geelong was ready, that is what it said.

We played perfect footy that day, up by 23 points at quarter time and then 52 points at the long break. When we played our best, no one could stop us in that year, and we happened to bring our best on that day. We smashed Port Adelaide, and the final margin was 119 points, a grand final record.

This is how easy it was. In the box, I recall the only decision of gravity after half-time being a debate over who we would have on the ground when the final siren rang, and we opted to have the older players on the field as much as we could manage it, because who ever knows if they will get another chance to savour that particular moment. It's unfathomable you could coach a grand final with an attitude like that, and it was actually hard to stay focused, to be quite truthful. Really, we were like a machine that day. You could almost feel the weight being lifted from not only the club, but its individuals, when we ran that lap of honour in 2007.

We kicked 24 goals, continuing that pattern of heavy scoring. Cameron Mooney kicked five and Paul Chapman four, while Steve Johnson completed his rollercoaster season with 23 disposals and four goals, a fabulous performance that earned him the Norm Smith Medal. I thought Matthew Scarlett was a little unlucky not to win the medal; his game from full-back was remarkable with 29 disposals and not conceding a goal to an opponent.

But Stevie's story was amazing; we had almost traded him a year or so earlier, and Collingwood might have taken him had their medicos not had doubts about his ankles. It makes me smile, that fact; if we had listened to our doctors about Brad Ottens when he was up for trade from Richmond, we might not have taken him, either. They basically said, 'Don't touch him.' He had a groin problem, and bad knees and a crook back, but some people just suit clubs, and Brad Ottens suited Geelong, and now he was a premiership player, too.

We celebrated at Crown that night, after a reception at Federation Square, and we stayed up in Melbourne, which was a pity since the people of Geelong were waiting. This is an awkward question for the club whenever Geelong reaches a grand final, because the whole event at the MCG finishes pretty late by the time the presentations are done, then there are the customary celebrations in the rooms. So by the time you reach the supporters' and sponsors' function – even if it is in Melbourne – it can be late. So I can understand the decision to hold the dinner in Melbourne, but all I wanted to do was to get back to Geelong to see the fans' reaction, because I loved the footy town that it was and remains.

It was a chaotic night with no apparent plan, just as it should be! Drawing upon my own experience as a player in a flag-winning team, I told the players to lay off the alcohol for a while so they could fully absorb the magnitude of what they had achieved. This was a complete and utter failure, to nobody's surprise! As I have said before, it is an emotional game, and there were plenty of emotions flying around that night.

Once I was given the podium, I asked all the staff to get up on the stage with me, taking much longer than the four or five minutes I had been advised to keep my speech to. They were chuffed to be acknowledged, and the crowd roared their approval for those people.

My point was this: it takes a lot of good people working together to win a premiership. I had told Brian Cook after the review in 2006, 'Don't pin it on one person.' And in 2007, the same principle applied, just as it would in different circumstances in 2008. That is my strong view about football clubs, that they are about the collective.

Mark Blake turned up, and earned himself a good reception from a sympathetic crowd, but he was shattered at having missed the game. It was strong of him; he showed that generally he was made of the right stuff, and he would have an opportunity down the track. As for me, I slept with the premiership cup, happy in the knowledge that I was a premiership coach for the first time, and one of my favourite photos is of our little dog, Bindi, sitting inside the holy grail.

At lunchtime on the Sunday we turned up at Kardinia Park to 30 000 deliriously happy people, a massive sea of people. We were introduced on the stage and interviewed by Billy Brownless, then on

Mad Monday, we hit the Lord of the Isles Tavern near the ground. It was the best week of my life; actually I had the best day of my life every day of that week. We had dress-ups and fines at Peter Burnett's pub on Monday, where the players made up stories about me and fined me anyway. Cameron Ling, the local boy who people were calling the Mayor of Geelong, was asked to don the mayoral robes. It was extraordinary, the release of emotion and the pure happiness.

At the Carji Greeves Medal function on the Thursday, I told the crowd that I had never realised exactly how much it would mean to me to win that flag. It was true, I found it hard to comprehend how important it was to me, and how much impact my first premiership as a coach had. As a player, you are ultimately responsible for your own performance as part of the team; as a coach, you are responsible for everything, and it is a much bigger achievement to coach a flag. That I learned in 2007.

Gary Ablett won the Greeves Medal as vindication for his wonderful season, and there was another big reception for Mark Blake, whom everyone felt sympathy for. About 1500 people linked arms around their tables and up on stage and sang 'We Are Geelong' as one. It was heady stuff. There was a parade through Geelong, and later Ron Watt, one of the coaches, texted a couple of mates at the little town of Bannockburn to say that he was bringing the trophy out to the pub there. Hundreds turned up, he said, because it was that kind of time.

Geelong had tasted the success it craved. Of course, we wanted more.

# 13

# HEARTBREAK

## 2008

No sooner had the celebrations of 2007 died down than Geelong had lost two premiership players, just to remind us all that the game moves very quickly. Steven King went to St Kilda, a disappointment to me but forced upon us, and Nathan Ablett walked out of the club, which was close to a tragedy. The trading of King was not a pretty situation and in the case of Ablett's departure at just 22 years of age, it remains one of the greatest regrets in all my years of coaching that I couldn't encourage him to stay.

The King scenario was linked to Mark Blake's future, because Blakey threatened to walk after being dropped for the 2007 Grand Final, meaning that we had to look closely at Kingy as one of our other ruckmen on the list. We had already offered King a contract for 2008, but then we withdrew it, and not surprisingly he was not happy. Blake had told us through his management that if King stayed, he would go, because he had missed the grand final and he wanted to find a club where he had opportunities. It was a nasty business, but it happens even more often today, with the players having more power.

I just wished that we had more options, but we didn't. And when we weighed up the two, Steven King was nearly finished, and he had endured more than his share of injuries, managing just 69 games in the previous five seasons. Mark Blake was six years younger and while he had a bit to learn, he was more durable and we knew that he could play at the top level because he had spent most of 2007 in the senior team already. Brad Ottens was our primary ruckman, so you were not necessarily going to be able to keep all three on the list.

I did not feel great about it; nor did Neil Balme and the others, but we had to make a choice and get rid of one of the players' mates, a player in King who was popular, a good bloke and a professional. We made the call, but while Mark played some good footy after that, he never quite let it go and I don't think there was as much warmth towards him from the other players, either.

Nathan Ablett's decision to leave Geelong came after just 32 games in three seasons with the club. In a sense it was not a surprise, since we had needed to work so hard to get him down to the club in 2005, but on the other hand he had just played at centre half-forward in a premiership team, and a great career was before him.

Nathan just would not take the step to full-time professional footballer. He loved playing, just loved the game itself, but hated everything that went on around football, especially the publicity and the attention, which spooked him. It goes back to his father Gary Senior's days of being so heavily scrutinised as a superstar player, I guess, and it probably shows why we all have to take our hats off to Gary Junior, in the way that he has handled the pressure of being the son of an all-time great player. Gary Junior battled his way through that issue and became an even better player than his father, in my opinion.

Nathan simply walked, and we could not convince him to come back in 2008. He had played seven games in 2005, another seven in 2006 then exploded with 21 games (and 34 goals) in the premiership year. He kicked three goals in the grand final and he was only 21 years old, straight out of a little country competition, but that grand final day – and night – frightened him away. 'Come and get a photo, Nathan,' the fans would say, and it was too much for him. By the time we got to him early in 2008, it was too late. He had made up his mind.

I will tell you, Nathan Ablett played like Wayne Carey, the former North Melbourne champion, and he could have been *anything* as a player. What we saw in those 32 games with Geelong was utterly raw, it was not even close to the full package. You did not have to teach Nathan anything, he just had it, and players like that don't come along every day. He had great hands, he was brilliant on the ground, and he could kick beautifully on either side, and he was a freak, Nathan. He could have been every bit as good as Gary Junior.

We made a mistake with Nathan after 2007, and it is a great regret of mine. When we won the flag, we should have hidden him away, maybe sent him off on a holiday for a few months, like my old teammate Leon Baker at Essendon used to do because he, too, disliked the spotlight that comes to footballers. We needed to be a bit smarter about protecting Nathan, because as a player in the reigning premiership team and an Ablett, he was always going to get the attention.

In July 2008 we convinced him to come back to training because he missed playing, but then he suffered an injury and at the end of 2008, he retired again. Three years later he bobbed up at Gold Coast with his brother, played two senior games for the Suns, then walked away again. It is a sporting tragedy, his story, and what a loss the game suffered . . . He is still only 30 years old; imagine how good Geelong would be with him and Tom Hawkins wandering around the forward line.

So 2008 started badly, which might have been an omen. Except that until grand final day, the season went brilliantly for Geelong. As a club, Geelong had not been one that could sustain domination of the competition; more so it bobbed up from time to time and then drifted away. Our task was to change that and I never sensed a grain of complacency when the players came back; they were hungry for more of what we had experienced in 2007.

We promptly won the first eight games of 2008 to set the pace. Harry Taylor had joined the club, and Travis Varcoe and Tom Hawkins were more firmly established, while big Tom Lonergan had returned to the senior team after playing in the VFL premiership in 2007. Lonergan had suffered an horrific injury, a near-death experience, in a marking contest late in 2006, leading to surgeons removing his right kidney. His return was welcome, and a feel-good story. He kicked 36 goals in 2008, playing as a forward, before he made his name later as a defender.

We were probably at our best in 2008, winning nine games by at least ten goals, flogging the opposition. Our only defeat of the home-and-away season was against Collingwood in round 9, a 90-point battering in our first meeting with the Magpies since the 2007 preliminary final. But we toppled Hawthorn, our major competition, in round 17 with Steve Johnson kicking the goal to seal it late. We reached the top of the ladder by round 3 and stayed there for most of the year, other than being overtaken briefly by Hawthorn mid-season.

The Hawks were clearly a challenger under Alastair Clarkson's coaching. Unlike Geelong, they had gone backwards to move forwards, picking Lance Franklin, Jarryd Roughead and Jordan Lewis in one draft (2004) and rebuilding their list, then reaching the finals in 2007, where Franklin kicked a late goal to win a final against Adelaide. Clarkson was in his fourth year and clearly they were coming, but at 17–5 over the season, they were a full four games behind our 21–1, which equalled the all-time record of 21 wins in the regular season set by Essendon in 2000, a year in which the Bombers won the flag under Kevin Sheedy.

In what remains a rarity, we were number one in both attack and defence, finding the balance that I wanted. Our percentage of 161.84 was the third best in VFL–AFL history, with only Essendon's 1950 team (162.24) and West Coast in 1991 (162.21) being higher. We scored heavily, managing fewer than 100 points in only three of the 22 games, and averaging 121 points per game. For context, Sydney in 2005 averaged 86.5 points per game when it won the premiership, to show how different the styles were.

In round 19 against Melbourne, our 469 disposals equalled the all-time record of disposals by a team in a game, set by West Coast the year before, as we kept pushing the bar up in that area. Our 242 handballs against Adelaide in round 14 was a league record, and we threatened it with 241 handballs against Hawthorn in round 17. To put this in perspective, Geelong averaged 412 disposals in 2008, the first time any team had hit the 400 mark, and almost 40 ahead of any other team.

These numbers were exploding in this period; just eight years earlier, in 2000, the great Essendon team had averaged just 338 disposals. It had not been my style, a high-possession game, but it had evolved that way as our players flicked the ball around to each other, working through the flooding that had been popular in the earlier part of that decade.

We savaged a few opposing teams, leaving people with the impression that it was all too easy, a notion that might have received a kick along when the television cameras focused upon me munching on a salad roll during the second half of the game against West Coast in round 13 at Subiaco. Geelong was 63 points up at half-time and two early goals in the third quarter meant the game was well and truly won, which was around the time I grabbed that salad roll.

Actually I had been doing it most weeks, but that was the first time that the cameras caught me, with Robert Walls, on Channel 10, enjoying the moment: 'I'll tell you what. I haven't seen *that* before.'

A lot was made of it, but quite simply, I was starving. It was a night game, and because of the preparation that goes into those games and the timing, you don't tend to have time to eat before the game, so that by the second half you are famished. So I just chomped away while I was watching the game, forgetting that the cameras might nail me. Cameron Mooney told me later that he had the football at one point and he could see me on the big screen and wondered, *What the hell's Bomber doing?*

Of course none of it was quite as easy as it looked but we had a great team, playing great footy, and we finished the home-and-away season with a 99-point win over the Eagles at Kardinia Park. Then we thrashed St Kilda by 58 points in the qualifying final, and overcame Western Bulldogs by 29 points in the preliminary final. By this point, we had won 15 consecutive games and were 23–1 for the season as we faced up to Hawthorn in the grand final looking to go back-to-back for only the second time in the club's history. The only time Geelong had ever gone back-to-back was in 1951–52 in an all-time great team coached by Reg Hickey, captained by Fred Flanagan and including the legendary Bob Davis.

We had the team to do it, and if anything, we were *better* in 2008 than in 2007. Famous last words, of course. We carried favouritism, we deserved it, and we thought that we were going to win. Our team was similar, with just four players different from 2007; Mark Blake earned a place in the side this time, replacing Steven King, and Harry Taylor came in for Nathan Ablett, while David Wojcinski and Shannon Byrnes missed out, allowing Lonergan and Varcoe to come in.

My notes to the players revealed a few injuries in the lead-up, with Tom Harley (knee swollen), Varcoe (ankle), Darren Milburn and Paul Chapman (hamstring soreness) and Joel Selwood (shoulder) all having niggles, and Milburn and Harley likely to need injections to play. Clearly it was a longer list than in 2007.

**General Notes/Talks pre-main skill session**

Harley – knee swollen. Inject mon.
Varcoe – ankle puffy.
Mackie – elbow hyperextended. non contact
Kelly – quad. download. 75%
Lonergan – weight loss.
Selwood. – shoulder. good range + power non contact.
cork R lateral thigh
Stokes. – groin. Signs good.
Ablett – groins. only minor.
Chappy. run at 90%
Milburn. Sore on Sat Am. Better Sun.
maybe inject Wed.
Wôjo – pulled up well.

Hawthorn was playing a defensive zone in 2008 that was referred to as 'Clarkson's Cluster', which was going to be an issue for us to deal with. In particular, we noted Luke Hodge's ability to zone off an opponent and win the football, which our opposition scout noted in the lead-up in his notes to the players and coaches: 'Hodge important/tag him, can't drag him away.'

What this referred to was that if you assigned an opponent to Hodge when he started at half-back and tried to lure him away from the play, he simply would not go there. This would prove to be critical in the grand final.

My notes made the point that the Hawks were number one in disposal efficiency, and therefore hard to get the ball back from, and that they averaged seven goal kickers, and were not necessarily a great stoppage team. They had high total marks, and liked to feed back into defence and switch the football when they had possession.

We wanted to beat the hell out of Hawthorn at stoppages and run the football hard and fast, as my note to the players said:

WE GET THEM BY

- KAMIKAZE BEST.
- PLAY ON FROM MARKS.
- Corridor ball WR

Our main match-up issue was sending Cameron Ling to Sam Mitchell in the middle, while we expected Gary Ablett Jr, who had finished equal third in the Brownlow Medal behind Bulldog Adam Cooney, to have Chance Bateman following him around. We asked the players to 'stop the fat side release', blocking up Hawthorn's switch, we wanted 'midfield outnumber', and 'fifth man in very important', to create a numerical advantage around the ball. The players were to be 'ruthless and disciplined' and to play a team game, so that they could 'be the best team'. We wanted the game on our terms: 'Play our WAY.' Our match day whiteboard implored the players to set another target for possession: 'RECORD POSSESSIONS??'

All of which was good in theory, but in practice, Hawthorn had other ideas. It is part of folklore that Alastair Clarkson had someone draw a shark on the whiteboard in the Hawthorn team room before the 2008 Grand Final, signifying the way to beat Geelong was to 'kill the shark', slow us down and take the air out of the football, just as the shark that cannot swim anywhere will die. That was their plan.

But what happened on the day is that we butchered our opportunities, of which there were plenty, and allowed them to dictate the way that the game was played. Then after we had left the door wide open in the first half, Hawthorn kicked four goals in six minutes of the third quarter and took us apart. We kicked the ball to Luke Hodge all day and watched him win the Norm Smith Medal. All day, we tried to get someone to Hodge, but we could not run him out of position, and the ball just followed him. He just goes to the ball, Hodgey; he is an outstanding footballer.

Hawthorn kicked 18.7, and we kicked 11.23, although 11 of those 23 behinds were rushed through by Hawks defenders as part of their plan. Geelong kicked 1.9 in the second quarter, which is inaccuracy in the territory of North Melbourne in 1998, when the Kangaroos handed Adelaide a premiership with 8.22 on the big day, a wastefulness that no one can afford on grand final day.

The first half finished with Cam Mooney have an angled set shot from close range after the siren that has become infamous. Mooney pulled the kick, and has since admitted that his mind was on other matters, notably that he would keep running and iron out

Grant Birchall, who stood the mark, as a show of strength: 'I was so excited about what was coming I tried to kick the leather off the ball. I kicked it off the inside of the foot and completely shanked it. It was by far the worst moment of my career.'

It did hurt us, that miss, and it is amazing how a shot after the siren can carry over into the break. So at half-time, I tried to sell a message about how we wanted to play the game, how to get it back on our terms, but we went unconventional that day for no good reason. We took shots when we needed to get the ball to players in the right position, which was usually standard procedure for Geelong. Brad Ottens running in and missing from virtually straight in front with a teammate (Mathew Stokes) wide open and available to him and in a better spot, was a great example.

At half-time, we talked about the poor conversion. I said, 'Look, we've got to find the easiest guy, in the best position. That's part of who we are and how we play.' I tried to remain positive. 'It's a close game. You wouldn't want to be anywhere else,' I said. But I was not getting much back from the players in that room, the vibrancy was not there, and I did not feel like they were engaged. At three-quarter time, after Stuart Dew's ferocious burst, our players were gone. We were only 17 points down at three-quarter time, which was next to nothing for a team with our firepower, but our players were mentally shot. I kept saying, 'Boys, *we're still in this*!' But the energy was not there that day.

Dew had been playing on Josh Hunt, and in that third quarter he had six minutes in which he kicked two goals and set up another for Cyril Rioli and had a hand in another for Mark Williams – four consecutive goals that killed us. That took the margin from 11 points to 30 points. We had learned with Josh that if he had a goal or two kicked on him he would be embarrassed and hard on himself, so it was best to take him off the ground for a few minutes while he had time to heal and gather his faculties. He was inclined to think about it too much for the next 10 minutes, as we had seen in the Nick Davis game in 2005. We got Josh off the ground, but it was too late to stop the momentum; Hawthorn won by 26 points.

I was not really angry, only really disappointed afterward, because we thought they had pinched one from us. I recall saying to the boys straight away, 'Don't let them beat you again, as long as you play.' I have never watched the whole game again on replay; it hurts too much, because I thought at the time that this Geelong team was good enough to win more than one premiership, and they were never going to get a better chance to do it. In a best-of-three format, I reckon we would have beaten Hawthorn every time, but on the day, they were better. That's footy.

We had 62 forward-50 entries that afternoon to 43 for Hawthorn, yet 11 goals was the best we could manage. I have a friend in football who kept asking for the next few years, 'Do you know that you're the only team to have 62 entries and lose a grand final?' Last time he raised it, I said, 'Are you gonna *keep* asking that?'

So why did we lose that grand final? Well, Hawthorn had an excellent team, first of all, and they did what they do. But it was about us, I have always felt. Killing the shark? Well it was certainly amazing, seeing the Hawthorn players go backwards to rush behinds, at one point Mark Williams actually kicking it back through our goals from a fair way out to stop the play and allow them to have possession of the footy.

The AFL changed the rules the following season, making it illegal to deliberately rush a behind when a defender was not under pressure because they thought it was a bad look. But the cluster was not something that we did not recognise: it was not a revolution in the game or a surprise to us on the day. Other clubs were using zones, too, but what we needed to do was move the ball properly, with the last option being to slow down and kick down the line.

The first option was to back ourselves. The idea was for us to make the ground longer and wider, get as many of our boys in play (positioned where Hawthorn needed to watch us), and if necessary, use the choice of a 45-degree angled pass. Better still, carry the ball over the zone and keep the ball moving with quick decisions. What we wanted was for the players to back themselves and execute. Needless to say, it did not happen.

Moving the football against a zone is about player management, freeing players up and getting as many of your guys into the play as you can. Playing against a zone defence, if you are ahead of the ball, you are out of play, just as if you are behind the ball and you are defending, you are out of play.

We used to work on the theory that you had to be careful not to move the ball too quickly in those circumstances, because you would shift the ball away from your teammates and force them out of play. So you had to wait for them, then use them, and sometimes you would wait momentarily, and then *boom*! That was Geelong's way. Get Andrew Mackie and Matthew Scarlett and others in the right position, then go.

So just a year after kamikaze football took us to the 2007 flag, we were already confronting a method to slow us down, and it was not the last cunning plan either, it must be said. Yet I don't believe that what Hawthorn did on the day in 2008 was the most significant factor in that result; it was about our poor conversion for one thing, it was about Geelong not having enough close games during the season for another, and it was a little sliver of complacency within the club generally, enough to cause a problem.

Poor goalkicking is a common factor among losing grand final teams, or even in drawn grand finals, and it has been going on since year dot. Who could forget North Melbourne in 1998, or the same club kicking 9.22 in the drawn grand final in 1977, when Arnold Briedis kicked 0.7 for the day? Further back, Essendon kicked a catastrophic 7.27 in the 1948 Grand Final against Melbourne, drew the match, then lost the replay. More recently Hawthorn in 2012 missed its last five shots at goal in a close loss to Sydney, and Fremantle's first grand final appearance in 2013 revealed early nerves that cost the Dockers dearly, kicking 1.6 in the first half and 8.14 for the day as they lost to the Hawks.

On this day Cam Mooney was our Arnold Briedis, at least in his own mind. Mooney was out of control with his self-blame, because while he missed some shots, his final tally was 2.3 and there were others – notably Brad Ottens – who missed easy opportunities. I made this point at the function that night, drawing from my theme of the year before, when we were all much happier, and I remember saying, 'It's no one person's fault. We win together, we lose together.'

We paid a price for having such a dominant year in 2008, with too many big wins, in my opinion, and we were not ready for a hard, tough contest with real challenges that Hawthorn undoubtedly provided. Of the 23 games that we won in that season, only two were by 10 points or fewer, and we had only lost that one game, against Collingwood, way back in May, almost four months earlier.

Because we were winning so easily, a lot of players stripped for every game, and there were some who were jaded by the finish line. After 2008, in fact from that day on, we resolved to make sure that we had enough close games in the build-up to finals, and by that, I mean that we orchestrated it. You *have* to do it when you are lucky enough to confront that situation. You need to train for it so that the players know what to expect, but it can be done. Regrets, we had a few!

As a club, Geelong expected to win that premiership and hubris existed in 2008 where in 2007, we made it up as we went along. This is evident in the preparations for grand final day and the after-match functions. In 2007, nothing was organised; in 2008, they wanted champagne in the rooms and people were given wrist bands to wear to the function, they had the dance music organised and all the alcohol that they thought was needed. The club did that, but they did not tell me, because they knew that I would have been upset. I preferred 2007, which was ad hoc. I believe in the idea that you do not assume anything in footy.

At the family day on the Sunday, I paid tribute to Gary Ablett Jr's game in the grand final, which was enormous. Gary could quite easily have won a Norm Smith Medal that day, just as his father did in 1989. I told the crowd that if we had more people with his attitude, we might have won.

I took the honest approach with the defeat. We stuffed up, so we had to face that; not make excuses. It might not have been what the crowd wanted to hear that day, but I said, 'I know that we let you all down yesterday . . . yeah we did, let's be honest, we did. We let you down. We have to live with that for the rest of our lives, and it'll only drive us to be better in the future.'

It's ironic, but I was on holiday in New York at the end of that season and I ran slap, bang into Craig Bellamy, coach of the Melbourne Storm who had suffered the same result in the NRL grand final, losing to Manly–Warringah. I knew Bellamy; we were both sparkies, and we even looked a little like each other. More to the point, we thought the same way and we had this long venting session about what it felt like to lose a grand final that you should have found a way to win. I did get something out of it.

Everyone was sad and disappointed, obviously, from players to coaches to staff to supporters. In the inner sanctum, though, we were not forgetting that in two seasons, Geelong had won 44 of 50 games, a record across two years that was basically unprecedented. I'm an optimist, and I knew we were doing plenty right. Plus, yet again, we had some anger to carry. Which is never a bad thing. Not bad at all.

SIMONDS

# 14

# NEW GEELONG

## 2009

Pain – both physical and emotional – is a part of professional sport, and we had endured more than our share by the start of 2009. But it wasn't a disaster; the 2008 grand final defeat drove Geelong from start to finish of the following season. We did not even have to mention it. Not a peep was said about it. The players, the coaches, the staff all carried it in the pits of our stomachs until redemption came.

It is always easier to get back on the bike when something is eating away at you. When a team loses as we did in 2008, having only lost a single game for the season prior to grand final day, no one wants a party. You force yourself to attend the official functions, get where you need to go, then jump in the car and go home and you cannot wait for the game to start again.

At Geelong in my time, we had the near miss against Brisbane Lions in 2004, the Nick Davis game in 2005, and then the heist by Hawthorn in 2008, and all were part of the journey. For me, after 2008 it was like, *Imagine if we only got one flag out of this group, that would be* old *Geelong!*' I wanted an *era*, not just a single premiership, even if 2007 was a drought-breaker. I felt – and the players did too – that Geelong's teams were better than a one-flag team.

Which meant that we were back to work in 2009 with vigour and energy. We had the same team with some tweaks, notably Shane Mumford, the big fellow from Bunyip, a little Gippsland town, came into the team as a ruckman when Brad Ottens went down with injury. Gary Ablett had an even better season than we had seen before and we drew improvement from some players around the edges, such as Shannon Byrnes, who had his best season.

Mumford had been a boilermaker back in Bunyip, and he played like one, crashing and bulldozing his way through traffic. He had ballooned to 130 kilograms when he first appeared as a reserves top-up player at Geelong in 2005, and part of his legend was that he had consumed 20 sausages at a 21st birthday party back home. But 'Mummy' worked his butt off when he came to our club after we asked him to get himself fit, and the Ottens injury allowed us to elevate him from the rookie list.

Geelong was so angry that year. We won the first 13 games straight, only falling in round 14 in a classic match at the Docklands against Ross Lyon's St Kilda. Hawthorn was suffering the dreaded premiership hangover, with injuries and poor form dogging the Hawks all year, but under Lyon, St Kilda emerged as the big challenger. The Saints started 2009 with a forward press that was new to the game in the sense that the zone they formed pressed up the field at the opposition, trapping you in the back half of the ground and often forcing turnovers. We had seen zones – the cluster from the previous year, for instance – but this was unusual, and it caught everyone else by surprise.

That is the way of AFL footy, where you are hunted. In 2007 we had shocked the opposition with the kamikaze running game, and two years on, a second method had emerged to counter Geelong's style. I have no doubt that it was targeted at us and it did worry me because it slowed us down. Neil Craig, the Adelaide coach, called it 'frontal pressure', while we called it 'The Squeeze', and others compared it with being marooned and then being pushed off the edge of a cliff. St Kilda swarmed at the opposition when that team had the football in defence, and ended up getting easy goals from the turnovers they forced, which was the polar opposite of the fold-back, flooding game that we had seen a lot of in the previous few years.

Fortunately by the time we met St Kilda in round 14, we had seen enough of the press to analyse it, because it was the talk of the competition. The Saints had also won the first 13 games in succession; they ended up winning 19 straight to start the season and 20 of the 22 home-and-away matches to top the ladder. Under Lyon, they had reached the preliminary final in 2008 only to be ousted by Hawthorn, but quite clearly they were now a force.

In particular, the Saints were tough to score against, putting together the best defensive record in more than 40 years of AFL footy. Their points-against tally of 1411 points at the end of the regular season, an average of just 64.1 points a game, was the lowest since the 22-game season was introduced in 1970, and the lowest average for a team since 1967. Lyon's team conceded 100 points in a game just once for the season, against Essendon in round 20, which is some seriously good defensive footy. As for Geelong, I knew that we needed to kick the football more against a press; when you kick and mark, it is more difficult for a pressing team to force turnovers through pressure, both perceived and real. Whereas if you handball a lot, they can charge at you and hassle your players into errors, the pressure building with each possession in a cumulative effect. It was an adjustment that we needed to make and yes, it slowed us down, but I would spend the next two years trying to make that happen.

The club had done some introspection in the wake of the 2008 grand final loss, and published a document to outline what it wanted to be. It is interesting, looking back at that document, which starts off listing 'Our Values':

**RESPECT** for our club, partners, communities and each other
**PRECISION** in every action and activity
**ADVENTUROUS** in mind and spirit
**CONVICTION** in our purpose and potential
**UNITY** through inclusion
**COMMERCIAL** but considered

The document went on to list the purpose of the club: 'We exist to instil a sense of unity and pride among Cats fans by providing a range of inspiring, exciting and entertaining football experiences.' It talked about our brand and DNA, and what drives us:

- Our essence, our soul and the sentiment through which we are all united is 'conviction'.
- What do we offer?
- We give absolutely everything we've got so Cats fans get the greatest opportunity to share the exhilaration of footy and express their passion for an Aussie tradition.
- We are Footy Full On.

The five-year plan talked about winning at least one premiership in the period 2009–13, and more flags than any other team. Under the section marked 'Our Vision', it stated:

- It is 2020 and we have won more premierships than any

other club over the past decade and are the most admired football club operator in Australia.

- We have become the benchmark for others to emulate, running smoothly and professionally with ample resources, international and internal experts and world-class facilities.
- Our players are considered role models for the code, displaying a conviction to winning and performance that is considered a religion.
- Our superb coaching and training practices set the style of play and we dominated on-field.
- We have a diversified business and expanded commercially into new product portfolios that are highly successful, ensuring robust, stable operations, the highest market capitalisation and a reputation for being innovate and commercially savvy.
- We have developed a core competency in providing unique, highly rewarding member experiences for members, resulting in the highest supporter and member base in the league.
- Our loyal supporter base are multi-generational and highly participative, with paid-up membership and sell-out crowds the norm.
- The club takes its core values extremely seriously and has an extraordinarily talented team that display: Respect for our club, partners, communities and each other; Precision in every action and activity; Adventurous in mind and spirit; Conviction in purpose and potential; Unity through inclusion; Commercial but considered; and models these values in everything we do.
- Iconic brands compete to sponsor us and align with our strong brand and exciting operational initiatives.

- Our working environment is energised, disciplined and a great place to be, and everyone wants to be part of it. Stable long-standing leadership and management are open to change, challenging thought and rewarding of effort and achievement.
- We are highly satisfied and stimulated and feel privileged to work for the club and be part of a supportive family.
- Quite simply we are the most highly supported, sought after and admired sporting organisation in the country – we are 'the team to beat'.

Clearly we had high aspirations, but so did other clubs, and in 2009 we were being challenged by the subtle changes in the game made by opponents intent upon bringing us down. Still, we went 18–4 for the season, the first time in league history that any team had won at least 18 games in three consecutive seasons.

We had begun 2009 with a strong win and some revenge against Hawthorn in round 1. This was the first time that the players' vow to never allow Hawthorn to beat them again after the 2008 Grand Final would be tested, and Hawks president Jeff Kennett poured petrol on the bonfire with his explosive interview on the ABC's *Offsiders* program on the day that we met in round 1: 'What they don't have, I think, is the quality of some of our players; they don't have the psychological drive we have. We've beaten Geelong when it matters.'

This was the genesis of the so-called Kennett Curse on Hawthorn and it was a stupid comment by a club president, an idiotic comment. As it was, we had made our vow not to let Hawthorn beat us again, so we needed no more motivation. The players were terrific when they came back after 2008, winning those 13 games on end. The closest we came to a defeat was against Western Bulldogs in round nine, when Brad Johnson had a shot at goal after the siren to beat us, but missed.

I was happy with that because it was a close game and we had held on, even though I made a comment afterward that I was unsure if we deserved the win. The fact is, it was close and we won, and we needed those games where the players were challenged right to the finish. Afterwards, I spoke to the players about that; about the whole club needing to be tested strongly sometimes.

The season came to its high point in round 14 against St Kilda, with the Saints being unbeaten at the time, too. We had drifted off form a fraction by then, and they beat us on Michael Gardiner's late mark and goal from close range. We ended up losing to Brisbane Lions the following week, too, and the players were cruising a little, I felt, waiting for the finals because we had already banked so many wins.

I had a crack at the players, told them that they had lost their mojo. Some negativity had crept into their mindset, I reckon, and they were thinking, *We've won one, if we get back in and lose again* . . . What I wanted was for them to take the game on, accept the challenges and run with them, and again, I reminded them that we were better than a one-premiership team.

In round 17, we beat Hawthorn when Jimmy Bartel kicked a point after the siren to break the deadlock in another great game in that growing rivalry. We had another close game against Adelaide in round 19, winning that by two points, again showing the importance of having close finishes, and similarly beat Sydney by less than a kick in round 20 at Homebush. Western Bulldogs, another emerging team, beat us by 14 points in round 21 and we would end up meeting them in a final.

The Hawks, meanwhile, became the first team since Adelaide in 1999 to miss the finals in the season after winning a flag. So our challengers had changed colours, but they remained significant. We beat the Bulldogs in the qualifying final by blowing them away early, then smashed Collingwood by 73 points in the preliminary final, when Paul Chapman kicked five goals and Cameron Ling closed down Dane Swan. Tom Hawkins, who had established himself in the team, also played well and we were headed to a third consecutive grand final – the second time in club history that we had managed to play on the big day three years in a row.

We would play St Kilda, the top team in the regular season, the Saints reaching the grand final for the first time under Ross Lyon. We also had the best player in the game, with Gary Ablett Jr winning the Brownlow Medal for the first time, polling 30 votes to win by a whopping eight over Chris Judd. Gary had finished third in 2008 (two votes behind Adam Cooney) and tied sixth in 2007 when Jimmy Bartel won the medal, so he was well and truly due.

I saw Gary Junior up close for long enough to know that he is a truly great player; even better, I believe, than his father, Gary Senior. A lot of people ask me for my view on this, and I summarise it by saying that if you want someone to bring people through the gate and have a highlights tape of sensational football, you would pick Gary Ablett Sr above any player in history. But I would then add that Gary Senior did not win a premiership, while Gary Junior has two to his name; Gary Senior did not win a Brownlow Medal against his son's two; Gary Senior won just the one best and fairest against Gary Junior's cluster of those gongs.

Gary Junior is the better player, the more consistent player in a team environment. With Gary Senior, Geelong won or lost depending on how he was feeling. He could win a game by himself, and he did that a lot, but if he played poorly, which he also did quite a lot, Geelong probably lost.

The first on-field issue that occurred in grand final week was the fitness of Mathew Stokes, who was carrying a groin strain that had occurred in the first final against the Bulldogs. Stokes would have been part of our best team, and would have returned for the grand final, but he told us in grand final week that he could not get up to play, despite playing 19 games and snaring 29 goals that year. I remember him being emotional when he spoke to me that week, and I told him how brave it was for him to say it. He was team first, Stokesy, and he didn't want to let us down; in the 2008 Grand Final he had played with a niggle, and had broken down. Meanwhile at the grand final parade, he told the media:

> To be honest, the whole reason I didn't play last week [in the preliminary final] was because of last year [in the grand final] and letting the boys down. I played probably two games I shouldn't have, where my groins just weren't strong enough. I shouldn't have played but I still did. I let my pride get in the way and this year I didn't want to make the same mistake.

Comparing our 2009 grand final team with 2008, Stokes' place would be taken by Shannon Byrnes. Tom Hawkins was now ensconced and he played instead of Tom Lonergan, and Josh Hunt had lost his place, while David Wojcinski, who had missed the 2008 Grand Final with injury, was back in the starting team by 2009. They were the three changes from the previous year, but we had very different opposition.

Corey Enright went into the grand final with a slight quadriceps strain, Tom Hawkins with knee soreness and Max Rooke with hamstring and knee complaints, but our injury sheet was not too bad. The bigger problem was dealing with St Kilda, which had lost only two games for the season, having progressed past the Bulldogs in the preliminary final. My notes, handed to the players in grand final week, show that we knew what was coming from the Saints:

- Game style quick and direct.
- Kicking team.
- Base game around defence.

They were not a team of great individuals, but they were definitely a great *team*, St Kilda in 2009, and the record showed that clearly. What we wanted on the day was for our players to attack, because against a team that pressed up like St Kilda did, you could be dragged into their style. Hence my notes said:

- Ballsy, brave, risky.
- Constant ball movement hurts them.

I asked the players to play on from marks at least 60 per cent of the time, which was a massive figure, but virtually necessary against St Kilda. We never achieved that, but it was a nice target to set, and we also wanted to put our own squeeze on St Kilda when we had the football in our front half. 'We own defender squeeze,' I wrote.

I wanted to make sure our forward-half players were not dragged up to the football, to keep our structure in place. We asked the players to restrict St Kilda's mark tally, which the Bulldogs had done with some success. We wanted Gary Ablett, who we knew would be tagged by Clint Jones, to take Jones deep into our forward line and we wanted Sam Fisher, the Saints' sweeping defender, to be made accountable, because he had a habit of becoming a nuisance.

We assigned Harry Taylor, only 23 and in just his second year at the club, the task of playing on St Kilda's captain, Nick Riewoldt, rather than Matthew Scarlett, who would play on Justin Koschitzke. Scarlett was too valuable to use on Riewoldt and he could set up so

**Attack – style, stats, set ups**

BALLSY, BRAVE RISKY.

- CONSTANT BALL MOVEMENT. HURTS THEM
  - KAMIKAZE
  - OFF LINE BALL USE.
  - ~~A~~ REVERSE LATERAL
  - BACK TO BALL FORWARD HB.
  - 1ST OPTION. PLAY ON FROM MARKS. 60%
- PLAY GAME IN OUR HALF
  'WE OWN DEFENDER SQUEEZE!'
  MAKE STK DEFEND: STAY HOME MARK INS. 50
  21/9 16/12
  LOWER VISION – HANG ON RATHER THAN DUMP!!

- MIDFIELD RUNNING PATTERNS.
  - HELP DEFENDERS AS WELL AS
  - PROVIDE MID OPTIONS 'A3!' JOEL COREY.

- ~~1ST OPTION: THROW IT AROUND~~.
  REPEAT OUTNUMBER.

18 STK PLAYERS IN OUR HALF
TARGET ZONE – KEEP POSSESSION 1ST.
✓ BALL USE. / FAT SIDE / REVERSE

much; plus if he played on Riewoldt, he would be dragged too far from goal. So Harry had the job, and a note I wrote to the players summarised his task. 'One day of your life,' it said.

At stoppages, we urged the players to use 'method, then talent', which is an indication of what we thought: that we had the more talented team, and that we needed to show that. I used those lines because the only way that St Kilda was going to beat Geelong was to take us out of our confident state, make it nearly impossible for blokes to get a kick.

Assistant coach Ken Hinkley's presentation to the players rated St Kilda and forecast the way we wanted to approach the grand final. He summarised his thoughts:

- Hard to play against.
- Let's attack them.

I coached the 'outnumber', which was about getting extra players to the contest, just having an extra player for insurance, even if we won the ball. It was about the next man in: 'If it's 13 versus 13, let's make it 14.' Nowadays of course, there are even more players around the football, but on this day, we wanted extra numbers to the football as much as possible. Above all, the players were warned that they could expect a messy game, that St Kilda would make sure that it was so. I wrote: '18 St K players in their own half.'

The press was difficult to beat, there is no doubt of that. To counter it, you had to slice through quickly, to have the guts to do that, but if you waited for a safer option, it only grew tougher. That is when you are gone, and that is what it was all about.

I thought that we would win the grand final, because we had the team to do it. We had only lost by a kick when we played St Kilda during the season, and I thought we were the better team.

We had more scoring power than St Kilda (second in scoring during the regular season, compared to their fourth), and a better balance between defence and attack.

We were well prepared but the job still had to be done, and it was a monumental struggle. St Kilda led at quarter-time, half-time and three-quarter time of that grand final, by a few points on each occasion. Lenny Hayes, their warrior midfielder, played a huge first quarter, which left us with a decision: whether to switch Cameron Ling on to Hayes and away from Nick Dal Santo, his opponent at the start. In this, we drew from the preliminary final, when the Bulldogs had switched their opponent for Hayes and then Dal Santo had got off the chain. We did not want that to happen.

Fortunately, we had Jimmy Bartel in the team. All season, we had practised using Jimmy as a second tagger behind Ling, who did it week in, week out. Jimmy was more than a tagger, but he took one for the team that day, and he calmed the Hayes influence a little, which helped us. He had a whopping 16 tackles and Hayes, who had 11 touches to the first break, finished with 24 for the day, winning the Norm Smith Medal. I rated Lenny Hayes, absolutely, and Jimmy's job was not necessarily to stop him; it was more to close down the way he was linking up forward of the play.

The rain came, and I was not happy about that. We were playing a team that we felt would enjoy slippery conditions more, although we had Geelong trained up to play in all conditions. As a team, you need to be able to win with 20 goals or win with 10, wet or dry. But the showers that swept across the ground were not necessarily welcome for us.

At three-quarter time, we were seven points down, but I still felt comfortable, and here was the difference: the players had the fire in their eyes, unlike 12 months earlier, when we were close enough to get over Hawthorn but without the mental capacity to manage it. We talked about what price we would have to pay, and how much the players were willing to put on the line. It was along the lines of, 'You play a lifetime to get into this position. Just play your best quarter of footy. It's what dreams are made of.'

As it turned out, the players had plenty in the tank that day. The last quarter belonged to us, and I am sure guys who had been there in 2008 were after redemption in that 30 minutes. Others filled roles around the edges. Shannon Byrnes, who had not played in 2008, was brilliant on the far wing in the last quarter, running off Raphael Clarke and dominating. We would not have won it without him. He was not our best player, Shannon, but in a team like we had, he was not necessarily covered by the opposition, and in good teams, everyone needs to be respected.

There were only three goals kicked in that incredibly physical last quarter but fortunately, they were all Geelong goals. Tom Hawkins got one early, then with a few misses, we drew level at the 21-minute mark. At 23 minutes came the key play: Steve Johnson extracted the footy out on the members' wing and squared the kick toward Gary Ablett in the centre square, a dangerous kick, and a very *Stevie* kick. Potentially, it could have lost us the game as it floated, and Gary waited under it.

St Kilda's full-back Zac Dawson came off his man, charged at Ablett and sunk a fist into the football, brushing it out of Gary's mitts. Who knows what would have happened if Dawson had made more solid contact on the ball; as it was, there was glancing contact, enough to bring the ball to the deck. Matthew Scarlett and his opponent, Justin Koschitzke, were right there, approaching the contest from the other direction.

What happened next goes into the annals of the game. Scarlett did not even bend over to pick the football up; an instant, he ran past Koschitzke and toe-poked it straight into Gary's hands, with Dawson's momentum having taken him past the ball. It was a little piece of genius; Scarlo has said since that no thought actually entered his mind. It was pure instinct by a great player.

Gary was free to turn and run, all the way to the end of the centre square, with Scarlett surging behind him in support, so close that Ablett actually thought for a moment he was about to be run down by an opponent. Gary, who at one stage veered to his right as though dodging a shadow, told Channel 7's *Game Day*: 'I can actually remember running inside 50 and thinking that he [Scarlett] was a St Kilda player and kind of baulking away from him. I think that's the reason I kicked it in the end. I'm sure I had 20 more metres to run and probably have a shot.'

Ablett's long kick landed at the top of our goal square, where Cam Mooney contested the mark, and going back with the flight like a madman, Max Rooke split the pack wide open and brought the ball to ground. Rooke had been like that all day, and Cam Mooney said later that he could hear the sound of his teammate's body crashing into St Kilda players, and that it has stayed with him. It actually scared me! He was a barometer for Geelong, Max Rooke, a spiritual leader for us and a wild animal on the field at times.

With his back to our goals Travis Varcoe scooped up the loose ball and handballed to Paul Chapman, lurking as the front-and-square man, and unmarked, just 20 metres or so from the big sticks. Chappy wheeled left and I knew that he would kick the goal. That is what Chappy does. He *wants* the football right then, he has no nerves, and he *wants* that kick for the win, just like Stevie Johnson does, and Jimmy Bartel.

Funnily enough, he had Jimmy Bartel wide open for a handball if he needed him, and he probably should have given the ball up, too, given that he was on his non-preferred side. But it was all perfect, really. We were a goal in front in the grand final with only three minutes to play.

From that moment it was about getting numbers to the stoppages, clogging the game up. After Rooke scored another behind, Scarlett rushed a behind for St Kilda that left us vulnerable again, just six points in front with a minute to go. In the box, none of us could get comfortable, and then Darren Milburn almost had his kick-in smothered by Riewoldt, after the umpire called him to play on!

Dasher's kick was long to the members' side, and if St Kilda marked it, the Saints still had a chance. Instead, Harry Taylor, playing his 43rd game of AFL footy, floated from the side and grabbed it. We had looked at shifting Harry away from Riewoldt, because we knew how much running that job required, and we pored over his GPS numbers to check that. Harry was young and inexperienced, but he showed that day what a great player he would become. He held Riewoldt to five marks and one goal, 13 disposals, and that was a significant win for Geelong.

The clock wound down from that moment, and as we ran the ball around the wing and Max Rooke marked Cam Mooney's kick up forward, giving us territorial advantage, we finally knew that we had the flag. In the box, I went crazier than I think that I have ever been in footy. On the commentary with Channel 10, Tim Lane had the call: 'It's OVER!! For the Cats . . . vindication has arrived.'

I never saw Max Rooke kick the last goal, which came after the siren had gone. By that time, I was up on the bench, jumping up and down and carrying on so much that I injured the knee of my board man, Alan Carter, quite badly. I hugged Brenton Sanderson, Ken Hinkley and the others in the box, and poor Carter was nursing a torn meniscus because I had slammed my chair into the side of his knee. It was not the first time he had become a casualty; around 2003 I had accidentally slammed the players' room door on his arm as he tried to follow the boys into the room. This time it was just such a release of tension after a dogfight of a game, such a relief to eke out the win.

Bob Davis presented the cup, which was appropriate, and Chappy won the Norm Smith Medal for his 26 disposals and three critical goals. Ironically, one of the comments that I wrote for the players in their match notes was: 'Team equals Norm Smith Medal.'

I did not want players thinking about individual glory; it was about making sure they did the right thing by the team, and what I liked about that win was that it was done as a team. In my press conference, I said that the beauty of the group was that while there were a few superstars – I named Ablett, Bartel and Scarlett as well as Chapman – the players all respected each other. It was a great thing for a coach to have, that bond and that respect within the playing group. It is a powerful thing; it is where you want to get to as a coach, but it's not all that easy to achieve.

He was a superstar, Chappy. When the big games and the finals came, I talked 'team first, team first', but I also knew that he would want to be best-on-ground, because that was the way he thought and operated. When he got that football from Travis Varcoe in the closing minutes of the 2009 Grand Final, I would have liked him to give it off to Jimmy Bartel, because that was our mantra, but I also knew that Chappy would think that he could kick it. Actually, he would *know* that he could kick it himself, and now, he had two premiership medals and a Norm Smith Medal to go with them, saying to the media, 'In the end it's not about the Norm Smith, it's about what we wanted to achieve. The Norm Smith's great, but you don't catch up with blokes who won other Norm Smiths. You catch up with your teammates who you win premierships with. That's something that we're going to have forever.'

We were lucky. I have said it in the past and I believe it, because in any game that close – Rooke's late goal gave the grand final to Geelong by a meagre 12 points – there are breaks. Tom Hawkins kicked a goal that brushed the goal post, unnoticed by the goal umpire. Chapman was feeling cramps in his hamstring at half-time, so we played him deeper, and he kicked the matchwinner when he might have simply broken down.

A bounce here or there went our way. St Kilda had 58 inside-50 entries, more than enough to win, and far more than our 42, but they kicked 9.14, wasting too many chances. As Ross Lyon said in his press conference, 'We left the door ajar, and they took the opportunities. It's pretty simple.'

But while it was a titanic struggle, I always felt like we could win, for several reasons. One was that, unlike in 2008, we had endured some close games during the season and won them. We knew what to expect and how to execute under extreme pressure. Secondly, I always felt that St Kilda did not have the scoring power to hurt us too badly, that the Saints would never get too far ahead even if they played their best footy. They kicked two goals in the second half and none in the final quarter, and that will not win too many grand finals for anyone.

Finally, St Kilda did not have the pain of recent defeat to draw upon that we had, and when I was asked after the grand final by the press whether the 2008 defeat had driven the players, I said that if they looked into history they would struggle to find too many teams in that situation who lost the second time around. It is just the way sport is.

Mark Blake now had his premiership medal after missing out so narrowly in 2007 and then being on the losing team in 2008, and Harry Taylor, Travis Varcoe and Tom Hawkins had their first taste of premiership success. Quite a few of the guys now had two; personally, I had five premierships – two as coach to go with three as a player. I told the media that I felt it 'only fair' that this Geelong team had two premierships, rather than just the one.

We won 65 of 75 games across the 2007–09 seasons with two flags, and I am proud that people loved the way that we played, even people who did not follow Geelong. We scored and we entertained, but it is worth remembering that it was not all about attack. I thought that our supporters really enjoyed watching us tackle and turn the ball over on the opposition, and we were an excellent defensive team as well. We played proper footy.

Our attack was built from our ability to win the ball, but also from our ability to win the ball back from the opposition. That was a major part of it, even if it was not so often acknowledged. We put ourselves in a great position to move the ball quickly, and on turnover, it was just *BOOM*! That is the essence of modern footy, and it would have been fun to play, too, which is important. Footy is a game, and it should be fun to play. As an observation only, I would say that with Ross Lyon's teams, I am not sure if they are so much playing footy, as doing a job. They come to work, they play their role.

When Geelong contended under Malcolm Blight, I would say that they were caught out of play too often; that is to say, they ran in front of the football too much, and their structure did not hold up if they lost control of it. They could not get back in time to defend, and they had a lot of players who would get in front of the ball: Paul Couch, Mark Bairstow, Peter Riccardi even had that habit, and playing like that allows teams to score too heavily against you.

The key to this is *transition*. When do you start defending as a player if you cannot influence the play, and when do you attack? If you are behind the ball and cannot get near it, you cannot influence the play, and that is what we talked about in my time at Geelong. When we had the ball, we wanted A3 running if you were out of the play (the 'A' was for attack, the '3' is for grade three, or top-level) and you needed to do that earlier than everyone else. Players needed to know when to set the defence, even when we have the football and vice versa; they needed to be ready to run forward hard when they sensed that we are about to get the ball back. The key was knowing exactly *when* to go. It is the real essence of football.

By dint of a lot of factors, we won that day against St Kilda and it changed everything for the footy club, I have no doubt. Had we lost, that would have been two defeats in a row and the old tags, the old criticisms, would have come up again, we would have reverted to Old Geelong. But what we wanted, as set out in the five-year document, was to create the best football club in Australia, as I mentioned to the press after the game.

In the New Geelong, we did not want to disappear after a couple of triumphs. We wanted a dynasty. We had aspired to be the envy of the competition, and right at that moment, I reckon we were precisely that.

# 15

# LEAVING

## 2010

The 2010 season, my eleventh at Geelong, began optimistically enough. We were the defending premier, going for back-to-back flags, a feat we had missed in 2008 when Hawthorn beat us in the grand final. We had some new players like James Podsiadly, who was a revelation despite never playing senior AFL football until he was 28, and we had a new skipper, because Tom Harley had retired soon after the 2009 Grand Final. Harley, a fine captain of the club, had confided in me several weeks before the grand final that he intended quitting. He told the *Herald Sun*, 'I physically can't meet the requirements to play, to see out a season, a full season in the AFL.'

Cameron Ling was appointed as the new captain, an easy enough choice given the leadership that he was already displaying under Harley, but it turned into a draining season for various reasons, not the least of which was that the AFL wanted to pinch the best player in the competition from our ranks.

The AFL had announced on 31 March 2009 that it was handing

a provisional licence to a Gold Coast consortium for a new club out of Queensland, and it had been public for some time beforehand that the league would expand into south-east Queensland and western Sydney with two new teams. The licence for the Gold Coast Suns provided that they would begin playing in the AFL in 2011, which made 2010 a busy year of preparation for the new Suns, who had the rights to sign a cluster of out-of-contract players from other clubs.

Karmichael Hunt, the rugby star and sometime Wallaby representative, had been signed, and Nathan Bock from Adelaide Crows, a 2008 All Australian, and it soon became apparent that their big recruiting target was Gary Ablett Jr, who was coming out of contract with Geelong at the end of 2010. Ablett was the reigning Brownlow medallist, and the rumours about offers – citing a huge contract of $10 million over five years – began late in 2009, following us all through the 2010 season like a big, black cloud.

I was annoyed by this right from the start, and a lot of people have assumed over the years that I was angry with Gary, but I was not. Of course, I could understand why Gary Ablett would take up a financial offer that amounted to twice what we could pay him at Geelong. Clearly he had every reason to accept an offer of that size.

But the truth is that I was annoyed with the AFL for creating a new club in its own image and then pinching a legend of *our* club, a player whose father was also a legend of Geelong and part of the story of the city itself. The Geelong Football Club is based on history and tradition, it is a unique part of the community in a provincial city, and I could not understand how it would be good for the league to take Gary Ablett Jr, a precious jewel so far as Geelong was concerned, away from the club and the city.

I did not get why people just accepted that as okay, to treat a foundation member of the competition like that. He was the best player in Australia, but was it good for football? I question that. Did it inflate the wages for all players and make life tougher for all clubs? I think so. I thought that the AFL was there to administrate the league, run the games every weekend, make sure people are communicated to and uphold the rules and regulations. That is what I thought; plainly I was wrong.

So while I was angry that whole year and it was seen as being directed at Gary Ablett, deep down it was City Hall and their new baby that set me off, and in the end, it caused tension between Gary and me. It started, I suppose, at Geelong's season launch, when I raised it in my speech. It was March, and Gary had spoken to the crowd at Crown and said that he played football for premierships, and I was feeling cheeky that night. Stepping up to the microphone soon after, I pointed out that '700 people in this room heard Gary Ablett say the only reason he plays is to play in a premiership, so Gary, you'd be more of a chance [here] than at the other mob that are offering all that money.'

It was not a serious statement, more a little dig, and I was not the only one to speak on the matter. President Frank Costa had talked earlier to the crowd about Geelong's strong culture: 'That's what makes this club such a great place to be, such a wonderful place to play footy and be part of the whole Geelong family – so that these boys won't want to leave because wherever they go other than here won't be as good.'

But it was my commentary that drew the headlines from a media hungry for information about the possibility that a player of Gary's magnitude might walk out on Geelong. It was a huge story, all along, and I can see exactly why. In the week of our first game I made the comment to the press that Gary 'probably knows what he's going to do', adding that we would just have to wait until he was ready to reveal the answer.

I talked to Gary a few times in that early-2010 period, and my theme was: 'Why not stay and have team success?' I know that Frank had put the same kind of situation to him, suggesting that with marketing money, he could make almost as much at Geelong anyway, even though we had no chance of fitting anything approaching a $2 million annual contract into our salary cap. Unless we shipped out a few players, that is, and that would have gone against everything that we had set up at Geelong.

A few rounds into the season, I told Gary that in the club's interests it would be better to either sign to play with Geelong or Gold Coast, to make a decision immediately. He said that it was not my business, and after that precise moment, I felt that he was probably going to the Gold Coast Suns. I also sensed that he was a little uncomfortable that having made the decision to go, he would be required to keep it quiet for almost a whole year, which is understandable.

I did not go out of my way to talk to him about it after that first meeting; we did not talk much at all. Later that year, Gary told the *Herald Sun* his version of the cooling:

> He grabbed me in his office for a chat, but it was more, 'Why haven't you signed for the club?' and I just said, 'To be honest with you, Bomber, I'm not that comfortable discussing it with you. I'm still working through that with the club.' I just felt that he's the coach, I'm the player. Contracts shouldn't be his role. But we had a pretty big argument there in his office, he walked out, I walked out, and he hasn't really spoken to me since, to be honest.

The story would not go away so long as Gary remained unsigned, so from the early part of 2010 right through the season, I would answer questions about Gary's future at every single press conference, so would every player at our footy club, and so would Gary Ablett himself. We were having a decent year – we won another 17 games and finished second, half a game behind Collingwood – but we could never escape the speculation, and it was a major distraction for Geelong.

To his credit, Gary kept playing well, but it was difficult for him, too, and there was some argy-bargy at list management level. We knew that Gary would almost certainly leave, and I *got* why, but Geelong felt duty-bound to make a counter-offer to a player of that quality.

I remember about three-quarters of the way through the season being involved in a list management meeting where the subject of Gary's contract came up, and there was frustration that, officially at least, we were unclear about what he was doing from the 2011 season. To that point I had no idea what Geelong had offered, which is how it works in modern footy; the coach could be the last to know, and other people are well-paid to handle contract negotiations. What I did know was that he was only getting about $500 000 a year with us, we did not have a player in the top 20 salaries in the competition, and that he was underpaid on the basis of market value. It was how we did things at Geelong.

In the meeting, I spoke up. 'By the way, what are we at? I hear this figure [from Gold Coast] of $1.9 million, but we aren't going to win, because the AFL's putting in $800 000.'

'We're at around a million,' the list management people told me.

I said, 'You are *joking*! So the Gold Coast offer is forcing us to double the pay of our highest paid player? What about the other guys, their salaries?'

We had strong parameters around our list management. All the players knew that they were taking an inferior contract in monetary terms to fit into a successful team and remain under the AFL's salary cap – at the time around $8 million. Gary was no different; he knew that he could get more money elsewhere, but he had also played in two premierships and been a big part of our successful culture.

When I found out what we were offering Gary, I said to the meeting, 'That's just not us.' From what I was told, if Gary signed with Geelong on the offer we had made there were likely to be two players who would need to be cut so that we could fit his contract into our cap from 2011. For the first time people at the club were prepared to go against our principles.

Brian Cook confirmed the final offer in an interview with Fox's *Open Mike* some years later:

> We ended up offering Gary $1 million a year (for five years) near the end. We were going to go outside of our (pay) bands, but we said, 'Look, we will get our money back from marketing and all that.' Our highest paid player other than Gary then was on about $500 000, maybe $600 000 max. But the offer he got (from Gold Coast) was much larger than that.

All of this stuff got to me in 2010, I must admit, and I made a few statements that, in hindsight, might have been a bit rash. There was the Carlton game in round 5, where we lost to the Blues, and the media asked me about Gary's performance, to which I said that I did not think he had a great game. I argued that his 32 disposals and two goals overstated his importance, and in the process gave the media another *Herald Sun* headline: 'BOMBER THOMPSON CREATES HIS OWN TURBULENCE'.

There were still more questions about the Ablett situation, to which I threw up the example of Joel Selwood, like Gary a dual premiership player already, who had recently signed a new deal to stay at Geelong. I noted that a lot of our players had stayed because they loved playing together and they loved playing for Geelong. Another headline bobbed up after that comment, and another round of speculation.

In the end, I think we all agreed that as much as we didn't want Gary to leave, we just couldn't pay him as much as the Suns. No one could have refused that offer. It's sad that AFL money lost Geelong's last Ablett.

The AFL was hellbent on this expansion into the Gold Coast and Greater Western Sydney but not much thought was put into the impact on the existing clubs, all of them battling for their existence in some ways. I could understand their thinking in expanding, but to be honest, it probably happened too quickly. Putting two teams into the competition over two years, 2011 and 2012, was a massive drain on talent and finances. I also think the draft concessions that were provided to the new clubs – Gold Coast had eight of the first 13 picks in 2010 – were a disincentive to the other clubs. It must have left some of them thinking, *What hope have we got?* I see that as a danger for football, because incentive is everything, and the popularity of the game is based around kids having a dream of playing.

Remarkably, Geelong kept winning most of the time, but deep down I always felt that we were struggling in 2010. We beat Hawthorn again in round 2, coming from four goals down at half-time to continue our dominance of that rivalry, and finished up winning 10 of the first 12 games, some by big margins. Key forward James Podsiadly, who had come to the club at 28, a mature-age recruit who cost us virtually nothing in terms of the draft, was one of the stories of the season. Pods had previously been on our fitness staff while playing with the VFL team, but he just demanded to be picked at senior level, and he could beat everyone at training, even Matthew Scarlett.

Yet the results on the surface covered up a pattern: we were losing to the teams who pressed up on us in the modern way, the method begun by Ross Lyon in 2009 that almost brought us undone in that year's grand final. In round 13, St Kilda extracted a little revenge by beating us at the MCG, and Collingwood, which had soared in 2010 on a forward press copied and improved from Lyon's model, beat us in round 19.

After finishing the season 17–5, we lost by four points in the qualifying final to the Saints, which made it tough for us, knowing that we would need to win three finals from there to win the flag. Cameron Ling appeared to scrounge a late, matchwinning goal for us in that final at the MCG, but the field umpire picked out a free kick against Cameron Mooney for falling into the back of St Kilda defender James Gwilt an instant before Lingy had launched his kick, and waved off the goal.

It was a devastating moment for us and for the supporters, virtually none of whom had realised that the whistle had gone. Our players had already celebrated the goal that seemed like it was the clincher. It seemed to me to be a rough decision, and when the press asked me about this afterwards, I encouraged them to 'write whatever you want to write, and write the truth about that last incident, that's all I'll say'. I did not want to blame the umpire, though, and I also told the players that they needed to turn up ready for a semi-final, or not at all, because we had fallen more than five goals down early against St Kilda. The way that we had started was just not good enough.

Footy had changed dramatically toward a strategy of pressing up the ground and attacking the opposition, with Mick Malthouse's Collingwood leading the charge now, dominating the season. It was all about combatting Geelong's game style, we knew that, and I wanted the players to *kick* the ball more, to cut down the kamikaze handball.

It was the way that I felt we could work through the presses because when a player marks the footy (rather than accepting a handball), the opposition cannot apply any real pressure lest he concedes a 50-metre penalty. In strings of handball out of defence, a pressing team can be relentless in its attack on the man and there is often a moment when the whole thing breaks down and the ball is turned over. Usually, it is a certain goal and Collingwood, as an example, was scoring heavily using the method.

My players could not accept that change was needed. They were playing how *they* wanted to play, not the way *we* wanted them to play. I tried to coach it, but I did not get the buy-in from the players, who were not convinced that the method that worked so well from 2007–09, winning two flags, needed to be altered. The players had been absolutely resolute in supporting me right from the start of my time at Geelong, even saving me in 2006. Now, for the first time, I sensed a pushback factor.

Hence, the source of more of my frustration. I was utterly worn out, and I had told the right people at the club that it was a fact. About halfway through the season I went to see Brian Cook and confided to him that I might not see out my contract, which ran to the end of the following season, 2011, that I was struggling to get through all the work, and that I was losing the players. I said, 'I'm not sure they're listening. It's going to be hard work.'

Coaching is very dull and tedious at times, and so many people expect so much of you that it becomes physically and emotionally draining. *All* the players need to be spoken to, and not just by your assistants, even though the assistant coaches pick up a huge amount of the workload. But the players still want to hear the message from the head coach, and it wears on you over time, because the demands are just enormous.

After the two premierships in 2007 and 2009, I began to receive invitations to have dinner with people in business, to speak to groups; I guess we had made a mark as a club and people wanted to hear about it. I wanted to do those things, too, pushing the club out in the public domain and growing it. But I also had to do my day job; I had to go home and watch the tapes and the edits of players and structures and opposition teams, and where was I going to get the time? I felt like the demands were only increasing, and that my life was being swallowed up.

If Geelong did not know that I was in danger of walking, then it should have, I reckon. That is what I will say. I felt that Brian Cook knew my situation, but he was not listening closely enough, or taking my concerns seriously enough. I remember him saying, 'You'll be right. You're like this every year at this time of year!' I said, '*No,* it's different this time.' At the end of the season he said, 'Just have a long break in the post-season. Come back after Christmas.' I said, '*No,* if you're going to coach, you coach.' I did not want to do a half-baked job; it was not my style and in any case, you cannot do it properly without putting in the time.

However in the meantime, there was another premiership to chase if there was a turn in our fortunes, so I kept my head down. We reached the preliminary final stage for the fourth year in a row and played Collingwood, but we were pretty much slaughtered that night. The Magpies were the best team in the competition by a fair way; they were ten goals up at three-quarter time before relaxing, and the final margin was a comprehensive 41 points. Collingwood went on to win the premiership after the first grand final against St Kilda was drawn, and the message was pretty clear; the forward press was the new method du jour and to beat it, change was required.

I remember Matthew Scarlett saying in the media straight after the preliminary final defeat that Geelong needed to come up with a new game plan, and that the old method was no longer working. To which I thought, *That's what I was saying all along*. The 2010 season was a failure of my coaching, because I just could not convince the players that we needed to change and worse, what we ended up presenting was the wrong way. That is one of the reasons why I ended up so tired. For the whole time I had been at Geelong, the players backed me and believed me, then all of a sudden in 2010 they wanted to be their own men. It comes from winning a lot, I guess, but it did not help any of us. For the first time but not the last, the media moved to declare the Geelong era to be over.

In the press conference that night after the preliminary final and the demise of our season, I mentioned that the players did not give me the buy-in that I wanted, and driving home from the MCG, I pretty much knew that I was done. Yes, I had a contract for 2011, but what would be the point of continuing if my heart was not in it? I had never bothered about contracts; did not even sign them most of the time, quite literally.

I had four consecutive three-year contracts in my time at Geelong, and the only one that I actually signed was the last of them, because the human resources people at the footy club made me sign. Contracts mean very little in footy, and I was always happy to have a handshake agreement with Frank Costa and Brian Cook.

I was dirty on the players and I told them that. I felt that under pressure, they kept reverting to their own way, handballing too much and trying to run the footy, which was the old-style Geelong. It did not work anymore against the better opposition teams. In 2010, Geelong averaged 209 handballs, ranked number one in the competition by a figure of nearly 20 per game, just as we were number one in 2007, 2008 and second in 2009. In 2010, our ratio of kicks to handballs was 1.04 to 1, meaning we handballed almost as much as we kicked; for a comparison, in 1990 the ratio of kicks to handballs across the competition was 1.9 to 1, almost double.

But to beat the press, you needed to break up your ball movement with a kick, to change direction, to slow down a little until the gaps appear. That was my theory, and a few years on, teams have adjusted, so that the forward press is not the big issue that it was back then. In 2010, it was new and the players were still working out how to handle it; we played the pressing specialists St Kilda and Collingwood four times that season, and lost every single time.

In the week after the preliminary final defeat, I attended the usual reviews and the draft preview talks, but I also went to see Brian Cook and told him that I wanted out. His first concern was that I was going to switch over and coach Essendon, where Matthew Knights had been sacked, and where my old club was looking for a new coach. There were rumours to that effect because the job was available, and the media was joining dots, although it was also well known that Essendon wanted James Hird to coach in a sort of homecoming.

I told Cook that I would not be coaching Essendon; that I was too tired. I said that the Geelong players had stopped listening to me, and that I was worn out from trying to change it. I knew that the list was in good shape, and that a change of coach would not be a bad thing after so long, more than 10 years. I also went to visit

Frank Costa down the coast. Frank had been at his holiday house in Aireys Inlet, and I met him halfway, at a coffee shop, finding him not angry with the news, although the Essendon rumours were concerning him. I said to him, 'Frank, I'm not going to coach. Geelong helped me be who I am, but I don't actually know if it's half-time in my career, three-quarter time, or whatever. I just don't know.'

I had also spoken to some of the Geelong players on my last day, guys like Darren Milburn, Matthew Scarlett and Corey Enright, and while I did not directly tell that I was leaving, they had worked it out; they knew. We had a few tears, but they understood what I was saying, and I remember Scarlett's sharp response: 'Are you coaching Essendon, or what?' I told him that I would not coach the Dons.

In the list management meeting earlier in the week, I had fought hard to keep Darren Milburn for one last year at 33, as well as Max Rooke and David Wojcinski. All of them were in the gun at that meeting, and it was one of those times where it was the list management people's show, but they still have to work with the senior coach, and if the senior coach wants something, who wins the battle? That day, I was in the mood to win.

A few people have said since that I did not want to face the notion of cutting my premiership players from the list, and that is probably where the stories come from, because that meeting, and making sure Dasher Milburn stayed, was about my last single action at Geelong. There is an element of truth in what people say. Dealing with those cuts would have been hard for me, because you fall in love with your players when you have success. They do so much for you. But it was not the only reason that I left; it was probably a small element of several reasons.

For instance the Gary Ablett story had grated on me, and with hindsight, Geelong probably should have done something similar to what Hawthorn did with Lance 'Buddy' Franklin in 2013, when he was targeted by Sydney under free agency. Hawthorn's coach Alastair Clarkson downgraded Franklin's importance to the team in that season, almost used him as a decoy so that the hit was not quite so fierce when it came.

Franklin signed with the Swans and walked at the end of 2013, straight after winning a flag with the Hawks. It was super-smart, because the Hawks had prospered anyway from being less reliant on a single player, and then they won again in 2014, the first year of his absence and made all the more ironic by the fact that their opponents on the day were the Swans, with Franklin as their star forward. I reckon that Hawthorn learned from what happened to Geelong with Gary Ablett in 2010, because we did nothing of the sort, none of the preparation for what eventuated.

It was a time of big change for Geelong. Gary Ablett signed a five-year deal with the Suns that was announced on 29 September 2010. Meanwhile after I spoke to Brian and Frank, Geelong announced publicly that I was pondering whether I would continue as head coach in the 2011 season, theoretically allowing a few days for the dust to settle. Frank Costa told the *Herald Sun*:

> Our hope is that as we get through next year . . . we can lighten his burden and get the assistant coaches to have a bit more responsibility. I'm hoping that he'll be able to run his responsibility for the property thing at the same time as still coaching. I think he could. Truly we don't know. It's one of those things where we wouldn't pressure him. He's such a good man and has been so good for us. He never talks about his contracts . . . so we won't really talk seriously to him until well into next year – but he knows that we want him.

It was 28 September, in grand final week, and Brian Cook told a media conference:

> The unfortunate reality is in our opinion, and we're not medicos, he's suffering some form of burnout after 11 years. He's reassessing his life, he's reassessing his future and we're caught in the middle of all that. I hope he coaches us next year but as I said, you would only want a coach who's completely committed to the cause and he agrees with that.

Cook was asked how he expected the Geelong fans would react:

> I think with surprise, I also hope with some empathy and understanding that coaching's a pretty tough job, and after 11 years of a pretty hectic journey we've been on, there's some burn-out here. I think people can relate to that. I hope they can relate to that. I think what has caused the issue for us is just the surprise element at this late stage. And it may be the same with members.

Neil Balme came closest to acknowledging the truth, that I had previously approached the club about my position for 2011:

> We think all our people are bulletproof so you don't think that they suffer from the normal things. But I suppose Mark has been indicating a couple of times that 'I'm not going to coach after next year' and these sorts of things he's been suggesting, and we're thinking, *Yeah of course! Why wouldn't you want to do this job*? So it does come as a shock, but I must say, I believe everything that he said. I mean he's not stacking on an act. I reckon he's a bit puffed out and he needs to think about whether he wants to have a crack at it. If he's totally committed, he'll get every support from here, but if he's not he probably won't do it. I reckon that's a reasonable position.

By this time, *The Australian* newspaper was already reporting that I would take up a job on the coaching staff at Essendon. Asked about this, Cook said:

> There's been rumours around for some weeks about this occurring, and we've approached Mark on that basis, as to whether the rumours were correct or incorrect, and each time Mark said they were incorrect. And by the way, the rumours were 'are you going to Essendon?' He still holds that position that he's not going to Essendon.

I am not about semantics, but what I told Geelong was that I was not going to *coach* Essendon, which I was not. On the same day that the press conference occurred at Geelong, Essendon announced that James Hird would coach the Bombers from 2011, so there was no head coaching job available. I was not interested anyway, and Essendon knew that; what *was* a possibility was that I would help Hird in a mentoring role, with Hird telling *On the Couch* that night that he would like me to come back to the club if I left Geelong:

> The job I've gone for is the senior coaching job, and they've spoken to me about a senior assistant who would assist me in certain parts of the role and I'm comfortable with that. I'd like to speak to 'Bomber' but I know he's got a contract at Geelong so . . . I think the rules pretty much say you can't do that.

Essendon would have known earlier that I was going to step down from the Geelong job, I have no doubt, but I did not tell the football club that directly and I never intended to coach Essendon footy club in 2011. They would have known because I had been talking to Essendon people. I am an Essendon person and I had friends there; I remember that David Evans, the Essendon president at the time, rang me a few times looking for advice that year about what the club needed to do in terms of coaching, using me as a sounding board.

I had invested in a parcel of land at Armstrongs Creek, near Torquay, with two strong Essendon people – Mark Casey, who is a coterie member, and Adrian Dodoro, who has been the Essendon recruiting manager for quite a few years. I was seeing them a bit in 2010, because it was around the time that the property was sold for the first time (the sale fell through later, when the buyer used a 'sunset' clause). I can actually remember talking to them about Essendon; asking them how bad it was inside and around the club.

Essendon was in big trouble, having sacked Kevin Sheedy after his 27-year reign, then appointed Matthew Knights, who had not particularly improved in his three years from 2008–10. The fan base and wealthy supporters were on the verge of revolting against the club; it was always going to be tough for Knights to follow a legend like Kevin Sheedy. I recall that one day, earlier in the season, myself, Dodoro and Casey were talking about that, and I told them that I might not coach Geelong in 2011, and their antennae clearly went up. They spoke along the lines of: 'You should be getting in touch with David Evans to see how you can help at Essendon.'

When I talked to Evans, he told me that Knights needed to go. But I told him that I would not coach Essendon; that if I did coach anywhere, it would be at Geelong. The fact is that I was not interested in coaching Essendon in 2011, but I do love the football club, and I was interested in helping them in some way if I had the time.

In my opinion Geelong should not have been quite so surprised when I quit. I had warned Brian Cook, a person I respect and with whom I had a close relationship. Other people at the club should have had an inkling, too, Neil Balme for example, but because I was contracted, and we were coming off the triumph of a second premiership in 2009 and still near the top in 2010, no one wanted to believe me or hear me.

While I accept that it can be messy when you leave a club, I believe that in reality, I did the right thing by Geelong by quitting. I am big on gut feel, and my feel was that I was finished at the club. My contract was worth around $700 000, which is considerable, and I walked away from that, never intending to coach an opposition club, and that is a lot of money to give up.

I just did not sense the energy to train a whole new group of blokes up, which was what we were confronting, and if someone had asked me right there and then, I would have said that I had coached for the last time ever.

The cooling-off period that the club had suggested in late-September ended with no change of heart from me, and on 4 October 2010, I sat with Frank Costa and Brian Cook at my final press conference at Kardinia Park to announce that my 11 years as coach of Geelong had finished. I told the media that Geelong was bigger than me, and that the administration would get it right. In any case, I said, Geelong was in a great position. I told them that the relentlessness of the job had taken a toll on my private life, and that 'there's a few things in my life I have to fix up'.

Cook put it all in a positive light, too, saying, 'It's an opportunity for the club to look at . . . a new era. Mark created history at this club and he will be remembered for that by a lot of people. We have all been on a magnificent, wonderful journey for the past decade, led by Mark. However, from today we are on a new journey.'

I had a great time at Geelong, and I loved the club and the city. We won two flags plus a pre-season premiership, and I left the club in a decent state, and a year later, I was rapt when the club won the 2011 flag under Chris Scott as the new head coach. I had no regrets, because I knew that my time as coach was done; in fact I was happy that the club had been able to move on.

In an article in *The Australian* after Geelong beat Collingwood in the 2011 Grand Final, Brian Cook made some comments that interested me. He said that my leaving had ended up being the best result for the football club, that Geelong had been invigorated by the change. It was not meant as a whack at me, and I did not take it that way. What I felt was that it bore out precisely what I had been thinking at the end of 2010: 'I don't think that if Mark had have stayed, we would have achieved what we've done. While it was a total surprise that he left, and it did rock us, in hindsight Mark made the right decision for us. In the end, there was too much familiarity between coach and players.'

Everyone in footy says that they want to leave their club in a better state than it was when they walked in, although not many people do. But Geelong is a powerhouse today compared to what it was in 2000, and I played my part in that growth along with many other people. It is a good feeling, and I feel a strong connection with the club even today.

Slazenger
Ford
GEELONG
GFC

# 16

# THE GAME

When you're a coach, you view the game itself differently. You need to understand the game as well as how to manage players and staff, deal with the trends, new rules and statistics, as well as seeing it all within the framework of your club, the AFL, recruiting and everything else that is part of the business of football.

As much as I love the game, it has taken a slightly crazy turn in recent years. That might sound old school, but even in this professional era the game needs to be fun for everyone involved, and it is not anymore. People spend far too much time at football clubs – I'm talking about players and staff – and too much of it is unproductive time. They are trying too hard, the coaches who operate like this. The game is meant to be fun, albeit serious fun.

Of course when I played, we were part-time footballers with jobs outside the club. Players now are paid well to devote their working lives to the game but it still should not be a chore to play footy. Kevin Sheedy ran a club that was serious in intent, but enjoyable to be around, and that is the kind of environment that I always tried to set up, at Geelong and later at Essendon when I went back. I wanted a relaxed, professional environment, where you worked hard and had some fun at the same time, and I wanted people to look forward to going to work. I wanted to create a place where everything that was done had a clear purpose.

I believe in looking after your people and that is a reflection of Sheedy's influence, and of the Essendon that I experienced in my playing days in the 1980s and 1990s. I often talk about the way people were treated in the great times at Geelong with Brian Cook and Frank Costa, and the different skills that the three of us brought to the table. My contribution was obviously in football, Frank brought the people skills and Brian knew how to run the place.

I was about training up people, developing players and showing them how we wanted them to play; I do believe there is a right way to play the game. Frank Costa was about people; Brian Cook used to say that he noticed a sign on Frank's office wall when he went to talk to him about being the new chief executive of Geelong, back in 1999. It read: 'Character first, talent second.' Frank taught us how to handle people, something he took to another level. He had been very successful in business, and applied the same principles to the football club. It was all about treating people well, and communicating with them so there were no secrets, and no surprises.

I learned a lot from Frank and I really admired Brian Cook, who knew exactly how to run a football club. Cook's speciality was business and communication; he drove the new professionalism throughout the club. He hailed from West Coast, and was part of the era when the Eagles won their first two premierships in 1992 and 1994, and I have heard it said that he brought the business plan with him and just changed the club name to Geelong, with subtle changes.

Brian was big on talent and coaching and I remember he came into my office one day and he said, 'Bomber, just tell the assistant coaches they'll be told whether they're going to be re-employed or recontracted by the first of August every year.' And I said, 'Brian, we can't do that. What if they're not going to get the job? We've got a month till finals and they're not going to be here!' He answered, 'I'll tell you what, they'll still want to do the job. And they'll probably do a worse job if they're uncertain about their future.'

Brian wanted them to have security and clarity in their employment. Within a game that has been described by one prominent former player as 'an industry full of frightened people', it was a masterstroke. That shows good management of a football club, and proper handling of people. I had never heard of anything like that previously, and I suspect it had never been done at a football club before, but we adopted it straight away at Geelong. We told the assistant coaches straight up whether we wanted them to continue the following year, and if they were being moved on, it gave them time to search for another job, putting them in front of the annual race for assistants' jobs.

We ended up doing the same kind of thing with the players; we set it up so that players at all stages of their season would get feedback from week to week and they knew what we were thinking about them. They were really clear on what they needed to fix, and if they did not correct the problem, then yes, there was a risk that they would not stay on the list. But they knew where they stood. The best example was ruckman Shane Mumford, who was enormous and unfit when he arrived at Geelong from Gippsland. We told him to get his condition right, and he went away and lost 20 kilograms by the next time we saw him. We were impressed. That's what young guys trying to make a mark need to do, so that the coaches say to themselves, *This kid wants to play.*

When I coached, I saw myself as a facilitator, rather than being the head of the team. Sure, I had the final say on everything, but if the players could come to a decision that I was happy with, that would be the best-case scenario for me. I wanted the players to eventually coach themselves, to show the way forward whether it was in a game, or the way we wanted to play, or even whether someone should stay on the list or get a game in the senior team. I wanted to be inclusive and I empowered people; I love that style.

There is so much to be done in a footy club that inevitably, certain tasks are appropriated by people underneath your rank. At Geelong, every person knew from their job description what their responsibilities were, and I let them have that responsibility, no question about it. If they did not do it properly, I talked to them, but they knew that they could make decisions without necessarily consulting me. They were allowed to get on with doing their job and doing it properly.

I coached with a defence-first philosophy, what might be called a two-way style in the vernacular. In my teams I wanted everyone to be an attacker, and everyone to be a defender, and just as importantly, we preached a team-first philosophy. There was no room for selfishness – there never is in good teams.

I never liked putting numbers back behind the ball, or flooding, although there is no doubt that like everyone else, my teams pushed numbers into defence to crowd up stoppages at times. But pure flooding with spare players in the backline was not my style; I used to argue about it with my assistant coaches. If we had two goals in a row kicked against us, the coaches would want to put a man back, or if we had a decent lead in the match and it was late in a game, they would want to send someone into the back half. This is commonplace in the modern game, because the copycats all do it now. Even Hawthorn, winner of a threepeat of premierships and a great attacking team, will do it.

I was not into verbal abuse of my players in the way that coaches throughout history have been; the days of the vicious invective seem to have virtually gone. Of course there are times when I needed to make a forceful point, and I can remember going hard at both the Johnsons – Jason and Mark – when I was an assistant coach at Essendon, early on. At the start of my Geelong days I went at David Mensch once, then when my assistants said that I had been too hard on him, I phoned back to the bench, apologised and put him back on the ground. Generally, it was not my style to be too harsh, and I don't see any real value in that kind of behaviour in the workplace.

I was always about giving people chances, and no doubt I was influenced by Frank and Brian in this. With some players, the performance might not be there, but the values were, and I believed that person deserved a chance. So I wanted my players to try their hardest, turn up, be reliable and seek the coaches out. If it wasn't working out for them, those players – the good people – would always get another opportunity. Of course there were some guys who did not want to train, who went out drinking, who blamed other people but still put in some good performances because they were talented, and they were the hard calls to make.

With the first category of players, when they were given a chance, they might work through their problem and play good footy again. This is where *values* are important in football clubs. Players with bad values rarely become better people but those with the right values have the potential to become better players.

It is an occupational hazard for a football coach that the players can make or break you. That is why you need to be prudent in what you say, and how you handle them, and a lot depends on the quality of the people. When he coached Western Bulldogs, my old assistant Brendan McCartney fell victim to the senior players and had to resign at the end of 2014. Brendan thought the young players were ready to take over the team, but he told me, 'I've been hard on the older players.' And the more he sensed the team coming under the control of the younger group, the older blokes fought to keep it the other way. He thought that he had it right but with hindsight, he should have talked to the board and told them, 'This is how I'm doing it.' Because once the board talked to the players, his position became untenable.

I did not like making games of football about the coaching, but I had some fun whenever I came up against the men in the opposition's coaching box who were good. Rodney Eade would try out different tactics and test you, while Mick Malthouse was basically the coach who cranked up the interchange rotations in the 2000s. Those frantic interchanges became an issue for us at Geelong, because we were desperately trying to create a one-on-one mentality, and Collingwood made it hard to keep track of where our opponents were. Interchange numbers skyrocketed in recent years to the point where the AFL chose to put a cap on them from 2016, but Malthouse's tactics caused a significant change in the game.

Ross Lyon was unique. Both at St Kilda and later Fremantle, if something was not working for him, he would change it, but overall you knew what you were going to get with Ross. His teams always struggled to kick enough goals, and when we played St Kilda in the 2009 Grand Final, I felt quite comfortable knowing that. I knew that Geelong could tough out a game if we needed to – we had that flexibility as a team – and then if the play opened up, I would encourage the players with a quick 'Let's go!' We wanted to run and take opportunities, but if we needed to get our hands dirty to just grind it out, then we could do that, too. Teams need to be flexible like that, because you never know what environment will be presented on a given day, whether it is windy, wet or the opposition tries to close you down.

Ross has a massive winning percentage as a coach: 66.7 per cent over 218 games with St Kilda and Fremantle at the end of 2015, which is highly impressive, higher than Tom Hafey (64.8), Allan Jeans (62.2), Mick Malthouse (57), Kevin Sheedy (57.8), David Parkin (59.3), Leigh Matthews (58.8) and Ron Barassi (54), to name a few legends of the caper, and fractionally ahead of his contemporary Alastair Clarkson (62). But he has not yet won a premiership, and in 2009, 2010 and 2013 he coached the losing team on grand final day, leading to some debate about his method. I rate Ross highly; if he has an issue, it has probably been with list management. I think part of being a good coach is playing your role in correcting list deficiencies. Fremantle had a shortage of tall forwards, so they went after Travis Cloke, Jack Riewoldt, Mitch Clarke, Charlie Dixon, Cam McCarthy and James Frawley. But much as the Dockers have tried, they have not filled those holes, and as the coach, Ross has to take responsibility for that.

Leigh Matthews would always test you, because he had such a great team with the Lions. It's interesting, Leigh was not a coach who tried a lot of different methods or strategies; he had the team to deliver what he wanted. What did Allan Jeans say? 'Good players make good coaches', and I think Leigh says the same thing.

Paul Roos coached the Swans in a similar style to Ross Lyon, who worked under him as an assistant at Sydney before graduating to head coach duties at the Saints. When the Swans were at their strongest around 2003–06, Roosy would tag six and seven of your players, and they were brilliant at creating a world record number of stoppages where they would bash you up. But because Roos liked to create a man-on-man game, you could manipulate the Swans and take their main players to places where they did not want to go, a point that Mick Malthouse made – Collingwood had a great record against the Swans under Malthouse. Mick would ensure that his players took their Sydney opponents to foreign places, extracting all their good, in-close players to the outside, and we tried all that, too. They would send half-forwards like Ryan O'Keefe up to midfield stoppages, and by the end, we decided to keep our own structures and allow that to happen, rather than always reacting to them. In the same way that it happened with Brisbane Lions, we eventually got the better of Sydney.

When I started coaching, there were people who thought they could win the game from the coaches' box, and I am not a fan of that style. I wanted us to have players who were on-ground coaches, little replicas of me, people who knew how I would think in certain situations. That is exactly how I trained them up to be, so that the Geelong players knew what I wanted to do and if they saw something happen outside of that, they would fix it.

It was the same when I played at Essendon under Sheedy; I was a little replica of Kevin and I knew exactly what he would want to do in every situation on the field. At Geelong, the players believed in the system, and we had the buy-in, as coaches call it, at least until my final year. This is hugely important, because in a big game or a final, if the players are in any doubt about what they are doing, or what the coach wants them to do, then you are in trouble.

At Geelong, we made it about us. Nowadays I see the young coaches come into the game and they are immediately trying new tactics or structures, then just as quickly, you can see them revert to the fundamentals, back to the way that they want to play the game. As a philosophy, that was important to me, from that time in 2007 when the playing group said to me, 'Let's worry about us.' From then on I would tell the players not to fear the opposition, not to talk them up or build their strengths out of all proportion. We focused on what *we* wanted to do, rather than fretting about the opposition.

A lot of time is wasted in watching the other teams at AFL level. Opposition analysis needs to be done, but not at the expense of developing your own plans. Every club has an opposition coach who studies what the upcoming teams do and do not do, and that's fine, but I learned from my early coaching experiences that I was receiving and passing on too much information. It is an easy trap for inexperienced coaches to fall into, and I think it would be the case in all the ball sports including soccer and basketball. Players do not want to know too much. If you give them too much, they will not absorb it anyway, which is the KISS principle: Keep it Simple, Stupid.

Self-focus took time to kick in at Geelong. Around 2001, when Brisbane Lions were at their peak and on their way to three flags, we encouraged our players to focus on the contested ball when we played them. We set up some stoppage structures to play against that great midfield group of Michael Voss, Simon Black, Jason Akermanis, Nigel Lappin, Luke Power and company, but we were too reactive. I was critical of the players because they were overly respectful to those star opposition players, and we were being beaten. In my eyes, initiative beats reactive every time, so I would get really angry when my people stopped playing and started to follow.

Back at the start of that process, we would last for 20 minutes against the warriors from the Lions. We kept drilling this into the players: 'We're learning our style of footy, it will take time to learn but we're going to repeat it over and over until we get there, even if we make mistakes along the way.' After a while, we could last until the second quarter before they smashed us, and eventually, Cameron Ling, Joel Corey, Jimmy Bartel, Paul Chapman, Gary Ablett, James Kelly and the others were able to get on top. Once we could beat Brisbane it was a big turning point for Geelong. From the start of my coaching run, we lost seven in a row to the Lions until we turned the tables one afternoon in 2004 at Kardinia Park. In a sense, they taught us how to play, because everyone follows the great sides and what they do. In the case of the Lions, it was about having big bodies around the football. I am a massive believer in that.

Around the early 2000s anyone could see that footy was evolving into a game with a lot of players around the ball. It's what Sydney, for example, did so successfully with strong midfielders, winning a premiership in 2005 and getting within one point of back-to-back flags when they lost to West Coast in 2006. Big bodies are still relevant today with all the crowding of players into small areas around the football.

I used business experience in my coaching, in particular the people management aspects, because really, the job is that of a manager. I have strong philosophies on purpose. For example, football departments at all clubs have grown a lot, yet everyone is just as busy as before, which is nonsensical. Surely when you employ more staff, the idea is to keep the incumbents fresh so that they are more creative, but what happens is that people just fill up their days doing irrelevant work to justify their positions and their salaries. It does not help anyone. It has *no purpose*.

I was never a fan of having a lot of meetings, especially long meetings. When I was coaching at Geelong (and then later at Essendon), my meetings were much quicker than what most modern coaches require. In season, everyone would come in on Monday mornings with the coaches and do a two-hour review of the previous game, then we would have a quick chat, a cover-off on who we needed to catch up with. For instance, I might need to go and see Steve Johnson about something or other. Later in the day, the line coaches would go through the video edits with their specific players. Technology can quickly give you an edit that shows every single act by a given player in a given game, and it is worthwhile going through that vision. The players did their recovery and then the coach would meet the doctors and fitness staff to talk about injuries, then it was time to start preparing for the next game.

I always considered training to be hugely important and of course, I am not alone there. From day one at Geelong in 2000, we trained as closely as possible to the way that we wanted to play, and the way that we played was how we trained. We had purposeful drills, which meant that you wanted to create the situations you had in a game, which was risky. Players can get hurt, and you don't want players not playing. It is one of my pet hates, having too many injuries.

The risk of hurting your own players in training is an ongoing day-to-day problem for all footy coaches but there is a way around it. We trained all our players and staff up to do competitive work on the track without hurting each other. Really, it's modified training, where the players are allowed and encouraged to go to the very point of the big tackle or the crunching spoil, then pull back at the end. Now, that is a hard point to reach, but it can be done. We always did loads of competitive work when I coached, because if you don't recreate the usual opposition pressure, you have players knowing where they want to kick the football even before they mark it, and it does not work like that in a game.

So in those training sessions, the man who was closest to the ball had the right to win it, and the bloke nearest to him had to concede it, which was a hard thing to teach. He was not allowed to smash into a teammate. There is an art to executing it properly, but sometimes players cannot help themselves; they are competitive, they might be half a second late to the football, but they still want the ball. We were happy with that in a match, but not at training. So the theory was, if you were not the first guy to the ball, just let the other guy have it. I'd say, 'You practise being second to the ball, and you guys around him, you practise good defensive decisions, because you haven't got the ball. Put yourself in a position to win the ball.'

Hawthorn is very good at it, I have noticed. If the Hawks win the ball, their method kicks in, but if the the opposition wins it, they defend strongly. It is the Allan Jeans mantra of the game having three distinct phases: they have the ball, we have the ball, the ball is in dispute. Sometimes Hawthorn can look like it has more players on the field than the opposition, and it would feel like that out on the ground, because they are so predictable to each other.

We practised where to run on the ground and we trained transition, teaching players what they should do when they had the football, and how to be predictable to one another. Everyone had to know what would happen. If a player had the football and was in trouble, someone has to be there to support him, which can only happen if you are predictable. In a game, that player will know what is about to happen, knows what his teammates are capable of doing, what they *will* do. At training, every kick had to be straight and I hated the receiving player having to wait for a kick. I'd say, 'Don't make him stop!'

I tried hard not to overcomplicate the ball movement; I did not want to fall into the trap of reinventing the game. Yes, you have to keep up with the trends but I never liked coaching tricks. For instance, if Gary Ablett was going to be tagged, some coaches might start him off the bench or take him off the ground three or four times in a quarter to break it. Kevin Sheedy would have done that, but I wasn't into it.

I was about the basics. On a Monday we'd have a light skills session, virtually a catch-and-kick, and I wouldn't bother with anything technical. Our main training was on hump day, Wednesday, right in the middle between the two games, then the players would have Thursday off. On that day I would generally go into the club, maybe for half a day, then take some work home with me. The notes for the week would all be done on that day, ready to hand on to the players.

We had a coach looking at the opposition; at Geelong, Ken Hinkley and Brenton Sanderson both did that for me over time. They might go to the opposition's game to watch it live. I might also go along, or might not. As I have said, I didn't want to overload the players with information, and I did change that opposition coach's role a bit over time. It is a frustrating job, because you end up watching a truckload of football and when it comes to match committee and then game day, often the coach won't listen anyway!

On a Friday afternoon we'd have a light skills session with a meeting beforehand, we might sit around in a circle and have a walk-through some set plays or stoppage set-ups, looking at how we needed to organise ourselves in defence if we were trying something different. We would talk about the match-ups for the game, because I always liked players to know who they were playing on, to allow them time to think and prepare. I was not one to leave that until the match day. Having said that, I was happy for players to do a 'handover' on game day if necessary, where they would change opponents because they were being taken out of position. My worry about players doing this is that it reduces the level of responsibility on a player if he has multiple opponents. He might think to himself, *I'll take your man, but I'm not going to worry about him as much as you did*. There is always someone who will let you down in that situation.

There are oodles of statistics quoted on games of football nowadays but like any numbers, they can be used to promote any argument. That said, I had a few favourites, some go-to numbers. I was happy to use the stats, but they had to be accurate and not subject to too much human interpretation, if possible. I talked a lot about forward-50 entries and back-50 entries, with the idea that we wanted 12 entries a quarter and less for the opposition. I looked at contested ball, specifically the differential, which is the number you will often see on the boards they hold up in the huddles at quarter-time and three-quarter time, 'plus five' or 'minus six' or whatever it might be.

Geelong was quite awful in the contested ball count in the first few years after I left the club, and Chris Scott gave the impression that he didn't care so much, which was interesting. The issue was addressed early in 2016. I think contested ball is still the key. It has always been the number one point. That is where the game starts, and no amount of webs or clusters or new innovations will change that. It is those critical balls during a game that you either win or lose. Good teams win them, and in this modern era, Hawthorn does that.

I looked at goals-per-inside-50 statistics, because they are a good measure of the efficiency of your ball movement. I quite often looked at scores from stoppages, or the differential of those numbers, too. Turnovers have become a huge part of the game as well, and I liked to watch the numbers for midfield turnovers and scores from turnovers. We also had our own numbers that are not part of the usual statistics that the public sees. We had a category that we called 'the ROS' (rebound, opposition get the ball and score) which measured how quickly you had set up a defensive structure, and how quickly your players got behind the ball after conceding possession. We also had 'the RES' (rebounds that turned into forward-50 entries) which showed you how well you were moving the ball.

Tackle counts are are much-quoted in the media nowadays, but at Geelong (and later at Essendon), we found it hard to measure exactly how important those numbers were. For instance, you can lose the tackle count but still have a great day, and I found it hard to get my head around that. I did not often push the tackle count with the players, although it was a statistic I would keep an eye on. The bigger issue for me was the count of *missed* tackles – that can never be good. For instance, in the 2015 Grand Final, West Coast only had a woeful 40 tackles on the day when they had shown themselves to be a good pressure team all year.

The game has changed a lot, even though the fundamentals are pretty much the same. The AFL tried a substitute among the four players on the bench but ditched that at the end of 2015, which I think is a good thing. With the sub rule, rotations went from about 50 to 110 per team, per game, in no time at all, which was out of control, and it took everyone off guard. Bringing it back to 90 per team, as the league has done for the 2016 season, is right. I side with the public on rotations; there are a lot of junk rotations – full-forwards coming off after a minute or two of the game – and I don't see how that is effectively managing players.

The best coaches now have what you would call 'play periods'. They will have looked at GPS data and worked out what an optimum play period is for each player, how long he can stay on the ground before the heavy fatigue kicks in. We tried to manage that, but it is not easy. Sometimes a player might ideally have an eight-minute play period where he does not touch the ball for six minutes, then he gets in better positions and starts finding the ball, and then he has to come off, much to his annoyance. The coaches will say, 'Hang on a second. Let's keep him going and we'll square it up by the end of the game.'

And right there is the battle between sports science and footy coaching. The good players will sense it. They'll think, *It's taken me a while to get into the rhythm of the game, but it's coming*. They hate leaving the field in that situation, and the coach would send a message to the player asking, 'When are you coming off?' But it is remarkable how often the good players just jump up and make a difference in games when it matters and it has nothing to do with their play periods.

Part of your job as coach is to keep analysing your list and working out what you need, identifying where the holes are, even if the actual recruiting is done by other people. The idea is that you retain a chance of either winning the premiership, or reaching the top four, or just making the finals depending on what stage your list is at.

You have to work out how to get the players you need, within a defined system.

Centralised recruiting, in the form of the national draft, does not really encourage development of players and the slow burn to success in football. I don't think the clubs in Melbourne, for instance, work on developing young players like we did in the past, because there is nothing in it for them. They cannot retain the players that they develop unless they choose them in the draft, and that's not always an option; it's dependent upon ladder position. So there is no incentive to build the game in a geographical area anymore – except for the interstate clubs with their academies – because the players that you find and nurture can be snapped up by an opposition club.

The draft is fine as an instrument of equalisation, but elements of the old zoning system from the 1980s also were very good. When I started playing, Essendon had Merrett and Hawker and Watson from the Wimmera zone and Vander Haar and Williams and others from Ringwood. Essendon put the time and effort in to find those jewels. I sense that grassroots connection has been lost in the era of the draft. So I was pleased when the AFL announced in 2016 that all the Victorian clubs were to be allocated a region in the state with the option of setting up academies, the same as happens in New South Wales and Queensland. There will be a bidding system for the players who graduate, giving the clubs an advantage but no guarantee of being able to draft the young player. I like that idea, although they need to do more to bring back the connection. At the moment they are spending millions of dollars in women's football, which is fine, but I hope they don't do it at the expense of the broader picture. There are kids out there in hundreds of clubs who need to be nurtured as well. Sometimes I think the AFL people don't get out of their headquarters in Melbourne's Docklands enough, quite frankly.

Because of the absence of zoning, the gap has increased between the top and bottom levels of the game, from my experience. I go out to footy clubs to train kids, and the children and their coaches have never heard of half of the drills and the ideas, because the investment has not been there. But if you go to a soccer club, their development program will have been run by an elite club, an organisation that is on the lookout for players. What does Manchester City do? It buys clubs around the world, puts training facilities in and develops players who might help the club down the track, Melbourne City FC being only one example.

I think one of the AFL's goals should be to capture the biggest portion of the elite talent in the country, to reach a point where most of the best athletes come to football instead of basketball, soccer and the rest, but that is a tough ask. Players are getting bigger money from soccer, in particular, plus they get opportunities that come from it being a big international game. The sport is putting resources into development so that soccer is a massive threat to the AFL's popularity, in my view, so they had better get it right before it's too late.

Australian Rules has Auskick which draws big numbers – around 175 000 participants per year – but from my experience, it's not well-planned in terms of the technical aspects of the game. They don't teach the kids how to kick the football, whereas in soccer, they start out dribbling, then add more speed and more pressure, a sort of graduation process. From what I have seen, that does not happen at Auskick or any of our junior programs. There are a thousand different kicking styles and some appalling standards. The kids don't learn about contested football, when they should be taught how to use their bodies to protect the football when they are after it. Marking contests should be part of training so that the standard improves over time. That's how we'll begin to close the gap between the grassroots and the elite levels of footy.

AFL clubs have to contend with all kinds of changes to the game and to the infrastructure around it. One of the changes that has made it tempting to seek a quicker rebuild is free agency for players, introduced at the end of 2012. I am not a fan, and I do not think the AFL needs it. Then again, I guess that it was inevitable with the push by the AFL Players' Association, who argued with some merit that young players were restricted in their movement at the start of their careers, and hence entitled to have some flexibility later. Restricted free agency kicks in after eight seasons in certain circumstances and is becoming more popular with players over time. Buddy Franklin was the first big-name player to jump, from Hawthorn to Sydney, but if you think about it, Chris Judd and Tony Lockett and others were able to change clubs prior to free agency, too. Players could decline to sign a contract; they could simply ask for a trade.

So from my experience, players were able to get to their chosen destination, by and large, before free agency. My problem with free agency is this: if clubs are going to lose players who are free agents after eight years, where is the value in taking a young boy in the draft and developing him? It goes against everything that I believe in, the notion of finding a player and developing him to be part of your own system.

I am thinking about Adelaide and its multiple-All Australian Patrick Dangerfield, who signed to play with Geelong from 2016 after eight seasons with Adelaide. If you look at Dangerfield, who is a sensational player, he took about three years to be a really good AFL player with the Crows. He was fifth in Adelaide's best and fairest award in his fourth season, 2011, so that was probably his breakthrough year. Four seasons on, he has gone.

Other guys might take five years to arrive as a fully-fledged AFL player – even longer if they are a bigger guy – and it is rare for them to just step in a be a star like Joel Selwood and Chris Judd did. So free agency just encourages clubs to be lazy, to pick up their guys and fill their gaps from other clubs without spending the time and effort on development. And that is a hit on the game, in my view.

Geelong went hard for Dangerfield in 2015 and landed the big fish, but I must admit I feel betrayed by what they have done, because at the same time, James Kelly and Mathew Stokes (to Essendon) and Steve Johnson (to Greater Western Sydney) were moved out, and they have been wonderful servants of the Geelong Football Club. I am already on record as saying that Paul Chapman, who went to Essendon from Geelong in 2014, should have had the opportunity to play out his time at Geelong, and I feel the same way about Kelly, Stokes and Johnson. These are multiple-premiership players, legends of Geelong, and they stayed at Kardinia Park through that period when all of them could have earned much more money elsewhere. It was how we managed people at that time. We had nobody on really big money and we stayed together for team success, we told those players to be loyal and that it would be reciprocated by the club, so they remained even when they might have extracted $250 000 a year more at another club. In Steve Johnson's case, he had a big offer from GWS only a year or so earlier, and he laughed it off and stayed put. It makes me sad to see those guys playing in different colours, especially when I see that Adam Goodes played out his time with Sydney, Matthew Pavlich and Aaron Sandilands are going again for Fremantle in 2016 and Shaun Burgoyne for Hawthorn. I cannot imagine the Hawks letting

Sam Mitchell or Luke Hodge play somewhere else, and that is my point.

People have said that Geelong needed a rebuild after missing the finals in 2015 for the first time in a long while, but who is to say that the Cats could not have won a flag by tinkering with the list they had? I don't believe they needed a rebuild, and what really annoys me is that for the club, it is a bit of history repeating itself. When I arrived at Geelong at the end of 1999, the former players were all at war with the football club, and I had to work hard to bring them back. The likes of Garry Hocking and Barry Stoneham were coming to the end, and we were careful about how they were eased out of the game. I think they were treated respectfully, so that they were ready when they did go, and that is crucial in a footy club.

You are dealing with people; what does Geelong not get about that? The danger is that in a football club, cancer can take over, people start criticising the bosses when no one feels comfortable. In that sense, a footy club is just another workplace, so what I feel now is that the legacy we created at Geelong in my time has been let go. I thought that some of it would survive, but five years on, it has disappeared, so it seems. Yet again, it is proof of what a brutal game it is.

Patrick Dangerfield might lead Geelong to another flag; he is certainly a special player. I will be happy if he does, but I still find it difficult to see why it had to happen the way it did, without consideration and respect for the loyalty those premiership players showed to the club when it really mattered.

# 17

# WITH HIRDY

## 2011–2012

Straight after I left Geelong Football Club for the last time, my then partner (later, wife) Jana and I went travelling overseas and I had a nice six weeks or so off, out of contact and away from football, drinking a few beers and pina coladas and fulfilling my dream of getting my life back. I had met Jana in 2006; she was a neighbour in Geelong, and we had been together ever since, eventually marrying in 2012.

When I arrived home in November 2011, Essendon people were chasing me about taking up a role with the club. I was interested, I don't deny it, because I cared about Essendon and I had left a job that was paying up to $700 000, but there was an issue about clarifying the role. To be completely comfortable, I needed a huge drop in responsibility and stress. Tim Watson has said that he initially understood that I would be the coach and it is true that is what they originally wanted. But that was not what I was thinking at all.

I could not have coached, because I was not 100 per cent into it, and you cannot run a football club in that state of mind. There is never enough time in a coach's life, and I'd probably had no more than two consecutive weeks off in my 11 years of coaching Geelong, which brings us back to my point about work–life balance and the toll that these jobs take on people and their families.

Essendon had hired Brendan McCartney, my old assistant from Geelong, as one of its coaches. Macca had not been offered the Geelong senior job after my departure; in fact Geelong wanted him to take up more of a development coaching role, so he had opted to leave and join the Essendon coaching group under James Hird. David Evans, the Essendon president, came to see me along with Ian Robson, the chief executive, and they made it clear that there was a place for me in the new structure for 2011.

The club was aware that Hird had never coached before – after his retirement as a player he had moved into the corporate world, working for Gemba, a sports and entertainment company – and they saw me as a good person to have around in those circumstances. I understood I was to be a kind of mentoring figure, someone in the background with knowledge and experience who Hird could turn to.

On 10 November, I turned up to watch training at Essendon Grammar and later that day, the club put out a statement announcing that I would be senior assistant coach from 2011. The next day, there was a media conference at the club where I was immediately under attack for switching from Geelong to Essendon. I was accused of hypocrisy given the way I had treated Gary Ablett Jr in his dealings with Gold Coast Suns, but to me, this was a completely different situation. I had stepped down from my previous job and had moved clubs for much less money, about $350 000 less. I said my decision was about workload and responsibility, not about money, and that I knew I could look myself in the mirror.

The people who spoke to me in this period – Evans, Mark Casey and Tim Watson – wanted me to oversee the football department, to make sure that the people in those roles were doing them properly. There wasn't a proper job description so the role was a bit grey but it sounded like something I could do without too much stress. The initial plan was for me to work part-time, perhaps four days a week. I was happy with the dip in responsibilities.

With hindsight, I probably should have just left Geelong and had a longer break from the game, but Essendon needed help and wanted help, and I cared about my old club. For me, it was about love of Essendon so I allowed myself to be convinced to look over Hirdy's shoulder. The club had sacked its coach, the supporters were in revolt against the administration and for a big club like Essendon, it had been a long time since any success had come – since 2000 in fact. The Dons had played a final under Matthew Knights' coaching in 2009, but were smashed in Adelaide when injuries meant they were without a ruckman. They then missed the finals in 2010. The club had won only 25 games in the last three seasons under Knights, who had two years remaining on his contract and had to be paid out when Essendon sacked him.

My old footy club was facing a significant challenge.

I was not meant to be just another assistant coach; the idea was that I would help Hirdy, keep an eye on him, but I was not necessarily there to attend all training sessions, meetings and games. That was my understanding of the role. To start with, I oversaw the training programs and looked at how Essendon was playing with regard to game style. I looked at how the coaches communicated with the players, how long the meetings went for, what was being said and done in those meetings and whether it was relevant to the game. I was on guard against unproductive work, which I openly despise. Because I had come straight out of a successful organisation that had won premierships and developed strong values, I was looking for ways to streamline the program and cut unproductive areas, improve efficiencies and help the Bombers.

After more than a decade at Geelong where Brian Cook, Frank Costa and others had set that club up so well, I was quite shocked at what I found at Essendon. The club had fallen miles behind the modern professional competition that the AFL, and in particular some of the top clubs, had become. I suppose the club had been purpose built for Sheedy's style over nearly 30 years. Matthew Knights probably wanted to change that but I doubt he was resourced to do so.

There were deep troubles. The players had no proper gymnasium or training oval for the summer, because the Essendon Cricket Club had access to the council-owned Windy Hill ground. Preseason training had to be done at Penleigh and Essendon Grammar School's grounds on a windy open surface; the players were expected to find their way to training at someone else's facility, then come back to the footy club and buy their own food, instead of having it prepared for them.

I saw players using wheels to mark out their own running tracks at 200 metres and 300 metres, just so they could do their run-throughs, and players warming up alone rather than in groups. If a drill went overtime at training, the coaches would feel the glare of the conditioning staff. Players were not allowed to do extra skills, extra weights, extra running. The club would change its training schedule to fit in community functions, which stunned me. At Geelong, football was number one. Everything else fitted around that. Our first hotspot at Essendon was the power struggle between the coaches and the high performance staff. We wanted to teach the players how to play; the HP people wanted minute-by-minute training. It was a conflict that needed to be fixed.

Essendon's problem was that the lack of success was building upon itself. When you are not playing well year after year, you fail to look outside at what other clubs are doing; you are not investigative or inquisitive when you truly need to be. Essendon had been swamped by the other clubs in the way that it prepared for AFL football and one of my tasks was to address that.

It was a big decision for a senior coach to drop back a rung like I did, and it's not necessarily easy to do. When we had our original talks, I was not even meant to be in the box on match days, but ultimately, I went to all the games. During the week and at games I watched the other coaches – Brendan McCartney, Simon Goodwin, Sean Wellman – do their own thing. If they asked me questions or wanted an opinion, I would help, but my style was to let them run the show. If they got it wrong, I let that go, because the key is to learn from errors. To me, winning every quarter of every match was not crucial; this was all about setting Essendon up properly.

I did bark at the players a few times, mostly when they stopped playing, and over-respected an opponent. Against better teams, there was a tendency for players to trail their opponents to the ball, to play reactive footy, and it annoyed me. That always got on my goat in my coaching days, because win or lose, succeed or fail, you must have a go. You must try to win, or *do something*, as John Kennedy Sr used to say. I hated players thinking, *I'm not going to make a mistake here, because I won't get the ball*. Or, *I'm going to make sure my man doesn't win the game for them, I'll stick with him*. You don't win games of football thinking like that. Think about the Matthew Scarlett moment in the 2009 Grand Final, when he leaves his opponent Justin Koschitzke, and makes the play with his little toe-poke. Initiative beats reactive.

I was finding my way back at Essendon, and I made the decision that I would skip a lot of the meetings. I'd just say, 'I'm not turning up to that one.' They would have a planning meeting to prepare for training, then actual training, then another meeting to review training. The doctors, fitness staff and coaches were expected to attend. It was out of control, and I told them that. I said to some of the coaches, 'I'll review training in the moment. It's not that hard to get around and make sure everything's done. You guys should start learning to do it yourself, because you will save a lot of time.'

When I first worked with Simon Goodwin, one of the main assistants, he kept coming into my office looking for approval for what he was doing, and I ended up saying, 'Stop coming in, mate!' I wanted him and the other coaches to make the call themselves, do what they thought was right. I allowed James Hird and the others to have their way and run their own race. That is why Geelong improved and the people grew. The people owned the team, they were accountable for it, and they were committed to it.

I spent quite a bit of time with James Hird in his first year as a senior coach. He had come back from the corporate world to do the job at Essendon but unlike a lot of the modern coaches, he had never worked as an assistant coach, so he was feeling his way in the job. Because he was a first-time coach, it should be no surprise that he did not know every single facet of coaching. But he did have good experienced people around him like Brendan McCartney, and everyone was there for him. Hirdy was impressive given his lack of experience; he could absorb and retain a truckload of information and he had a great capacity for hard work.

The reality was, though, Hirdy was learning. For instance, I felt that he took *too much* advice. There is an element to Hirdy that I observed where he would listen to me, then listen to someone else, and the most influential person in that discussion would end up being the last person who offered an opinion. Sometimes it seemed like he was looking for the next person until he found someone to confirm his own opinion.

Hird's instinct as a coach was to attack, rather than defend first, the same way he played the game and more in the Kevin Sheedy mould. Brendan McCartney and I both spent time trying to convince him to focus more on defence, and he jumped on board with us, although deep down he wanted to attack and score heavily. It was healthy debate, in my opinion, it wasn't as though Brendan and I said, 'If you don't teach defence, we won't work here.' I said my bit, Hirdy did his thing, and we had four years of gradual improvements in the points-against tally. We were coming from a low point in 2010 under Matthew Knights, when Essendon was smashed for 109 points a game, the worst defensive record in the competition.

The administration was building a new facility at Tullamarine and planned on moving away from Windy Hill. Although I spoke up about the need to have one venue for all our facilities, I could not see the need for Essendon to move from Windy Hill, our home since 1922 and formerly our playing arena as well. The decision had been taken before my time; the football club had endured years of shared management, with a bowling–croquet club and a cricket club also using the facility, and the ground itself was far too short by comparison with the venues we played our games on.

Personally I thought the problems could have been sorted with the club remaining at its spiritual home. The cricket club had already agreed to move to a new facility built in Ascot Vale at the football club's expense, and the ground could have been tilted slightly which, in combination with using some land at the eastern end, would have made the ground big enough to practise on, mimicking the bigger grounds that we played on. As for the bowling club, they had been at the Essendon Recreation Reserve even earlier than the football club, and understandably were unhappy with moving, but surely something could have been arranged. I thought Windy Hill could have been a wonderful venue with some money spent on it. It reeked of history, and it already boasted a swimming pool, the social club and the hall of fame. However the club thought otherwise and driven by chief executive Ian Robson, forged ahead with the plan to build a new elite training and administration facility at nearby Tullamarine, costing $20 million.

At the time, Robson talked up the proposal: 'We know that we've fallen behind. Does it guarantee premierships? No. But it gives us the best chance. There's no salary cap in this space. We could have come up with a solution for five to ten years but we wanted to be a bit braver than that.'

Essendon needed an injection of cash for the building project, and so I set about raising money in consultation with Bruce Heymanson, who was the number one ticketholder at the time. We did a roadshow together; we travelled around, and I did talks for clubs and sportsmen's lunches. Once at the Athenaeum Club in Melbourne I did a talk and a question-and-answer session for about 30 people around a table. Heymo was pretty excited when he rang me that night: 'You know we just raised $400 000 in a day from people who aren't even connected with the club?' The two of us raised more than $1.5 million, I reckon, and it was a lot of fun. Sadly, Bruce has since passed away.

So 2011 was a decent year, Hirdy's first as coach and my first back at the club. We won 11 games and played a final, losing comprehensively to Carlton in a knockout game, but showing some improvement. We beat Geelong, and they went on to win the premiership in Chris Scott's first year as my replacement, and we beat Sydney in a memorable game when Adam Goodes missed a shot on the siren at Etihad Stadium that would have won the game for the Swans.

The Essendon playing list was okay, and my thought was that we should continue to pick up young boys and develop our own, to disregard what number the draft pick was. Recruiters have to find players who fit the game plan, the club values, and in this case, who fitted Essendon; by the end of 2011 we had identified that we clearly did not have enough elite, hard-running athletes, aerobic monsters. We had no run in the team, and Adrian Dodoro, our head recruiter, knew it and I wrote my own plan for the kind of players to be integrated into the club, based on three criteria:

- Football aspects, which covered skills
- Physical aspects, which talked about body size, ability to play with injuries and so on
- People aspects, which was about personal traits

We were also about what type of person we were recruiting, and essentially we wanted combative people, a balance between rule-followers and risk-takers. I have always been slightly in favour of risk-takers in that equation. I like people who have values in terms of respecting the team, people who know how to defend. We didn't want the guy who would think, *I won't handball to him, I'll have the shot at goal*. I wrote out the plan, and told Essendon that every player we brought to the club should be looked at against those criteria.

Not that it was a full rebuild – our list was okay. I just wanted Essendon to improve each year by adopting good principles and procedures. In good teams, people make good decisions, but why do they make good decisions? They make those decisions by doing it together, as a team, by being fully aware of what the plan is, and by making a commitment to do the job properly, stay on plan.

I believe Essendon was happy with the progress and we had put plans in place for the future, notably in the conditioning area. Then the club hired high-performance coach Dean Robinson in August 2011, a decision that would have ramifications for a long while.

I knew Robinson, of course, because he had been my conditioning guy at Geelong from 2007 to 2010, which included two premiership years. I had the utmost respect for him, although we had lost him in the middle of the 2010 season at Geelong when he was headhunted by the new Gold Coast Suns club. I remember asking the Geelong players what they wanted to do, whether Dean could continue until the end of the season, but they wanted to make the change immediately so he left mid-season.

In 2011 Essendon had parted with fitness man Stuart Cormack who had previously worked with the West Coast Eagles, and was looking for a replacement. Around the same time Dean, who called himself 'The Weapon', had a falling out with the Suns and was heading back to Melbourne, and he rang Brendan McCartney to see if there was a possibility that he could come to Essendon. He'd heard we were looking and said he could be available.

We were already looking at other people, so I didn't offer the club an opinion, but then the other candidates fell through. We missed out on Chris Dennis, who is the strength and conditioning coach at Geelong now. He had a good set of skills, he was a Victorian boy, and he was half-interested in returning from his work in Europe, but eventually he said no. We were also keen on Darren Burgess, who was at Liverpool in the English Premier League. He was planning to come home to Australia, but he was not ready to do so for another year. I really liked his ideas, but he ended up joining Ken Hinkley at Port Adelaide in 2013. Once a few from the short list had dropped out, I put up the The Weapon's name.

'This guy is here, he's good, but he needs to be managed well,' I said. 'He's not your normal sort of bloke, he's quite different. But he is quite talented.'

In the light of what occurred over the next couple of years it has been said that I brought The Weapon to Essendon outright, but it was not that simple. I did rate him highly, and I still do, but he was just one of the people we talked to. I knew what we would be getting with Dean so I didn't even sit in on his interview process. I was happy when Essendon gave him a three-year contract at the end of 2011.

Robinson liked big bodies, which he made no secret of. He told the *Herald Sun* in 2012:

> It's a contested game and bigger bodies handle contests, handle hits and handle collisions better. All you've got to do is look at NFL, league or union; the size of the bodies are bigger because they're bigger hitting games. Therefore, the energy cost coming out of the hits you take in AFL cause a large amount of fatigue.
>
> The least-fatigued side, at the end of the day and the end of the season, is going to win. Being fit and strong and having a body that can handle collisions is going to allow you to carry less fatigue and perform at a higher level. It's not fitness. Fitness is probably the same, or very similar, across the league if we were to $VO_2$ max every side. It's the ability to recover and reduce fatigue, and having a bigger body will do that in my opinion.

> That's why I believe Essendon wanted me to come here. You don't want them carrying non-functional weight. It's power-to-weight ratio that we're ultimately talking about.'

Our idea was to make our players strong and as dynamic as they needed to be; the program would be individually planned to maximise the ability of every player to cope physically in the game. The new players, those who came into the club like striplings, needed the most work. We felt that we needed to put 10 kilograms on some of them.

The first pre-season in 2011–12 was hard; the next one was even harder. It had to be. We openly talked about the need to increase the strength of our players, especially the midfielders, and that notion came from Geelong. At Geelong, we would beat up the opposition. That had not been the case at Essendon, and it needed to change. The Cats had a kind of licence for players to go into the centre bounces and it became a badge of honour for the players once they knew that they had graduated, that they could stand up to the fierce in-close contests that occurred once the umpire bounced the football in the middle. At Geelong, we trained our midfielders to be the best contested ball team, able to win the football in heavy traffic, take the hit and go again and again. It was part of the recipe for our success.

Essendon also hired Stephen Dank in that 2012 pre-season to run our sports science department. Dank was recommended by Robinson but I had never met him until the interview process. He was a qualified biochemist who came to be referred to as a sports scientist, the generic term. He hailed from Toowoomba in Queensland; his resumé carried a Bachelor of Applied Sciences, majoring in biochemistry and microbiology, from the Queensland University of

Technology and he had a Master of Pharmacy from the University of Sydney. He was a businessman who ran a series of anti-ageing clinics, and he was into sport.

Dank had made his name in rugby league; he had worked as far back as the 1990s with St George, then Manly in the NRL, and more recently with Cronulla Sharks in the same competition, as well as spending some time in 2011 working with Gold Coast Suns. In the NRL, he had a nickname of 'The Pharmacist' and his practice of using calf's blood to treat injuries and his use of DNA profiling on athletes had attracted some attention in the sports industry. To that point, he had never been in any trouble with sports authorities – or none that we knew about. Dean Robinson wanted Dank at Esssendon. They were friends; Dank had stayed with Robinson at his home when they were both working with the Gold Coast Suns.

The Weapon also wanted Suki Hobson, from Geelong Football Club, as head of weight training, which Essendon agreed to. Already there were signs that rather than Robinson being managed, he was being treated like a god by our club. I would never have given him so much power, as much as I respect him.

Robinson wanted Dank to handle sports science, including recovery and GPS data, WADA compliance, food, rehabilitation and training loads. Paul Hamilton, the head of football, Danny Corcoran, who at the time was people and development manager, James Hird and I interviewed him. In the interview, I found Dank charismatic, confident and interesting. He was good company. But I was sceptical about hiring him, and I told the club that, as did Corcoran. In particular, I could not see why we needed him; at Geelong, Dean Robinson had managed those areas and it had not been a problem.

Danny had previously run football at Essendon before becoming chief executive of Athletics Australia and then the Melbourne Rebels rugby union club. He returned to Essendon in 2010 as part of the gathering together of a new group that included Hird and myself. He had a wealth of sporting experience and he had read about Dank's use of exotic substances in his time in the NRL; he had also interviewed Dank for a high performance job at the Rebels a couple of years before, and was not impressed. Corcoran told the club that Dank was not needed in that role and I agreed with him. I thought that Robinson could handle those areas himself, as he had done at Geelong in my time there.

But Danny and I were not making the decision. I was an assistant coach, and he had his quaint title of people and development manager. I was never in a position of power where I could say, 'No, this can't happen.' It was happening above my head and while it was frustrating, I had chosen that path of less responsibility, so all I could do was to say what I said: that I thought that we had the skills in place through Dean Robinson to perform the tasks that Dank was hired to do. I did not think we needed him.

Essendon hired him anyway. The Weapon definitely wanted Dank, and I believe Hird wanted a better supplements program.

With hindsight, Bruce Reid, as the club doctor, should have been involved in that selection process. Afterwards, when the trouble blew up, I remember wondering whether those of us who were in the interview had asked Dank the right questions. Stephen Dank never told us that he wanted to embark on a big program of injecting players; we spoke to him in the interview more about what he had done in the past. He talked about high performance and what was required, but looking back, I can see that we asked the wrong questions. We did not find out what his passions were, or what he intended to do if he was hired, and in the end, he did what he wanted to do; he did not do what we hired him to do. The whole thing was allowed to happen and it was not managed properly. The program ended up being top-heavy in the sense that there were too many chiefs, and not enough Indians, if I can put it that way. Stephen Dank was not an Indian; he was a chief.

Dank believed in what he was doing at Essendon in 2012, and he was a great salesman and a smart guy with lots of business interests. He was a great talker and he loved sport and I liked his company. You could hold a conversation with the guy, he was so personable, and even though AFL was not in his background, he quickly came to know a lot about the sport. But reluctance was still my gut feel.

The 2012 season began with a flurry. We came back fit and strong, and won the first four games before losing in round 5 by a single point against Collingwood, then won the next four on the trot. So through nine rounds we were 8–1, equal top on the ladder with West Coast, and absolutely flying. Through 15 rounds we were 11–4 and still in range of the top four, while Jobe Watson was having a career-best season on his way to the Brownlow Medal. Our recruiting had been good, the coaching structure was settling down, the football department was working much better and the new game plan that had been introduced had started to kick in. The players knew what they had to do, and those things were becoming habitual.

Essendon was happy with the changes that had been made, especially with the conditioning. I remember we all went to David Evans' house for drinks and finger food one night, and I saw Robinson being the centre of attention, and just raised my eyebrows. He was a guru in the club's eyes, but Essendon was prone to looking for saviours. People were calling him The Weapon and talking him up, and I remember thinking, *Don't pump him up too much!* Robinson didn't need talking up; he needed someone to keep him focused on what he was doing. He would admit, I am sure, that he could get sidetracked. He was an outstanding operator, but he needed managing.

Dank was a problem for us from the start and while we did not know about the scale of injections of players at that point, I sensed that there were issues. To my eyes, the areas that he had been hired for – the GPS, the food – were on the backburner and the supplements were taking up all his time.

Bruce Reid, the club doctor with 30 years experience, came back from Christmas holidays on the Murray River in the 2012 off-season and discovered that the new sports scientist was giving the players a peptide called AOD 9604, originally created as a fat-burner but by repute, also helpful in healing damaged muscle and cartilage. Before the break, Reid had already felt marginalised when he learned that without his approval, Robinson had ordered a supply of Tribulus, a herbal supplement taken in tablet form, to give to players. Reid was worried about the WADA status of Tribulus and had phoned Dr Peter Harcourt, the AFL's chief medical officer, to inform him. Harcourt confirmed that it was not banned.

After he discovered the injections of AOD 9604 being given without his consent, Reid went to James Hird and me with his worries, and we organised a meeting with Robinson and Dank. We needed to have a process in place, something that was adhered to, where someone managed the program and took into account the health and safety of the players. I spoke along the lines of, 'Let's have a system. If it's going to happen, then let's have nothing illegal, let's get it approved first. If you don't show us the approval, we don't do it.' So everything the players were given had to be WADA approved, and Bruce Reid, who was also at the meeting, had to give his approval first. We nutted out a protocol for future injections, with players having to give their consent, and we asked for proof that the AOD peptide was within the WADA guidelines.

Sometime later, Dank told Essendon that AOD 9604 was approved by WADA. It was at training at Victoria Park, I was out on the track, but I remember being told that Dank had the approval. There was a sense of celebration among a few of us, given that by then, our club doctor had questioned it and we had started to wonder. Personally, I was sick of hearing all the talk about the supplements program given that, to me, it was not worth the trouble. Surely, it could not be more important than training and preparing for games. That's what I felt.

In the end, I believe Hirdy wanted a proper supplements program, and that he wanted Dank to push the envelope while remaining within the WADA guidelines, just as other clubs have done. Personally, I was not especially interested. Supplements and peptides – they are not my thing.

I believe if we had known the level and magnitude that Dank went to, then we would have moved him on earlier. Dank and Robinson did not even call them peptides; they called them amino acids. I did not think for one minute that the players were being given prohibited substances or breaking the drug code. As has been revealed since, James Hird emailed Robinson, who had sent him the new guidelines, after our first meeting:

> You know my thoughts on supplements.
>
> 1. It must not harm the player
> 2. It must not be illegal (according to WADA and the AFL drug guidelines)
> 3. We must get player consent

Once Bruce Reid had contacted Harcourt, the AFL appeared to think the drug code was being broken at Essendon. That was the sliding doors moment in the whole scenario. Had the AFL responded with a different mindset – even come into Essendon to sort it out with us, to see what was actually happening – a lot of what followed might have been avoided. But the AFL managed the situation like a policeman; what it did was to take some blood samples from Essendon players, and send them off to Germany for testing in case they contained prohibited substances.

The samples returned negative readings, but for us it was a lesson in how the AFL runs its business. It showed us that the league is not into working with people to head off problems. I suspect when Reid notified Harcourt of his concerns about Tribulus, all it did was make the league suspicious. Yet if the AFL was so worried about the health and wellbeing of the players – as it has said that it was – then surely something should have been done straight away? I must say, I wish the AFL had done something.

By this time, Bruce Reid was concerned about AOD 9604, and on 17 January 2012, three days after the meeting where the protocol was formed, Reid dictated his now-famous letter, addressed to head of football, Paul Hamilton, and James Hird, full of frustration and typos:

> Dear Paul/James
>
> I have some fundamental problems being club doctor at present. This particularly applies to the administration of supplements. Although we have been giving supplements for approximately three months, despite repeated requests as to what exactly we are giving our players and the literature related to this, have at no time been given that until last Sunday. Last week the players were given subcutaneous injections, not by myself, and I had no idea that this was happening and also the drug that was involved.

It appears to me that in Sydney with Rugby League the clubs do not answer to the governing body (e.g. A.F.L). It seems that their whole culture is based on trying to beat the system as are close to the edge as one can. It is my belief in A.F.L that we should be winning flags by keeping a drug free culture.

It is all very well to say this is not banned and that is not banned but for example, the injection that we have given our players subcutaneously, was a drug called AOD/9604, is an Oligomeric Pepitide. The drug is derived from the growth hormone. The molecule has been constructed so it has removed what we call IGF-1, which is part of the growth hormone that causes muscle and organ growth and bone length and photosynthesis.

It is at the moment used for fat metabolism but also bone strength in children and may have some side effects that may be beneficial in bone growth. This to me just seem ludicrous at this stage where the only trials I have got are on how to lost weight and fat around the abdomen.

If we are resorting to deliver this altered growth hormone molecule, I think we are playing at the edge and this will read extremely badly in the press for our club and for the benefits and also for side effects that are not known in the long term, I have trouble with all these drugs.

I am still not sure whether AOD/9604 is approved by the drug authorities in Australia at this stage. Just because it is not classified as illegal, doesn't mean that it can be used freely in the community, it cannot. The other interesting thing about AOD/9604, is that its market in America is in body builders. This also should raise a red flag if we are worried about perception.

When it comes to Actovegin, this has been used around the world for many years. There is some flimsy evidence that it may help in speeding up the healing of tendons when they are damaged, though after speaking to radiologists, the recent opinion is that platelets and one's own blood, probably does a better job.

We are claiming that we should use it as a recovery agent. To me it seems ludicrous that a few mls of calf's blood spun down, is going to give you a concentration of growth factors and other factors that would speed up recovery.

I am very frustrated by this and now feel I am letting the club down by not automatically approving of these things. I need to collect my thoughts as these drugs have been given without my knowledge.

I am sure Steve Danks believes that what we are doing is totally ethical and legal, however, one wonders whether if you take a long stance and look at this from a distance, whether you would want your children being injected with a derivative hormone that is not free to the community and whether calf's blood, that has been used for many years and is still doubted by most doctors, is worth pursuing.

Kind Regards

Dr Bruce Reid

M.B.B.S.

Senior Medical Officer

The letter was addressed to Hird and Hamilton but it was never acted upon. Hirdy said later that he could not remember seeing it, and the same for Hamilton, another sliding doors moment in the whole sorry affair.

None of this was public at the time, although behind the scenes, there were rumblings all along. In January, a delegation of our players had met with Hird and Jonah Oliver, the club psychologist, expressing concern about the sharp increase in injections. Mark McVeigh was particularly upfront in the talks.

On 8 February, Dank gave a presentation at Windy Hill about the peptides and other substances the players were given, and consent forms were handed out for signing. There were four substances on the consent form: AOD 9604, Thymosin, Tribulus and Colostrum. Dank told Jobe Watson that there was a 'bad' form of Thymosin, and a 'good' form, and that he was taking the good type, meaning the form that was not banned.

The protocol that we agreed to was not followed, because Dank did not listen to us. In the lead-up to the Anzac Day match against Collingwood, players were treated at HyperMED, a clinic in South Yarra, and one player complained to Bruce Reid that he had a sore backside from being injected. Reid was angry again, and another meeting was called with Dank and Robinson.

This time, I spoke up, and I went hard at Dank, saying something like, 'We can't inject without the procedure in place. We can't do it.' I yelled at him, and Bruce Reid demanded that records be kept of the injections, a job that was given to Dean Wallis, who was working in the footy department. We went away from that meeting in the belief that everything would change, but it did not. A few weeks later, I heard about Dank injecting a player in his office, downstairs at Windy Hill, and we had a third meeting.

On that occasion, I was not far short of going berserk, accusing him of being out of control. I was sick of it; we were all spending too much time on an issue that, in my view, we should have been finished with. I told Dank, right up close to his face, 'This is bullshit!' I was angry, Bruce Reid said that my face was contorted with rage. We insisted that he stop injecting players altogether. I had had enough by this point, but he was a confident man, Stephen. He said, 'Okay, son.' But this did not stop him. Amazingly, he kept going and the changes that should have happened as a result of that meeting did not come. The majority of the injections stopped, we felt, but not all.

Dank was disorganised, the way he operated, and when we asked him for a spreadsheet and some records, he took weeks to do it, and he would say, 'I forgot to bring it up, son.' And we would say, 'Well, just go down there and *pick it up*.'

He was also injecting a few club staff with various substances for sleep problems, weight loss and the like, which I did not know at the time. I had none myself. It was not a great look for the club, but in the end, I can understand how it happened because Dank was a great salesman, promising 'I can fix this, I can fix that.' And his anti-ageing clinics had never been busier; people want to stay young forever. At the clinics, he would have supplied quite a few different products to the public because they didn't have to comply with any code as sportspeople do. In any case, those injections were not relevant to the broader issue and should have remained personal between Dank and the staff members involved; they did not, of course, as we would find out later.

There were big issues within the club long before any of it became public. There had been a meeting during the 2012 season where Bruce Reid had suggested to the club that it remove Dank and Robinson. Although I was not at the meeting, James Hird has said in interviews since that the notion could not be pursued because Ian Robson told them that the payout would be too steep.

One factor that is super important in footy is keeping your best team on the park. It is easy to say but harder to manage; if you look at the premiership team every year you will find that they are close to their optimum in terms of personnel. Look farther down the ladder and you will see teams devastated by a run of injuries. The variation that teams get in injury levels is ridiculous.

Injuries are controllable in football, at least to a point, in my opinion. By and large, you are best to let them heal naturally, not taking shortcuts. Of course you cannot stop the impact injuries, like a guy wrecking a knee in a tackle. They are controllable to the extent that you need to be careful what you are doing as a coaching group in terms of player loads and drills. At Essendon, the loads were not controlled properly and I don't think the coaches had the feel for getting the right level of physical contact at training. You cannot be a good football coach until you develop a feel for training loads.

What you need is for the coaches, the doctor and the high performance people to come to a resolution about players and their ability to get on the park. You need to have trust between these people and you cannot have the senior coach riding roughshod over the others with the decision. The players themselves will nearly always want to play. But sometimes it is neither in their best interest nor the team's, which is where the right process and the trust comes into play. And if you don't practise properly with contact work, training has no real purpose. At Geelong, we had all this down pat, but it takes time.

There is always a reason why players get soft tissue injuries, the same as there is a reason that teams lose matches. In footy, I think we have a history of not being able to train big guys properly, for instance. Look at Geelong in 2015, when Nathan Vardy, Dawson Simpson and Hamish McIntosh were all suffering breakdowns.

I just think we have to factor that in – in the modern game, there might be 70 stoppages, and the ruckmen have a physical wrestle at every single one of them, plus they are jumping into contests with their eyes on the ball. It is not easy, and we expect too much of them. They need a training program that is totally distinct from other players, but no one has worked this out yet.

At Essendon from 2011 on, we talked a lot about injuries, because I had my views that teams often get it wrong. I used to tell Hirdy not to worry about it too much himself. 'You'll get 22 players to deal with, just manage them well,' I'd say. 'Let the doctors do what they do, let them make decisions, and don't put pressure on them.' The same goes for the physiotherapists.

As for our 2012 season, it all came crashing down in the last two months as our players broke down one after the other. We lost the last seven games in a row that year, and missed the finals altogether, finishing at 11–11. We suffered more than 30 soft tissue injuries to players, a blight of hamstrings and calf strains that killed us. It was the result of training hard under Dean Robinson, preparing for what was coming. If you play a game of contested footy without having the endurance to take the hits, you are going to fade out, so to me, it was fine. It was not a one-year plan. It was about seeing how long the players could tolerate it.

I felt that we did not make good decisions together, pushing the players too hard, trying to win every minute of every game. I could see straight away that Hirdy was playing guys who were sore. Back at Kardinia Park, I had learned to leave injured players out, because playing injured often delays the healing process. I learned the hard way, from the experience of failing because in the end you break people down, and it catches up with the club. The players, of course, always want to play.

So what happened at Essendon is that someone like Jake Carlisle would play, because the coaches saw that the team looked better with his name on the whiteboard, which was about the look, rather than the long-term benefit. The doctors should be saying, 'He's about to break, give him two weeks off.' Because you do not look good if you overtrain players and they break down. Later on it would happen with Paul Chapman, and Tom Bellchambers lost a year because of it after he had stress reactions early in a season.

A coach should be demanding that the players' standards are high, that they do all they can, without playing people who are injured. It is about management of players. If two or three are tight or overloaded or sore, you rest them. I know that all clubs send players out with niggles all the time; that is a fact of life. But there is a line to be drawn and too often, clubs get on the wrong side of it. At Essendon, we pushed the players too hard from 2011. Jason Winderlich was an example of a player who could not handle it, Scott Gumbleton was another and David Zaharakis could be put in that category as well. Winderlich and Gumbleton have retired; Zaka had knee tendinitis in 2011 but was made to play and ended up missing a lot of footy.

The good players felt obligated to play, and that is a mentality that goes back a long time at Essendon, I discovered. But I always felt that when the game got faster and smarter and we got more reliant on team rather than individual brilliance, everyone had to be able to pull their weight. In the modern game, the required level of fitness is higher. You can't afford to carry blokes anymore, and players need to be healthier to be on the park than they were before. You have to know where the line is with injuries and niggles, and not cross it. My philosophy was to select healthy and fit players.

Of course this issue is complicated by the fact players want to play, and some can actually get through games when they are badly injured. At Geelong, Matthew Scarlett played a few times when he should not have, but he had proved to us that he could do it. One day, his back was so sore that he could not even bend over and he still played. All week at training he said, 'Just play me, I'm not going to accept not playing.' Jimmy Bartel was the same; he would play with a broken leg if you did not stop him. Which is where the coaches have to be prudent with selection.

We were careful with concussions, even before the AFL tightened the rules on players returning from big hits. Unless a player was right, we would not play him. Even with flu, I preferred not to play a guy until his body temperature was back to normal. The fact is, those guys do not play well. They might train well and look good on paper, but they cannot sustain it in a game. The players are all the same – they just want to play.

So at Essendon throughout the 2012 season our injury numbers were astronomical: 30 hamstring strains (three times the AFL average), eight calf muscle strains and eight quadricep nicks. A total of 258 matches were missed. Everyone blamed Robinson for the problem. When you are training for an endurance base, as we were, it cannot be done in a single year. It is a three- or four-year program, because the players need to grow accustomed to it, and after some time you can push them harder, and they adjust. That is where we were at.

Essendon was looking for a scapegoat, and The Weapon was almost sacked towards the end of 2012. Personally, I did not think it was his fault, and I told him that. To me, the heavier training loads that we needed to enforce were always going to lead to a few injuries. Not only that, I felt that the way we had managed injured players had caused a few recurring problems which had nothing to do with the programs that Dean had put in place. I just felt it was part of the process and that it would sort itself out, but I think Dean could read the play; he probably thought he had merely done what Hirdy and the others wanted him to do, and had grown a bit paranoid because the same thing had happened to him at the Gold Coast, where he ended up out the door.

Dean should have been closely monitored, and also supported. Essendon needed to talk to him, and help him through. It should not have been about letting him do his own thing and then criticising the results. They should have said to him, 'No, Dean, let's get your job description sorted out, this is what you're responsible for, let's make sure you're doing that. We're going to be watching.'

It was not my job as assistant coach to do that. It was Paul Hamilton's job because Dean reported to Paul. In the end Hirdy was at odds with The Weapon whose personality did not suit James. Dean was not an Essendon type of person, he is more of an outback New South Welshmen, a country boy, and he could be a bit weird and a bit nerdy. And it was a key part of Paul's responsibilities that he managed the coaches, the doctors and the head of high performance, all areas where there were plenty of egos flying around. When there was trouble, he should have been talking to James, and if it was not resolved, he should have involved Ian Robson.

Nobody got to the bottom of what had happened with the injuries in 2012, they were content just to play a blame game. When they asked for an external review of the soft tissue injury crisis, they never asked me what I thought. I would have told them that it was not Dean Robinson's fault, that it was much broader than that.

By season's end, Paul Hamilton had quit as head of football and Danny Corcoran had taken over, back in the job he had performed so well more than a decade earlier. Danny had endured a shocking year; his wife and the mother of his three children, Maxine, had

# FOOTBALL DEPARTMENT

## March 2011

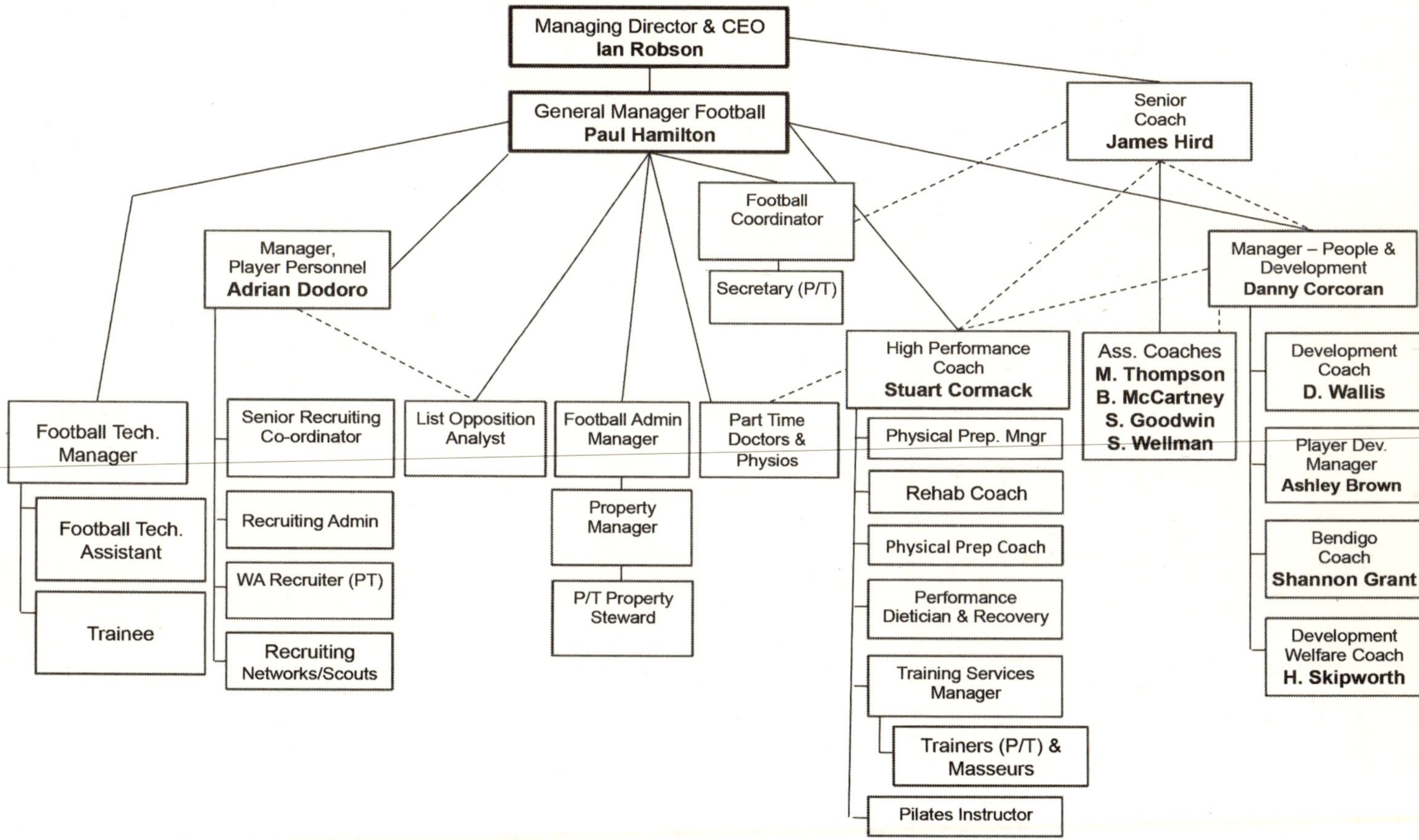

fallen ill at the end of September 2011, and was diagnosed with brain tumours. Maxine Corcoran, who had represented Australia in athletics, died on 30 November 2011, so that when a lot of the dramas occurred with Dank and Robinson at Essendon, Danny was away in France grieving.

In the independent report into Essendon's management that came a couple of years later, former Telstra boss Ziggy Switkowski would heavily criticise the set-up of the football department at Essendon, in particular the dual roles of Hamilton, who was a former player, and Corcoran. Danny was meant to be hands-on and Paul to manage up, but I never thought Hammo was the right guy in that job; he stewed over decisions in his office, struggled to have hard conversations and to ask for money for things that were not already in the budget. I said as much to David Evans, several times.

We all let the the players down, I believe. Paul was in charge of the medical staff and the conditioning and sports science staff; that is how it was in the structure. James Hird as head coach needed someone in that head of football role who he trusted, someone with a good eye and a hard nose. Hirdy should have been more on top of Hamilton and Hamilton should have been better at his job, too, just as Ian Robson, as chief executive of the club, needed to be across these things.

Stephen Dank also left the club at the end of 2012. He was about to become a household name and his face would adorn the television news most nights.

A few years on from all this, the *Herald Sun* published a front page story that really annoyed me. It made a link between Geelong and Dank in 2009, a premiership year. The story related to Actovegin, a calf's blood extract used in the treatment of muscle injuries, being sold to the club by Stephen Dank. The inference was that Geelong might have been up to no good as well as Essendon.

The truth was, Geelong had bought Actovegin from a company in 2009, and had previously used Actovegin in 2007 when Max Rooke had a run of hamstring tears. It was not a prohibited substance, so there was no issue at all, but what really interested me was the line in the story about Dank approaching the club to have an ongoing relationship, and what had occurred after that. Geelong's statement read:

> In 2008 or early 2009 Stephen Dank's professional services were recommended to the club. Our then assistant general manager of football operations Steve Hocking met with Dank in regard to this, but after that meeting the club decided not to engage Dank's services. At no time did Dank have a position with our club.

And right there is the difference. A similar situation had arisen at two different AFL clubs. Dean Robinson wanted Dank involved. One club went through a process, and said no and the issue never even reached the level of the senior coach, which was me at the time. The other got excited and ran with it. What happened with Stephen Dank and his injection program at Essendon in 2012 could never have happened at Geelong when I was there. At Essendon, it was an accident waiting to happen.

# 18

# TUMULT

## 2013

I knew something bad was coming. On 5 February 2013, I was in Dr Bruce Reid's clinic in Richmond having my bad back checked when I got a phone call to say that Essendon was holding a media conference to announce an inquiry by the Australian Sports Anti-Doping Agency (ASADA) into our conditioning program of 2012. President David Evans had given me a heads-up a few days earlier: something big was looming, but my back was bad, a disc problem that had to be scanned that morning, followed by a trip to Reid's clinic for some further treatment and advice.

Media people had been sniffing around Essendon, and we had endured the troubles over the program internally in 2012, so I think deep down, we all knew something was about to happen.

But at the same time, when I heard that the club was to be investigated by ASADA over the supplements program of 2011–12, I still felt that nothing illegal had happened. I remember thinking, *Perhaps it was unethical, but I haven't seen anything that breaks the WADA code*. I certainly knew that the club had not intended to break any rules and I also could not accept that Stephen Dank would be stupid enough to intentionally flaunt the rules.

Overall, I took the company man's view of things. I thought we were innocent until proven guilty of breaking the drug code, and knowing Stephen Dank, I could not see him being foolish enough to go over the line. If he did, he was going to get caught, so if he did, I thought, then it could only be because he was mistaken about the status of a substance.

At the media conference, David Evans said that some checks of the supplement program had revealed 'concerning' information, and James Hird said he believed all was above board. 'I'm very disappointed – shocked is probably the best word,' he said. 'I believe we followed processes, we put in place the right sort of processes. My understanding is we worked within the framework given to us by the AFL and WADA. I'm shocked to be sitting here.'

The same day, Essendon stood down Dean Robinson, which I thought was unfair, because I felt that The Weapon had done what he was required to do by the club. We had gone down a path of making our players stronger, we were getting results, then we changed course. To succeed in football, you need to think strategically and stick with your plans, and it might be a five- or six-year plan, but you do not go changing the coach, changing the running program or the weights program mid-stream. It is one of my pet hates.

From 5 February, it was a free for all. One player, Kyle Reimers, who had been delisted by Essendon at the end of 2012, gave a television interview in which he talked about the injection program and mentioned the consent form that the players had signed, which was the start of the tumult. Two days after the press conference the big sporting organisation heads including the AFL's Andrew Demetriou stood with federal government ministers before the media to release the Australian Crime Commission's report into drugs in sports, the so-called blackest day in Australian sport. Both the NRL and the AFL were engulfed in this, and for the media, it became the biggest story in the business.

David Evans called in Ziggy Switkowski, the former head of Telstra, to undertake an internal report into Essendon's structures. Switkowski was not asked to determine if illegal drugs were used in 2012; that would be left to ASADA and its investigation. His job was to look at the internal processes of the club that led to the issues, and in May, he made a series of recommendations and criticised the 'lack of clarity about who was running the football department' under the Danny Corcoran–Paul Hamilton situation. The line that Switkowski took in his summary jumped out at everyone, and has been quoted back one million times, it seems:

> In particular the rapid diversification into exotic supplements, sharp increase in frequency of injections, the shift to treatment offsite in alternative medicine clinics, emergence of unfamiliar suppliers, marginalization of traditional medical staff etc combine to create a disturbing picture of a pharmacologically experimental environment never adequately controlled or challenged or documented within the Club in the period under review.

Ian Robson stepped down as chief executive in May, soon after Switkowski's report was released. Robson said he had to take responsibility for the problems: 'The CEO must be accountable for everything that happens within his organisations. Coaches cannot bypass him, and boards must work through him.'

What Switkowski had said was true, in the sense that the checks and balances were clearly not there at Essendon, but I hardly felt we needed an internal inquiry to tell us that. It was blindingly obvious. Switkowski interviewed me, and I told him that.

What we really needed at the time was for David Evans to sit down with everyone and ask what happened. But in the end, I am not sure that Switkowski's report actually helped the club, because by giving it to the AFL and making it public, it fanned the flames that were already burning. It certainly helped the AFL's case.

I thought something was wrong with the way the club was handling the situation, that it was not defending the staff or talking to us. I cannot remember the board ever sitting us down as a group, talking to us about what happened. I convinced David Evans that we should get someone in from outside; someone who knew about handling a crisis like this. He said, 'We've done that. We have Liz Lukin.' But Liz, a public relations strategist, would not talk to us either, and her strategy was that Essendon should roll over. It was all about *the look*.

At this point I just wanted to talk to someone so I rang Warwick Hadfield, a journalist friend who had been my media manager for a while at Geelong, and asked him if he knew anyone. He was shocked at what I said. Like everyone else, Warwick, who is into politics and sport, had thought we were completely at fault. He came up with Martin Hardie from the School of Law at Deakin University, and Bruce Francis, the former Australian cricketer.

Martin had done a PhD on drugs in cycling and he came to the club as a consultant but he was moved out after a while. He has continued to do a lot of work behind the scenes and has been a good supporter.

By this point, the headlines were screaming about so-called Mexican drugs, about AOD 9604, Thymosin Beta 4 and Hexarelin, substances that had never been talked about in AFL circles and there was a fair bit of scaremongering happening. And once Switkowski used the words 'pharmacologically experimental environment' we were considered fair game for everyone to take a swipe at us. Trial by media was rampant, and from then on, the public perception was that we had cheated.

It was a horrendous year, an awful time at the club. We were working half days at the new headquarters and taking work home. I could not stand being there. I did my work then escaped, and tried to read and study and work out what exactly was unfolding in front of our eyes.

Back then, a lot of the focus was on the AOD peptide, the use of which no one at Essendon ever hid. AOD 9604 was on the consent form that the players signed, and the ASADA investigator told our players that it would never charge them with taking that substance. An experienced doctor with expertise in that area, Andrew Garnham, told our players and their parents that, in his view, it was not dangerous to their health, not performance-enhancing, and that he had been told by ASADA in February 2013 that it was not prohibited.

Jobe Watson went on television and said that he took it at Stephen Dank's behest, and he was just being honest. But after his interview, Jobe went to play a game in Perth and was roundly booed by the crowd. Yet through all that, the AFL *never* came out and supported Jobe, even though it knew that ASADA would not prosecute any case against players who took AOD 9604.

It got really ugly. On 22 August, a woman calling herself 'Sarah' and identifying herself as an Essendon player's mother called into Triple M radio in Melbourne. Tearful and angry, she unloaded:

> It's all right for James and the board of Essendon to say they have not cheated. The whole question is not about cheating.

> The whole question is about morals, it's about ethics and it's about the trust that the parents put on the club.
>
> For him to be used and to be injected with substances that may not be illegal but could be banned for substances that are labelled not for human consumption or not for human use and for the club to completely disregard it and to inject my son, I find appalling.

I don't believe that the so-called Essendon mum actually existed; I think whoever it was duped Triple M, and in the process, hurt the club's case, because that was the type of environment we were working in. The club asked all the parents, and they all denied involvement in the call to Triple M. Meanwhile, 'Sarah' was nowhere to be found.

There was a public relations war with both sides of the argument landing blows, and as for AOD 9604, it was never actually the big story that was presented. Stephen Dank had a notion that it could be a winner in the treatment of athletes in the repair of injured cartilage, tendons and bone. Above all, he is a businessman, searching for new products that would help in the fight against fatigue and injury in sportsmen. He had also told us that WADA did not consider it prohibited in 2012, which Andrew Garnham believed, too.

The players battled on bravely through the tumult around them in the 2013 season. Essendon won the first six games of the season despite the disruptions, and 13 of the first 17 rounds. Through round 17, we were second on the ladder behind Hawthorn, and we were set to play the Hawks in round 18 at Etihad Stadium.

But the pressure was incredible and that was where friendships began to splinter. The day before the Hawthorn game, James Hird came out in the *Herald Sun* and said that Andrew Demetriou, the league chief executive, had tipped off David Evans about the

ACC's interest in Essendon, in a phone call made to Evans during a 4 February meeting at Evans' home. If that was true, Demetriou may well have broken the law. He denied it, as did Evans.

It drove a wedge between Evans and Hird, who were longtime friends. While they embraced before the Hawthorn game in a public show of faith, it was a bad night for the club. Hawthorn smacked us around, Lance Franklin kicked eight goals, and in the rooms afterward, Evans broke down and needed medical attention. I never saw Evans in the rooms, but by then, I had lost faith in his handling of the situation; the path that he was taking with the AFL was too passive. I thought that the club was being hammered, while declining to fight back.

Soon after the Hawthorn game, Evans stepped down as president. I respect David Evans, and I know he was put in a terribly difficult position in that year, but James Hird and I both wanted someone to fight for the players. We had visited Paul Little, a businessman who was on the Essendon board, and another board member, Paul Brasher. We told Little that we were concerned about the way the club had managed the situation, and he and Brasher acted on it. I wanted more support for the football department staff – 33 of us – who had been left hanging by all the allegations and the headlines. They helped set up meetings with staff members and provided support, whereas previously, I'd had a business card left on my desk with a note saying, 'If you need to talk, call us.' It was an online counselling service, hardly what was required.

Paul Little had been an Essendon board member for several years, and the managing director of Toll Holdings for 25 years; he was one of the richest men in Australia. He assumed the chairmanship of Essendon on 29 July 2013, taking over from David Evans, who became the latest person to lose his position over the 2012 program, following Dank, Robinson, Hamilton and Robson. I was glad that Little stepped up and he addressed the media:

> I wish it had been under more favourable circumstances but that's the way things are. I would like to confirm that David Evans has done a marvellous job for this football club. David will continue to help and assist me in my role as chairman and obviously [in] coping with the demands of the current investigation that is underway.

The Weapon had departed late in the season, having been stood down in February. I'd said, 'Why not pay him out?' I am told he had less than two years of a $290 000-a-year contract remaining. But Essendon held out. As was typical of the way things were happening, The Weapon took court action against the club and Essendon had to cough up $1 million, about $600 000 more than the payout would have been. And he was never charged with anything.

The AFL had asked ASADA to present an interim report in August so they could get a glimpse of its ongoing investigation into what had happened at Essendon, clearly with the finals in mind. ASADA had not had sufficient time to reach a conclusion on whether Essendon's players had breached the drug code, but in light of what Switkowski had said, the AFL was not about to let us take our place in September action.

I wanted someone to actually start fighting for us, and Little had a problem with the club's passive stance, thinking we had been too compliant previously. I wanted someone to defend the staff and defend the players, and while I did not know Little well, I thought that he would do that. I thought that someone needed to say, 'We'll give our players the support that they need until they're proven innocent or guilty, and we'll deal with it then.' I could not see why anyone would manipulate the result, or reach a verdict before finding out what had actually happened.

The players started to feel the heat, and our results slipped away. After that round 18 defeat by Hawthorn, we only won one more game, against Carlton by a goal in round 22. A 14–8 record and seventh place was a great leap forward from 2012 in theory, but in practice, the AFL was about to stick a bomb under us.

Early in August, the AFL received ASADA's interim report, which by nature, was not finalised, but nevertheless had some explosive allegations within it. Then on 13 August, with three games of the season remaining, the AFL charged Essendon and four staff members – James Hird, Danny Corcoran, Bruce Reid and myself – with bringing the game into disrepute. I was shocked, because I had been led to believe that I would be in the clear.

Paul Little had called me and said that it looked like I would not be charged, then at eight o'clock the night before the charges came out, I received another call: 'Looks like you *will* be charged.' Where does the responsibility end and how do you determine that? I felt like I was a long way down the line in terms of involvement in supplement programs. Quite honestly, it would have looked better if *everyone* responsible was charged, but of course, that was not the case. In fact, people with just as much responsibility as me were *not* charged.

The AFL knew what my involvement was. I was in some of the email chains, but I never replied to any of them, and I was not included in quite a few of the meetings with regard to those matters. I was not interested in it. I had not seen an injection given; I was not at the meeting that was held at David Evans' home in Hawthorn when Andrew Demetriou allegedly returned David's call, the day before Essendon asked ASADA to hold an inquiry. David

Evans originally told me that ASADA might not even interview me, although in the end, they did. After that, my solicitor had said, 'You shouldn't have a problem again after you are interviewed.'

The AFL's charge sheet was colourful; it contained the full text of Dr Bruce Reid's letter of the year before, which had not been public before. It pointed out that 'a convicted drug dealer' in Shane Charter had been used to source peptides, and put forward information about some Melanotan, a tanning substance, that James Hird had received from Robinson for self-injection. It alleged that several staff members had been injected with Hexarelin, a WADA-banned peptide, by Dank in 2012.

The charge sheet also stated that James Hird, Danny Corcoran and Paul Hamilton had all been present at a meeting at the AFL in 2011 when concerns were expressed by the AFL's integrity officer, Brett Clothier, about the growth of peptide use in the game, and warned that peptides represented 'a serious risk to the integrity of the AFL'. No charges were brought against players; for the first time, the AFL admitted that there was no case against the players who used AOD 9604.

Specifically from my point of view, the charge sheet referred to my role in Dean Robinson's employment by the club as high performance manager in 2011, despite what it called 'significant concerns about the way Robinson had conducted himself'. It mentioned that I had not ensured sufficient employment checks were made on him. This was interesting, because the Gold Coast Suns, a club virtually run by the AFL itself, had hired Robinson in 2010 and used his services in 2011, not so long ago.

The charges also alleged that I, along with Hird and Corcoran, had 'failed to act' when Suki Hobson, our weights coordinator, had informed us that vials of the WADA-banned peptide Hexarelin were being stored by Dank at the football club. While the charge sheet acknowledged that I had in May 2012 'resolutely advised Dank that injecting of players was to cease', it alleged that none of the people at that meeting with Dank and Robinson had informed the players that this was the case.

There were 34 pages of allegations, text messages, emails and bombshells on that charge sheet. The hearing was set down for 26 August at the AFL headquarters in the Docklands, which meant we all had all of 13 days to prepare. Many people were already saying that our destiny had been decided, including Tim Watson, my old premiership teammate, on radio:

> The AFL operate as well, in fact even better than a political party the way that they operate – the way that they leak out information. They conditioned, I think, the general public a while ago to this whole idea that points were going to be taken away. I think they've already determined in their own minds, even before this report was handed down . . . that would be the punishment that was actually afforded to Essendon.

The day of the so-called hearing arrived and I hated every minute of it; I objected to it on principle. It was called a 'hearing' by the AFL, but in reality, we were in different rooms with our lawyers and people kept coming in and out, and I had two Queen's Counsels and their assistants, plus two solicitors helping me. I had resolved to fight. My position was that my place in the whole regime had been well down the chain of responsibility. That was my beef, that there was no opportunity for me to tell my side of the story. If the AFL Commission had all sat down, heard our perspective and judged us on that, then I would have had no issue with the procedure, but that is not how it happened. It was not about fact finding, it was about *negotiation*. It was about how much guilt we would accept.

With hindsight, I believe the case against Essendon should have been heard by someone other than the AFL Commission; it should have been an independent body outside the competition's structure. We never felt like we were getting due process in that case, especially since to that point, the players had not been charged with any breaches of the WADA code. We just did not know whether doping had occurred and our feeling was that it probably had not. Nobody knew.

The hearing went for two days, and I went in to face the music knowing that overall, I could have done more to stop whatever happened in 2012 at Essendon. I was able to list up to five instances where I had *tried*, including the two meetings where I got stuck into Stephen Dank. But I have always owned up to the fact that I could have done more; we all could have gone harder. I have never shied away from that.

But it became apparent over the two days that the AFL wanted me to pay some kind of price. My penalty looked like being $40 000. My QC said, 'You've got to accept some responsibility.' And I said, 'Well, I do, but $40 000 is too severe.' We actually felt that if it went to court, I might be able to escape with no penalty at all.

I think they were playing us off against each other, saying things like, 'Danny Corcoran is close to signing.' I can remember walking out of my room and heading into the others, asking them what they were thinking. I can remember hearing people yelling at Hirdy, who held on for a long time. Those two days crushed him.

Dr Bruce Reid would not bargain at all, indicating that he would head to court to have the AFL Commission disqualified from hearing the case. That left myself and James Hird, and Hirdy was resisting, big time. I heard rumours that they went hard at me as bait, so they could get Hirdy to come along too.

I could not understand how one day I was looking at no penalty, then the next day, the lawyers were saying, 'Hey, $30 000 is not that bad.' We spent two days haggling about wording and money, when I felt like we should be arguing about whether I was guilty or not guilty.

I was not going to roll over until James Hird did, and once he agreed to accept a penalty, I went with him. A court action might have cost hundreds of thousands of dollars, and the lawyers were saying, 'Take the thirty [thousand dollar fine].' I found it hard, because principles went out the door for expedience. People say things like 'You'll get over it.' But you *don't* get over it. I was annoyed, and I signed an agreement that I did not really believe in. Then again, had I gone to court on my own, I might have looked silly. I was less than happy with the process, and while I accepted some responsibility in terms of the process that was run, I hated the fact that we never had a chance to defend ourselves.

They took us into the Commission's room to put it in writing, and Mike Fitzpatrick, the AFL Chairman, asked me if I had something to say. I had nothing to offer at that point, because the deal was done. I said something like, 'You're asking me *now*?' In the end I accepted a $30 000 fine from the AFL, but I argued a lot over the form of words that suggested I failed in duty of care to any player. In my case, I was so far down the chain of responsibility that it did not apply. 'Don't pin that on me,' I said. 'To allow the program of injections to run, yes I'm guilty. I let it happen, didn't do enough. But no more than that.'

James Hird and Danny Corcoran also accepted penalties as well as the club itself, while the charges against Bruce Reid were dropped later. Essendon was kicked out of the finals – the first club in history to have this inflicted upon it – and fined $2 million. The club would be listed as finishing ninth on the ladder, and also had its first two picks in the 2013 and 2014 national drafts stripped. Danny Corcoran was suspended for six months and James Hird for 12 months, with the coach saying afterward, 'I am deeply sorry for what happened at our football club in 2012. I do take a level of responsibility for what happened. I should have known what was going on, I should have done more and I'm very disappointed that I didn't.'

The document that I signed that day read as follows:

> The AFL and Thompson agree that in 2011/2012 the Essendon FC implemented, while Thompson was Senior Assistant Coach of the club, the Program, which was experimental, inappropriate and inadequately vetted and controlled.
>
> It is agreed by the AFL and Thompson that:
>
> - he contributed to EFC's failure to take sufficient steps to ensure the health, welfare and safety of players in relation to the Program;
> - when he became aware of facts that suggested that unsatisfactory practices were occurring, the action he took was not sufficient to stop those practices;
> - he did not take sufficient steps to avoid there being a risk that players could have been administered substances that were prohibited by the AFL Anti-Doping Code and the World Anti-Doping Code and any such risk is an unacceptable risk;
> - as Senior Assistant Coach, he shares responsibility for the inadequate governance and oversight within EFC's football department in relation to the Program, and in consequence, Thompson accepts that Essendon FC breached Rule 1.6 of the AFL Player Rules.

Sanction

The AFL will impose a $30 000 fine.

The AFL and Thompson consider that the best interests of the game and its supporters are served by a resolution of this matter now given Thompson's willingness to accept responsibility as described above.

The AFL acknowledges that:

- No breaches of the AFL Anti-doping Code have been established to date;
- To the best of the AFL's knowledge and belief, Thompson and the Essendon FC did not set out to implement a supplements program that would result in players being administered WADA prohibited or harmful substances; and
- Mark Thompson's willingness to resolve the matter as described above is appropriate action by him in the circumstances.

The huge effect that the events of 2012 and 2013 had on the people involved cannot be underestimated, and to me, that was the biggest story of all, the human carnage, the feuding, the leaking and the nastiness. I fell out of love with the game for a while, and it left me with a lot of bitterness, not just toward the AFL, but toward people at Essendon. Had the AFL not suspended James Hird for 12 months, leaving the club without a coach, I would have moved on. I'd had enough, and I was set on leaving the club and to be honest, I don't think the club would have cared if I'd left and Simon Goodwin had taken over for a year. There was tension between Essendon and myself, because I had challenged them during the whole controversy, urging them to fight for their staff, and they were annoyed with me. But Hird had said that I was the 'obvious' choice to replace him, since I had not been suspended, and I knew that the club needed me to help for 2014.

Sean Wellman is an example of the toll that the whole sorry saga took. The effects went far beyond what anyone on the outside realises. Sean was an assistant coach, and a good one, in 2012–13, but when it was alleged in the media that some of the staff – including Hird and an unnamed assistant coach – had been injected with Hexarelin during 2012, it implicated all of us. Wellman was mortified and so was I, because neither of us had taken injections. Later it emerged that the stories referred to Simon Goodwin, who told the ASADA investigators that he was never told that he was to be injected with Hexarelin, which is banned by WADA. Hird also denied that he had taken Hexarelin, but the headlines were large, and the mud was sticking.

Sean Wellman left the club over that. A couple of years earlier, while assistant-coaching at Melbourne, he had been through a similarly nasty scene when the Demons were fined $500 000 for engaging in conduct prejudicial to the AFL's interests in 2009. Melbourne was never found guilty of 'tanking', or deliberately losing games, but it was punished all the same, and Sean knew only too well how dirty the game could be.

While we all fried in the Hexarelin allegation, he said to David Evans, 'What are you going to do about this, David?' Sean wanted the club to put out a statement to say that he was not implicated. But Evans and Ian Robson said, 'Give us a week.' Nothing happened, so we went back to them. 'Give us some more time,' they said. It was a terrible look, the fact that staff were having injections of substances that were banned by WADA. It was not illegal to do that, but it made Essendon *look* like drug cheats, it left a stench, and Essendon should have acted earlier on that once it became public.

The players are the important people here. They were the ones who were subjected to the injections, they had to deal with the uncertainty later, they had ASADA people telling them how dreadful the substances were, how it could affect their unborn children. They saw all the crazy headlines about the exotic drugs and the dangers of side-effects on their kids. When I think about it, I am not sure how, as an industry, we all let that rubbish happen in front of our eyes. I don't get how human beings could inflict that upon anyone.

The pressure that was put on those young men over more than three years would have been virtually unbearable. They were told to tell the truth, and they told the truth. They could hardly have been more compliant with the ASADA investigation at Essendon. They were thrown out of the finals in 2013 having earned the right to play in them, then charged by ASADA, cleared by an anti-doping tribunal, then put on the rack again because WADA appealed. Ultimately a court in Switzerland would suspend them but all the while, the issue had hovered over them. I called it a Perfect Storm.

And it would get worse. This was only the beginning.

# 19

# IN CHARGE

## 2014

Essendon announced on 10 October 2013 that I would be its head coach for 2014 only, replacing James Hird until his suspension was complete. I could not say that I was keen to begin with and neither was the club, which was angry with some of my behaviour. The acting chief executive, Ray Gunston, and a board member Chris Heffernan actually told me that, that they did not want me. My inclination was to walk away.

James Hird went off to study in France; his suspension would end on 25 August, meaning that he would not coach any of 2014, although if we made the finals, he would be back from overseas. Paul Little and the board had offered him a contract extension, meaning that he would automatically resume the senior coaching job in 2015, so I was being offered what amounted to a fill-in position, which I accepted.

It was not even close to a fait accompli that I would be the coach.

But at the Crichton Medal night, Simon Goodwin and I handed out the trophies because Hirdy could not be there under his suspension terms, and when I was introduced, the crowd went nuts. I remember looking down at Ray Gunston, who was up the front of the function, and he was saying, 'You've got no choice here, mate!' The supporters made the decision for him there and then.

The role could easily have given to Simon Goodwin and I think he would have done a decent job of the coaching. But he would have had to step straight down again in 2015 when Hirdy returned, and that would have been hard for him as a first-time coach. In the end he left the club anyway, taking up an assistant's role with Paul Roos at Melbourne, with the promise of a head coaching position beyond that. I know that Goody was upset with me, which is okay, but I don't think it would have been a great fit for him in 2014 at Essendon in his first senior job and with the whole ASADA business hanging over the players and the club. I could not see any winner there.

The players also drove the decision to go with me as Hird's replacement. I am not sure what they said to the football club, but I know they kept ringing me. I remember Jobe Watson saying to me around that time, 'We only want you to do it if you want to do it. But we'd love you to do it. You've got to be into it.' I felt a sense of duty, and I did not want to let the players down, so in the end, I agreed to coach, even though my salary was the same as what it had been as James' assistant, about $350 000 less than my last salary at Geelong, four years earlier. There was not even a proper negotiation, I just copped it. Sadly, the club did not really appreciate this, as I found out later.

I remember going to the board and asking them, 'How do you want me to coach the team? Give me some guidelines, potential outcomes.' They had nothing for me on that score, so I had to do what I thought was right. Fundamentally, it was about defence, or *better* defence. Essendon had been a poor defensive team for quite a few years, and I went to Plan A just as I had done at Geelong. I wanted to make Essendon a hard team to play against, make them accountable through the midfield. We ended up conceding 79 points a game, our lowest for many years, and fourth best in the competition.

Fortunately, I hadn't told the club that I had been planning to leave at the end of 2013. But the board and the administration were less than happy with my behaviour, including some of the criticisms of Essendon I had delivered over the ASADA case and over list management. The coaches had been led to believe Brendon Goddard would be given a three-year contract when he was picked up from St Kilda on free agency at the end of 2012; at the last minute this became four years at big cash, and I spoke out about that (although to be fair, Brendon has been a good player at Essendon). Again, I felt the process had been flawed, that we were not necessarily all on the same page.

Overall, 2014 was one of my best years of coaching, I think, especially given the circumstances. It was not pretty. The ASADA case hung over the club all season long, with the players receiving show-cause notices, one step short of a formal charge, on 12 June. There were two bouts of federal court action from Essendon and James Hird against the AFL, challenging the legality of the original investigation. Those cases were lost, and they delayed the charges against the players even further. We did our best to shut out the external matters and get back to playing football, but it cannot have been easy for the players.

As for ASADA, we did not even talk about it, other than to do some planning in the case that the show-cause notices arrived. To their eternal credit, the players kept their minds on the job. And we deliberately made it fun, and made it different – I was more open than I had been at Geelong. I wanted to give something to the fans, give them more value for money, let them into training, let them into how the team was coached, the players' feelings and thoughts. I used the after-match media conferences as a vehicle and appeared on Fox Footy's *AFL 360* program. That was a big change for me compared with the way I'd worked at Geelong, where I only did the minimum requirements of media and largely kept to myself.

Ironically, I found that I enjoyed that open-book atmosphere and the players responded in a relaxed, professional environment. We moved away from some of the stuff we were doing before I took the job, so we had short meetings most of the time, and everything we did was meant to have purpose, and I think the players picked up on that. It was a completely different training program, with the same goals but with some pressure. I would scream a lot, try to create confusion and frustration, get them yelling at each other. That is what I wanted to see. That is how I wanted them to train, in that environment of chaos like a game, and they loved it.

I worked on their mentality, too. Essendon's players were not as resilient and as ruthless as they should have been, in terms of being a top-four team or a premiership team. I wanted them to understand what they did when they played well, and remember how they felt, almost to bottle it. 'Let's get back there, where we want to live, where we love it,' I'd say.

The thing is, footy had ceased to be fun for Essendon players in 2013, and we had to try to change that in 2014, even though there were a million distractions. We took up a casual version of the

Leading Teams model, and we talked to each other with openness. Players were allowed to talk about it if they were struggling, and they were offered suggestions as to what they should do about it. Jobe Watson as captain was excellent as an example; he told everyone that he needed to improve his defensive work.

Jobe was a ball watcher, a see-ball, get-ball player, and he could be caught out by an opponent at times. When you have your best player and your captain saying that kind of thing, it is a real advancement for the group. The players' state of mind had been more like 'I don't have to do anything, because I'll get away with this or that.' But we asked them to have hard conversations, and if something went wrong in a game, to have the courage to speak up, and they embraced it.

We had our moments in that year. We lost to Hawthorn in round 2 when we were in front with a minute left – Cyril Rioli kicked a late goal to beat us. We played some solid footy up until 12 June, when the show-cause notices arrived for the players from ASADA. The players were stressed about it, obviously, and a few days after that we lost in the last 30 seconds to Melbourne when we had been in front. Christian Salem got the goal to kill us there, and I held the players back for 45 minutes afterward, telling them that the ASADA matter was no excuse for us to lose.

Jobe Watson's long-term hip injury was another drain on the club, although in other ways, it presented opportunities. When Watson ruptured his hip tendon – a weird injury – I actually took it as a positive, because Jobe had been *everything* to Essendon, quite literally. Jobe Watson is a natural leader, a great leader and captain, and he was not one to ask for help in doing that job. People always came to him and he responded. The club needed someone to represent it; who else would you ask? So when I came to Essendon,

I could see that he was doing it all, and he needed some more help. Hence, with Jobe missing a stretch of footy, it allowed people like Dyson Heppell and Michael Hurley to step up as they needed to do.

I loved that year of coaching. The three years without the responsibility in 2011–13 had been good for me. I was cooked by the time I finished at Geelong, but I sank my teeth back into coaching in 2014. I felt that I had a chance to make a difference at Essendon. We were not going to win a premiership; we did not even know if we would have a team by the end of the season, because of the potential for charges by ASADA, but I took the job on and tried not to worry about the possible conclusions too much. My attitude seemed to rub off on the players.

Toward the end of the 2012 and 2013 seasons Essendon players had fallen away, physically shot and full of injuries, but we were determined to stay to the bitter end in 2014. From rounds 16 to 18 we won three on the trot, beating Port Adelaide by two points at Adelaide Oval in an amazing contest that really showed what our revised game plan was built on. We defended extremely well, and we shut down their run. That was the season under coach Ken Hinkley when Port stunned everyone with their speed and ball-carrying ability, but we sent Jason Winderlich down the back, a smart player who caused the Power some issues as a spare.

I took solace from excellent improvement from a group of players like Michael Hurley, who we used down back as opposed to centre half-forward previously, and Paddy Ryder, who had his best season in the ruck, while Dyson Heppell was developing into a really high-quality midfielder. By the round 22 win over Gold Coast up in Queensland, we knew that we were safely into the finals.

By then, James Hird was back from France, his 12-month suspension completed, and he came back to the club. I said, ‘Come back and find a place. But it's not going to be in *my* office! It'll have to wait until we're not playing anymore.' We did not want him to come into the coaches' box, because the media focus would have moved straight to him, which was not good for the team. It all worked fine – Hirdy came to training and helped out where he could.

In the elimination final against North Melbourne we had a 27-point lead at half-time and we were playing excellent football until the Kangaroos rained seven goals on us in the third quarter. They ended up beating us by two goals, but there were many positives for Essendon. Joe Daniher, for instance, kicked four goals in his first final as a key forward at just 20, and 22-year-old Dyson Heppell had a terrific game, too, as a midfielder, while Zach Merrett played his first final as an 18-year-old. We could have won the game – possibly should have – but we moved away from what we were meant to be doing, which was a concentration thing. Essendon still had a propensity for running too far in front of the ball, and it returned to bite us in an elimination game.

This was the end of the road for me, but I was proud of my work. I must admit that some of that year was about proving myself again, because people at Essendon thought I was lazy. I actually felt a lot of people were overworking at the club, going to meetings that did not help anyone, and I took a different path. My idea was: do your job properly, then go home. Every night when I left the club, I would poke my head into the office of the fitness and high performance people, and I'd say, 'Turn your computers off and go and inspire players and talk to them. You can't do it from in front of a computer.'

Off the field, James Hird's decision to appeal the federal court case against the AFL was in the headlines. The club was not happy about it; they wanted to find a way to move on, since the players still had the ASADA investigation sitting over their heads, and they knew that the court action would delay it even further. James's wife, Tania, also had a crack at the AFL and Andrew Demetriou on television, and there was speculation that James could be sacked by Essendon.

As for me, I was done unless there was a radical change. There was some speculation that I might go and coach the Gold Coast Suns, who had removed Guy McKenna from the head coaching role. Then on the day of the Crichton Medal, Essendon seemed close to sacking James.

I don't know why Essendon acted like that, but I do know that some tension had built up between James and the club over the previous months. On 2 October, the day of the best and fairest, they were looking for me to come to a meeting, and I just made sure that they couldn't find me. I could sense that they wanted to feel me out, ask if I would consider coaching in 2015 if they moved against James, so I simply did not answer my phone.

However I knew that I was required at the Crichton Medal at Crown that night, and they nabbed me just before the count. It was the same situation that I found myself in way back at the end of 1998, when Essendon wanted to sound me out and possibly move against Kevin Sheedy, and I did not like it. I never, ever said 'yes' to the coaching job for 2015. What I actually said was, 'You shouldn't be asking me that!' At this point, James was still the coach of Essendon, and I wanted him to go on as coach. Paul Little had kept ringing me and I ended up saying, 'Don't do it that way.'

There was no way I would do it like that and and no way that I would have taken the job. *Don't come near me while he is still officially the coach of Essendon.* That was my position.

Hirdy had some bitterness towards the board, and the feeling was mutual, I think. They had fallen out of love to some extent. Paul Little and the board seemed annoyed that James had pursued his legal action, but in my opinion it was his right to do it. Ultimately, he would have felt alone, unwanted when he came home from France. We will never know if he was a good coach or not. He never had the chance.

At the Crichton Medal, I asked everyone to stand up – the players, the staff, the players' partners – to celebrate a good year, a season of improvement. I told the crowd that they had the power, that the game belonged to the people. I said that Essendon was trying to build a great club again, that having been 'splintered' at the end of 2013, it was coming back together. I praised Paul Little for what he had done, fighting for the club. I said that I had been told by Essendon that 2014 was not to be a 'gap year', and that the team had indeed made strides; many players had their best season.

Then I got to my own situation, which was where I ran into a spot of bother up on that stage. I wish that I had worded it in a different way, and I know that it caused James Hird to think that I was pitching for his job. But I told the crowd that I had loved coaching, that the players had been responsive, but 'the thing I'm really struggling with right now is taking a step back'. At this point, sections of the crowd started to interject, especially when I mentioned the Gold Coast Suns.

I told them that I had not talked to the Suns, which was true. Then they started yelling out '*Noooo*' when I said, 'The plan was to leave after this year.'

I responded, 'I don't really *want* to.' Then there were cheers from the floor. I said that I did not want to go because I loved the football club and I loved the players, but that 'I can't do a job that doesn't actually fill the needs'.

To me, stepping back into an assistant coach's role in 2015 after coaching Essendon in 2014 would have been going backwards. I had done it once, when I left Geelong, at a time when I was tired and stressed and I needed a break, but this time I had my teeth into the senior coaching job, and I knew that it would be too tough to go backwards in a professional sense. That is what I meant on Crichton Medal night, but it was not interpreted that way. It was an awkward way of saying goodbye.

My comment that night about having my passion for coaching was taken by the media as interest in the Gold Coast job, but in fact, I was just putting out the bait, intentionally. I wanted to let the AFL know just to see if they would interfere, given that they are effectively the owner and operator of the Gold Coast Suns, and I knew that I was not exactly popular down at AFL House. At the time, I still had not paid my $30 000 fine to the AFL.

I was never going to coach the Suns. Jana and I had been married for two years, and I was not going to take her up there after a really difficult couple of years at Essendon. I never spoke to them, although I know they spoke to friends of mine. I did not want to coach the Suns and I probably would not have coached Essendon, either. Did the AFL intervene and blackball me from getting that job, as some people have speculated? I cannot say for sure, but I do find it strange that the Suns never found me, never actually came to talk to me. I know that they called Michael Quinlan, my manager during my time at Geelong, but I'd come to the view that the AFL just did not want me coaching a club that it virtually owned, and Rodney Eade, a very worthy candidate, picked up the job. I was disenchanted about footy and to coach, you have to be in the right state of mind, which I was not.

In October, Essendon announced that James Hird would resume

his contract and coach Essendon in 2015. They made the deal with Hirdy, so they needed to stick to it, I thought, but Essendon was having trouble being truly inclusive. In my opinion, if they had sacked him, it would never have stood up in court, removing a coach because he pursued his legal rights.

As for me, I was in Playa del Carmen in Mexico with Jana, which must be *the* best place in the world. We drank piña coladas in the pool and hardly got out of the water from day to day. I had not paid the AFL fine and this was causing angst back at home, but Essendon owed me money, and they would not pay it until I signed an employment release form. My plan was to use that release money to pay the fine, and the AFL knew that, but it was withheld over a few details.

At one point the AFL rang Essendon and told them to pay me out. 'Hurry up and do it,' they said. But it still was not done. I was transparent about it, but there was a point where I did not want to pay that fine at all. It did cross my mind, but common sense prevailed in the end. The whole thing was a bit hard to swallow, that's all.

In November 2014, ASADA issued infraction notices to 34 past and present Essendon players for breaching the drug code, specifically naming the banned Thymosin Beta 4 peptide as being used. In February 2015, the AFL's anti-doping tribunal found the charges were not sustained, and the players were free . . . for the time being. Already two years had passed since the day that Essendon agreed to cooperate with ASADA, and the players had a little celebration at Crown. I went and had a few beers with them, and they were relieved and excited. A new season was upon them, but WADA decided to appeal to the Court of Arbitration of Sport. That knocked the stuffing out of them, and 2015 was destined to be another write-off, this time with James Hird in charge.

On 18 August 2015, James Hird resigned from the Essendon coaching position, acknowledging that his departure was the circuit-breaker that was required for the club to go forward. The players had succumbed by this stage, slumping to 5–14 in the season. They had been thrashed by 112 points by Adelaide a couple of days earlier.

That night, I went to see James and Tania at their home, and we tossed around a few things. Hirdy was still unhappy with what I had said at the Crichton Medal in 2014, but I told him what had happened and how it unfolded. We were fine. I said to him that I knew it was coming for him. We all knew that; even he knew by then. We were all stamped over this affair. There was too much power and influence lined up against us and the media would not allow him to coach on. In fact, if you asked every single media person whether James Hird could continue, they would have said 'no'.

We had three years of total hell, and we had supported each other through that. He lost Simon Goodwin and myself, two of his lieutenants, and had to coach in 2015 with a new bunch of assistants and an inexperienced new chief executive in Xavier Campbell. During the year, I had said on television that Essendon was drowning, and while I was criticised for saying that, it was true. In the end, it was only a matter of *when* James would be removed and at that point, it became better for the club that he did go. The AFL, the media, the footy public were not going to get off Essendon's back until it happened.

I spent the year observing from the media benches, working with Fox Footy and 3AW and giving talks, keeping my head down where possible. I did not go to Essendon's 1984–85 premiership reunion, which caused a stir, but I did not receive the invitation. I know that people rang me after this was mentioned on *AFL 360*, and they invited me, but by then I had other plans; I was catching up with some people that I had not seen for a long time. Plus, I did not want it to be about me, and if I had walked in to that function, on top of everything that was going on at the time, it would have been. I will go to the next reunion, for sure. I love Essendon, and I am fine with Geelong, too.

In 2015 as WADA and ASADA sorted out whether the Essendon players were guilty, I spent a lot of time on the speaking circuit, and I made a habit of asking everyone in the audience to put their hands up if they thought that Essendon had cheated. Usually I would get an 80 per cent response, so I knew what people were thinking. We had been branded by that point.

It is a vicious world, I have learned, and there was no one to protect me other than myself – I was never in any boys' club; I am an independent and I felt like one of the few people out there who was defending Essendon. A story did the rounds that I had a drug habit, and it hurt. It is a horrible world sometimes.

My observation is that Essendon has suffered since the departure of Kevin Sheedy and has a long way to go before they get back to being a great club again. The club needs to improve its communications, it needs to work on becoming a good place to work again in what amounts to a people business. What happened with ASADA put the process back a little further. But I do hope that Essendon finds greatness again.

In January 2016, the Court of Arbitration for Sport in Switzerland upheld WADA's appeal and suspended the 34 players for two years. Taking into account that some voluntary suspensions had already been served, the players would be left out of football for the 2016 season. The CAS report pointed to the secrecy around Essendon's conditioning program, in particular the failure of the club to produce records to defend itself, and the fact all the players bar one did not declare any injections on the doping forms when they were drug-tested in that period. The court convicted the players on its 'comfortable satisfaction' that TB 4 was used, using a circumstantial case.

Twelve Essendon players would be suspended plus a number from other clubs, and Jobe Watson's 2012 Brownlow Medal would be the subject of speculation, too. It was a devastating verdict, and at the time of writing, some players are pondering an appeal to a Swiss court to clear their names. I am glad they want to appeal; I thought the CAS verdict was disgraceful. The players have been fingered for dishonesty but the truth is they were the most honest group through the whole process. The one-size-fits-all aspect of the finding is hard for me to comprehend as well, because there were clearly some players who must not have been injected with either Thymosin alpha or Thymosin beta, yet all 34 have copped a suspension. I don't get how one-size-fits-all can apply when you are talking about people's careers and reputations. Jobe Watson was forced into a situation where he handed back his 2012 Brownlow Medal, a dreadful outcome in my view.

The AFL Players' Association and others have questioned whether the WADA code fits a team sport like AFL footy, and I agree with them. I don't think it works for us and I note that when the AFL's anti-doping tribunal sat in judgement of the Essendon case, it found on the players' sides. No code would be so hard on itself but at WADA level, it is all black and white. The American professional sports don't follow WADA and I can see why they don't. Because if a player buys a sports drink from a shop and finds there is something illegal in it, that is not worth a two-year suspension. If you have a Sudafed or make a mistake with a painkiller, it should not be categorised as drug cheating. The Essendon situation was a test case for footy, and I think the WADA code failed.

Around the same time as the CAS verdict was released, WorkSafe Victoria fined Essendon $200 000 for breaches of the Occupational Health and Safety Act relating to the 2012 conditioning program, charges that were not disputed by the club.

Three-and-a-half years down the track, and it's still not over. I wonder if it will ever be over for the people involved, particularly for the players. On a personal level, it has taken a heavy toll, and I'm still confused and angry about the denial of justice. Quite frankly, I am left with more questions than answers. Some of them are below, but there are so many I could fill pages and pages.

- After president David Evans gleaned information about the supplements program from James Hird, Bruce Reid and other Essendon staff members in February 2013, what information forced him to take the dramatic step of virtually self-reporting to the AFL?
- What discussions led Essendon to the point where Dean Robinson was immediately dismissed?
- We know it was Lukin's idea to commission an independent report on Essendon's management and governance of the situation. But what instructions were given to Ziggy Switkowski, and what rules and restrictions were set for him? Why was only some of his report made public, including the sections with inflammatory words that made Essendon look even worse than it actually was?
- Wouldn't the report have been more useful had Switkowski interviewed the physiotherapists and high performance staff who sat right near Stephen Dank's office at Essendon, people who could have provided relevant information?

- Why didn't Essendon's management simply gather the staff in one room and ask what happened with the supplements program, instead of relying on outsiders like Switkowski to ask the hard questions?
- Why did Essendon not defend itself on the allegations relating to AOD 9604, given the explosive reporting that was done on this topic in the media? This, despite a reputable doctor telling the players and their parents that the supplement was not dangerous to their health, and that ASADA did not consider it to be a banned substance under the WADA code.
- Why was there such mystery surrounding AOD 9604? Why did the club never find out exactly how many injections were given, leaving the way open for wild speculation?
- Why did the AFL not intervene to defend Jobe Watson, a player who merely told the truth? He admitted to taking AOD 9604, a substance that was *not* prohibited.
- How could Liz Lukin advise that James Hird should stand down as Essendon coach early in the 2013 season, when the investigations had not been completed?
- Why didn't Essendon act to clarify the situation when the media reported that Stephen Dank had treated staff with various substances, an allegation that had nothing to do with the investigation?
- Why did Dr Peter Harcourt, the AFL's chief medical officer, not come straight to Essendon to look into the supplement program when he was alerted to its existence by Dr Bruce Reid, rather than ordering blood tests be sent to Germany for analysis? Why didn't the AFL, if it suspected Essendon was cheating with performance-enhancing drugs back in the 2011–12 pre-season, come into the club and stop it right then and there?

- If people like James Hird and myself, alleged to have been involved in a program that brought prohibited supplements to a football club, were truly guilty of that charge, why were we allowed back into football at all? James returned from a year off and was offered a two-year extension, and I coached in 2014 while he was away. Were we scapegoats?
- Why weren't those of us who were punished allowed to present our side of the story to the AFL Commission? Instead of finding ourselves in a position of negotiating our penalties, why was a proper hearing not conducted? Why couldn't we defend ourselves in front of a neutral panel?
- Why were certain people at Essendon charged and not others? Why were David Evans, Dean Robinson, Paul Hamilton, Ian Robson – people who left the club – not charged, yet people like James Hird and myself were?
- Finally, I would like an answer to this: what would the AFL do differently next time (in circumstances where there will hopefully never be a next time)?

Answers to these questions would make a difference to my understanding of what happened and why, but it wouldn't change the biggest story of all: without a doubt, it's the human carnage that this situation caused. Essendon made mistakes; we all did. So did the AFL, in that there were people who could possibly have put a stop to the damage much earlier. So many friendships have been broken over the whole thing, and good people have been lost to the game. Down the track, I know that the AFL and its clubs have to start working a lot more closely together. They have to be more transparent. The AFL must trust its clubs and the clubs must find a way to trust the AFL. Bridges need mending, and quickly. Some lessons have to be learnt from this sorry mess.

# 20

# REFLECTION

I have never stopped loving the game, but it is the game itself that holds my affection, not so much the the nastiness and the noise of what happens around it. As I have said, the politics can be suffocating, and people can get carried away with themselves under the microscope that is trained on footy.

There will always be a bit of the football coach in me, because it is in my DNA. It is there in the way that I watch the game, and there's still a bit of the competitor within me too. I try to work out ways to beat certain styles of play. In 2016, for instance, we have this frenetic ball movement, some of the quickest that we have ever seen, and it is exciting to watch. Western Bulldogs, Adelaide, even St Kilda are taking amazing risks in the way that they move the ball up against the usual defensive zones. I wonder whether that method will stand up, ultimately, or whether those teams will come undone, concede too many goals because of the level of risk. It's fascinating to see it unfold.

I still love watching the game, even in an era where a lot of people complain about the congestion around the ball. It *is* a problem, I will grant that, but I tend to look more at ways around it and solutions, and I enjoy watching teams try to break the stranglehold and move the ball out of the quicksand.

People have speculated that there will be zones introduced, with a certain number of players to stay in certain areas. For instance, you could mandate that each team must have four forwards inside the 50-metre attacking zone at all times, with a free kick or some kind of penalty if they did not. It is worth trying, I would think, in a pre-season competition at the very least, but I do foresee a more radical solution.

I would have fewer players on the ground; if I were running the game I would reduce the teams from 18 down to 16 players each on the ground, with six players on the bench. That is the only way that you can make a dramatic change in style. So basically teams could start with five forwards and five backs, and there would be more interchanges so you would be sharing the load among your players, which would be good. I think that might make the players last longer at full tilt, and the intensity would be incredible. We would see more one-on-one contests, which is what we want. There would be tired teams, and fresh teams, and you would get plenty of goals. If you had an injury or two, that would be well covered with six on the bench, and therefore injuries would not be such a factor in deciding results.

It has been done before, of course, in other competitions. The rugby sevens concept is an example, and while that is probably too big a reduction – from 15 players down to seven – it is a hell of an exciting game to watch! In Australian football, the old VFA in Melbourne, forerunner of the current VFL, used to have 16 players a side on the ground rather than 18, and the ball zinged up and down pretty quickly.

At Geelong when we were at our best, we would train 12 on 12, and that helped to teach us the style of game that we wanted to play, the kamikaze game. We worked out that it was the right number for our levels of fitness and for our ball movement. It was perfect. I would love to see the AFL do something like that.

I was pumped to see teams jump up and tackle Hawthorn's dominance in 2016, denying the Hawks a fourth consecutive flag. Usually, as we found at Geelong after the 2007–09 run, the opposition teams change up something and find a way to make life difficult for the dominant team. That is what I look forward to in footy, because the Hawks have changed the game a bit with their possession of the football, and someone will change it again, because that is the nature of the game. A Thomas Jefferson quote, one of my favourites, comes to mind: 'If you want something that you've never had, you've got to do something that you've never done.'

Zoning is quite popular as a defensive mechanism in the modern game of AFL footy, but you can slice through a zone with good kicking. Essentially, that is what Hawthorn does when it has the ball but as an opposition team, you can do it to the Hawks, too. For instance when Hawthorn played 'the Cluster' around 2008, we relied on having 18 players being in the right positions. If you are a good kicking team and you reset your forward line early, and make sure that not too many players are up in the middle of the ground, it creates holes in the zone, and you can cut through.

West Coast's zoning in 2015 became known as 'the Web' and when it failed in the grand final, a few people took it that zoning as a philosophy was not the answer. That is untrue. Hawthorn was playing some zone too; the difference is that if Hawthorn is zoning, they also have key match-ups that they stay with. In the grand final, for instance, James Frawley stayed with Josh Kennedy, the

Coleman medallist, and played superbly. The problem with West Coast's zone was that it left certain dangerous players free, notably Cyril Rioli, who won the Norm Smith Medal without having a hard close marker at all, all day.

For any team playing Hawthorn, you are better off training your players up for the type of footy that you will get in September. In West Coast's defence, the zone was what they were accustomed to, and maybe they had not played man-on-man all year. If you try to switch on the day, the players can panic.

What I expect to see is that teams will try to play *like* Hawthorn, which is the way of sport. In the 2000s when we could not beat Brisbane Lions, we copied them. The first step is usually to make a statement, something like 'Let's make it hard for them to score.' The next step is getting over the hump. Hawthorn is a great team; it is not as though the Hawks can just be shut down or pressured out of their game style. They can grind it out with the best of them. Just look at the 2013 and 2014 grand finals, against Sydney and Fremantle, two of the hardest, grinding defensive teams, sides that can bully a lot of other teams around the football. Hawthorn had it covered and they stood up for longer. They just have so many scoring options. With forwards, I always liked clever people, guys who were tricky and dangerous, and Hawthorn has those guys in Luke Breust and Cyril Rioli and Paul Puopolo. They are players who can bob up and make something happen, which is exactly what you want.

Hawthorn is the template for how clubs should approach the game. It's easy to forget the club was in dreadful strife for a few years, in the period before Alastair Clarkson was appointed for the 2005 season. In his first two seasons, Clarkson finished fourteenth and then eleventh on the ladder. Getting back to a position of authority is not about going backwards to move forwards, as is often said. It is about getting things right, which is what Hawthorn has done, and what we did at Geelong.

The notion of taking your pain and intentionally sliding down the ladder for better draft picks was popular a decade ago, but Hawthorn is an example of why you do not need to bottom out. The Hawks have played finals in nine of the last ten seasons including four premierships, and still show very little sign of wavering. The same could be said of Sydney and Geelong; the good clubs seem to find a way to replenish their lists while still being competitive on the field.

I am a strong believer that deliberately going backwards is not the way to go, because it is based on a myth: that the best players always come from the top picks in the draft. The reality, and it is very clear, is that you can get a good player with any number. There are dozens of examples of players who were delisted by their original club, developed from a rookie list or taken with low picks in the draft who have become very successful. The pick number is unimportant.

At Geelong, we used some early picks for Joel Corey and Jimmy Bartel, but we had cracker years in 1999 and 2001 at the draft, which was good timing for me as coach. In my first year we picked up Cameron Ling, Joel Corey, Paul Chapman (pick 31), Corey Enright (pick 47), then in 2001 we got Gary Ablett (father–son), Bartel, Steve Johnson and James Kelly. Tom Hawkins and Matthew Scarlett also came under the father–son rule. And there you have the basis of the three premiership teams at Geelong. And we never had too many early picks in the draft. Joel Selwood and Andrew Mackie were top 10 picks but Mathew Stokes came off the rookie list, Tom Harley came in a trade for pick 37, Cameron Mooney for a flutter of picks including Leigh Colbert, and Matthew Egan from Oak Park.

It is true that the old father–son rule, where a club only needed to give up a third-round pick to get a player, was kind to Geelong. Gary Ablett (pick 40), Tom Hawkins (pick 41) and Matthew Scarlett (pick 45) were good examples, and the league eventually changed the system to make it tougher, bringing in a bidding system. Clubs who want to take a player under the father–son rule now have to work harder, but I wish they had not changed the rule. I like what it stands for.

It is the same with the veterans' rule, which made it much easier for teams to hold on to their older players. Under the old rule, a club only needed to declare half a veteran's salary under the cap; now it is much harder and more complicated.

When I had a team that was not really in contention, it was not about winning or losing or the score. It was about how I wanted them to learn to play. We tried to win every game, never under-prepared, and looked to get the points every time.

A rebuild in footy can take up to seven or eight years, but the problem is, clubs are not prepared to ride it out. If you look at Geelong, we took from my arrival in 2000 to win the first flag in 2007, then ultimately won three premierships in 2007, 2009 and 2011. There is your evidence. At Melbourne, where the league ended up fining the club $500 000 for conduct prejudicial to the interests of the AFL (but not for tanking), they ran out of patience. Carlton is in that situation now and I will not be the slightest bit surprised if they jump early and change their coach again in three years. I really hope not for Brendon Bolton's sake.

It shouldn't be so hard to be patient. Hawthorn took four years for Clarkson to get them a premiership, and Clarkson himself has admitted that the prize came earlier than he expected in 2008. This is why I was pleased with Richmond's response when the speculation came about Damien Hardwick's position in 2015. Brendon Gale, the Richmond chief executive, actually came out and called it 'bullshit', and that is how it should be. Clubs need to guard against knee-jerk reactions but in truth, it has been happening for years because it is an emotional game, full of passion and argument. The best clubs remove the emotion and make calm, rational decisions, but that is not easy to do in the competitive football environment.

The game has been part of most of my life and will continue to be, I would imagine. With my senior coaching days done, I am trying to work out my own future, and it is tricky. It's hard to replace the vibrant, competitive environment of an AFL club, and I still have not nailed down where I fit in now, to be truthful.

I would like to start an academy for young players, and I also have this idea of what I call 'coaching the coaches', where I go into footy clubs and make sure the right systems are in place. I've started doing this, and I'm keen to see how it progresses because trying to bridge that gap between the grassroots and the elite is something that interests me. I can see myself working with young coaches, showing them *how* to coach, because it's a huge job. The coach is the most important figure in any footy club. It is the coach who has the most influence, working with the players day after day as he does.

When I visit footy clubs to do talks nowadays, I see a lot of junk training, people working with outdated methods. What they need to be talking about is playing football with lots of people around the ball, but there is no training being done for that. This is not the fault of Australian rules coaches; they just don't know what to do. Soccer is full of that type of coaching, where players are trained for spatial awareness and positioning. I have seen it firsthand.

Part of me feels hypocritical to be working in the media; I have had stints with 3AW and Fox Footy. I was vocal about not liking some of the things that were said and written during the whole Essendon saga and I don't like how certain stories grow legs. I know journalists are doing a job but I hate how it is so difficult to get to the actual truth of certain matters when they crop up.

Having said that, at Fox in particular I have enjoyed being in a good team environment. I would like to think that I know the game well and am prepared to express my opinions, so perhaps I can find a niche, a role, a place where I feel that I fit. Leigh Matthews is one commentator I really respect, because he can strip back an issue and explain it clearly and concisely, and he does not have agendas behind what he says. There's no group-think for Leigh, and that is the way that I would like to operate in the media, too, as an independent. No agendas, no bias, no looking after your mates. After 35 years in the game, I am happy to call it exactly as I see it.

I know that I was a good coach, and the dominant era of Geelong shows that. I had success because I was more observant than people thought I was, and because I could work out quite quickly what was important and what was not when it came to the game itself.

In terms of my method, I was not disrespectful to people who worked with me, and that was helpful. I am not necessarily a great communicator in a general sense, but when I communicated as a coach, I did it well. I could explain matters to a group of people and they have told me that I made sense.

I am a team person, and I know that in football, you need to make the big decisions together. Sure, have your own opinion, and maybe work towards that in the meetings that you need to have, but other people need to be involved too. Some coaches do not allow others into the picture, and when the pressure comes, they go off by themselves. That approach does not work.

I let people grow, just as Kevin Sheedy did with me. My assistant coaches were each given an area to handle and they owned it, the same as the players owned their roles. If someone made a mistake, he knew I would not be jumping down his throat. The only time I would criticise players was when they stopped playing, whether it was through fear or intimidation or whatever else it might be.

I look closely at other coaches and while there are lots of ways to give a rating for how a bloke is performing, the best way of all has nothing to do with win–loss records. It's about how his players are tracking, whether they are improving year by year. Good coaches draw out that improvement and it is not difficult to track from within, either. You write down why you recruited a player in the first place, and what areas need addressing, and then you cross-reference back at a later date. It will show you how your own program is working.

I hark back to something I wrote in a report for Essendon in 1997. I was new to the coaching game, but almost twenty years later, I still stand by it: 'Teach, don't command or judge.' Simple. Give people chances, don't judge them too quickly, and make sure you provide them with pathways for learning how you want them to play.

I lived by that in my life as a senior coach, and it's the best advice I can hand on to a coach of any team, at any level. As the old proverb says, 'Give a man a fish and you feed him for a day. Teach him to fish and you feed him for a lifetime.'

# ACKNOWLEDGEMENTS

It's been good for me, looking back, to see what I've achieved. Only recently I've realised how lucky I have been with the timing of major changes in my life. The book has given me the opportunity to reflect on those who I have learnt from and who have helped me along the way, in footy and in life. To all of you – you know who you are, and you're part of this story – you've been amazing role models, influenced me greatly and taught me how to teach and to be a leader of people. I haven't been an easy person to work with or live with, so thanks for putting up with me. From the bottom of my heart I sincerely thank you all for the roles you played in my life and story.

To all the teammates I've worked with – so many great men who committed their life to the Essendon Football Club and together reached the pinnacle of success. We always played in finals, won premierships. We worked hard, always striving to be better, doing things we had never done before because we were desperate to get something we had never had before. Without their help I would not have played a single game of senior football, not won premierships, not gone on to coach anywhere and Geelong might not have won three premierships and created legends of the game. A big part of this book and my story is a direct result of my ex-teammates who had a massive influence on me. I loved playing with them, loved our skillful style of play, loved our combativeness and fierce battles with the other clubs, loved winning games, loved the premierships I got to play in. I thank my teammates for the wonderful memories.

Thanks to my crew of players at Geelong who are now heroes and champions of the game. I am very proud of their success, and the fact that they remained respectful of the game, and to the supporters and staff at the club, and most importantly to each other. We won with class, respect and humility. I love the words in the club song, and for a period of time we really were 'The Greatest Team Of All'. I really missed the Geelong Football Club after I had left, especially the players who are just good solid men, now my mates. I have an incredible level of respect for them and that will remain forever.

I want to thank the current players at Essendon for being so honest, respectful, resilient and tolerant throughout the supplement investigation. I'm saddened that it has affected their ability to play as a champion team and that after four years, we still haven't found out what really occurred. And I'm sorry I could not have done more to make it easier for them to just play the game. Finally, I am sorry for not being able to do more to prove their innocence as I honestly believe they have done nothing to deserve the treatment they received. Nobody has been treated worse in football in all the years I've been involved in the game.

I need to thank Kevin Sheedy for giving me opportunities, firstly to play and then convincing me to take up coaching. Kevin shaped who I am more than any other person. I've always felt him looking out for me along the journey and that has comforted me. I'm really glad he chose to look after me when he had many others to choose from. Thanks also to Denis Pagan for giving me my first coaching opportunity outside the Bombers which was an incredibly worthwhile experience. At Geelong, working alongside Brian Cook and Frank Costa was one of my masterstrokes of timing and decision making. They were great to work with and to work for, and I learnt so much from both of them. I cannot thank Brian and Frank enough for taking a punt on me back in 1999.

A few special mentions. David Wheadon was my first mentor back when I started coaching and taught me lots about not only the game, but how to teach it. Brendan McCartney was the first person I employed and he finished the same day as me as well; he was my rock and a great coach of football. Stephen Wells and I fought and argued a lot, but together we selected good people who could play the Geelong way. We all made great memories and still have a good laugh. One of my favorite people to work with was Steven Hocking, the toughest conversationalist I've ever meet. He won every time; he was always right. He just got things done and was so disciplined, tough and fair. He was perfect in that football admin role. There are so many other people deserving of mentions, but I cannot fit you all in.

To my family – thanks for the sacrifices you made along the way, for putting up with my moods and for the support you've shown throughout especially when the tough times were present. I know I've been hard work at times.

Thank you to my wonderful children Lauren, Michael and Daniel. I missed part of your lives but you have turned out to be wonderful people, and thanks must go to your mother, Annette.

Another special person who influenced my life has been Jana. We shared some amazingly fun times together and I coached some of my best years with her by my side.

And last to acknowledge is Martin Blake, who at times I'm sure thought he had the worst task in the world in co-writing my book, as did editor/sounding board, Andrea McNamara. Without their patience, organisation, getting me into line and most importantly connecting with me, the book certainly wouldn't have happened.

# NOTE FROM THE CO-WRITER

Bomber Thompson has done pretty much everything in Australian football, which is why I jumped at the chance to help him write his autobiography. We were already acquainted, of course, from his time coaching at Geelong, when I was writing footy for *The Age*. While Bomber was no one's idea of a media groupie, we got along well.

Piecing together the book was a lot of fun. We had lunches at his cafe in Port Melbourne and at his home, where he whipped up delicious pulled pork buns. He came to my home, too, and we talked footy a lot over six months or so. Bomber loves talking about footy: how to play it the right way, how to prepare for it. I truly hope that some aspiring coaches read this book because it offers up so much.

Bomber has kept a lot of stuff, and he produced old game plans, a submission that he prepared for a coaching job more than 15 years ago, a sports psychologist's notes to him as a player, game notes handed to Geelong players before the three grand finals he coached and newspaper articles that he liked, including one of mine! When he told me that he had been a quick player in his time at Essendon and I expressed doubts, he found a printout of times for the 20-metre sprint from around 1988, with him quite close to the fastest! Point taken.

Thanks go to Bomber for his honesty and for the laughs, and to his parents, Bruce and Patricia, who loaned us a raft of old photographs and cuttings. Thanks to Andrea McNamara (publishing consultant), who was a constant source of ideas, advice and encouragement to both Bomber and myself, and to Tracey Jarrett for making it all happen as well as to Ben Ball at Penguin for giving us a shot at this.

While writing the section on Essendon's drugs scandal, Chip Le Grand's book, *The Straight Dope*, was invaluable with its diligent recording of the events that engulfed that football club from 2012 onward. It is a fine piece of journalism, a deserved winner of the 2015 Walkley Book Award and the William Hill Australian Sports Book of the Year. If you want to know more about the saga, look no further.

Thanks to the newspapers (*The Age*, *Herald Sun*, *The Australian*, *Adelaide Advertiser*) I borrowed bits from, and to the AFL and Geelong's websites, which were helpful. I thoroughly recommend a website called AFL Tables, which has an enormous amount of historical information on games of footy, is totally free and does not even carry any advertising. I used it all the time to take Bomber back to games in the distant past.

The idea of this book was to put a full stop on Mark Thompson's coaching career. It is quite some career, too, certainly worth reflecting upon. I would love to see him coach again, but he insists that he won't, pointing out that the job is all consuming. His influence on the game is monumental.

*Martin Blake*

# CAREER HIGHLIGHTS AND STATISTICS

**ESSENDON PREMIERSHIP PLAYER**
1984, 1985, 1993

**ESSENDON PREMIERSHIP CAPTAIN**
1993

**GEELONG PREMIERSHIP COACH**
2007, 2009

**ESSENDON TEAM OF THE CENTURY**
Interchange bench

**ESSENDON BEST & FAIREST**
1987, 1990

**ALL AUSTRALIAN**
1986, 1990

**ALL AUSTRALIAN COACH**
2007, 2009

**ESSENDON CAPTAIN**
1992-95 (69 games)

**PRE-SEASON/NIGHT SERIES PREMIERSHIPS**
1984, 1990, 1993

**GEELONG PRE-SEASON/NIGHT SERIES PREMIERSHIP COACH**
2006, 2009

## MARK THOMPSON THE PLAYER 1983-1996

| Season | Premiership season | | | | | | Pre-Season/ Night Series | | State of Origin | |
|---|---|---|---|---|---|---|---|---|---|---|
| | Mtchs | Wins | Losses | Ties | Gls | Brownlow medal votes | Mtchs | Gls | Mtchs | Gls |
| 1983 | 2 | 1 | 1 | 0 | 1 | 0 | 0 | 0 | 0 | 0 |
| 1984 | 20 | 16 | 4 | 0 | 4 | 0 | 4 | 1 | 0 | 0 |
| 1985 | 23 | 20 | 3 | 0 | 5 | 1 | 1 | 0 | 0 | 0 |
| 1986 | 22 | 11 | 11 | 0 | 2 | 6 | 1 | 0 | 1 | 0 |
| 1987 | 18 | 8 | 9 | 1 | 16 | 4 | 1 | 0 | 0 | 0 |
| 1988 | 0 | 0 | 0 | 0 | 0 | 0 | 2 | 1 | 0 | 0 |
| 1989 | 10 | 7 | 3 | 0 | 0 | 3 | 0 | 0 | 0 | 0 |
| 1990 | 24 | 18 | 6 | 0 | 7 | 3 | 3 | 0 | 0 | 0 |
| 1991 | 9 | 3 | 6 | 0 | 6 | 0 | 1 | 0 | 0 | 0 |
| 1992 | 21 | 12 | 9 | 0 | 5 | 1 | 1 | 0 | 0 | 0 |
| 1993 | 21 | 15 | 5 | 1 | 2 | 5 | 4 | 0 | 0 | 0 |
| 1994 | 13 | 7 | 6 | 0 | 1 | 0 | 1 | 0 | 0 | 0 |
| 1995 | 11 | 6 | 5 | 0 | 0 | 0 | 0 | 0 | 0 | 0 |
| 1996 | 8 | 5 | 2 | 1 | 1 | 0 | 1 | 0 | 0 | 0 |
| TOTALS | 202 | 129 | 70 | 3 | 50 | 23 | 20 | 2 | 1 | 0 |

## MARK THOMPSON THE COACH 2000-2010; 2014

| Club | Season | Position | Wins | Losses | Ties | Matches | Players Used |
|---|---|---|---|---|---|---|---|
| Geelong | 2000 | 7 | 12 | 10 | 1 | 23 | 37 |
| Geelong | 2001 | 12 | 9 | 13 | 0 | 22 | 34 |
| Geelong | 2002 | 9 | 11 | 11 | 0 | 22 | 37 |
| Geelong | 2003 | 12 | 7 | 14 | 1 | 22 | 35 |
| Geelong | 2004 | 4 | 16 | 9 | 0 | 25 | 35 |
| Geelong | 2005 | 5 | 13 | 11 | 0 | 24 | 37 |
| Geelong | 2006 | 10 | 10 | 11 | 1 | 22 | 37 |
| Geelong | 2007 | Premier | 21 | 4 | 0 | 25 | 31 |
| Geelong | 2008 | 2 | 23 | 2 | 0 | 25 | 31 |
| Geelong | 2009 | Premier | 21 | 4 | 0 | 25 | 33 |
| Geelong | 2010 | 3 | 18 | 7 | 0 | 25 | 35 |
| Essendon | 2014 | 7 | 12 | 10 | 1 | 23 | 35 |
| TOTALS | | | 173 | 106 | 4 | 283 | |

# PICTURE CREDITS

All AFL images are used with the permission of AFL Media, and the photographer credit is included where the information is available. Every effort has been made to trace and contact copyright holders. If there are any inadvertent omissions, please contact the publisher with revised information.

Chapter 2: Kevin Sheedy watches from the bench during a 1980's VFL match. (*AFL Media*)

Chapter 3: Footy cards from the 1980s.

Chapter 5: Simon Madden with teammates including Mark Thompson (right) in the rooms after winning a 1989 VFL match. (*AFL Media*)

Chapter 6: With Gavin Wanganeen, holding aloft the Foster's Cup trophy after beating the Tigers at Waverley Park, 20 March 1993. (*AFL Media*)

Chapter 7: Assistant coach of the Bombers, at the 1998 round 15 match between the Bombers and Port Adelaide. (*AFL Media*)

Chapter 11: Leaving the field after the three-quarter time break during the Round 6 match against the Tigers at Telstra Dome, 6 May 2007. (*Lachlan Cunningham/AFL Media*)

Chapter 14: Addressing his players at quarter time during the round 8 match against the Kangaroos at Skilled Stadium, 16 May 2009. (*Lachlan Cunningham/AFL Media*)

Chapter 16: Working out field positions during the round 9 match against the Hawks at Telstra Dome, 25 May 2003. (*AFL Media*)

Chapter 17: Addressing the media as head coach, James Hird, looks on during a media conference at Windy Hill, 7 December 2010. (*Lachlan Cunningham/AFL Media*)

Chapter 19: During the elimination final against North Melbourne at the MCG, 6 September 2014. (*Justine Walker/AFL Media*)

# INDEX

## G